VOLUME 48   SEPTEMBER 1979   PAGES 1–290

BOSWELL'S PAOLI

By

JOSEPH FOLADARE

TRANSACTIONS

The Connecticut Academy of Arts and Sciences

Published for The Academy by

ARCHON BOOKS   Hamden, Connecticut

Copies of the *Transactions* of
The Connecticut Academy of Arts and Sciences
may be obtained from

ARCHON BOOKS

The Shoe String Press, Inc.
995 Sherman Avenue
Hamden, Connecticut   06514

Library of Congress Cataloging in Publication Data

Foladare, Joseph.
Boswell's Paoli

(Transactions–The Connecticut Academy of Arts and Sciences;
v. 48, p. 1– 290)
Includes bibliographical references and index.
1. Paoli, Pasquale, 1725–1807.
2. Statesmen—France—Corsica—Biography.
3. Corsica—History—18th century.
4. Boswell, James, 1740–1795.
I. Title
II. Series: Connecticut Academy of Arts and Sciences, New Haven.
Transactions; v. 48, p. 1–290.
Q11.C9   vol. 48, p. 1–290   [DC611.C8315] 081s
ISBN 0-208-01765-8   [944'.945'0340924] [B] 79–1242

Litho printed and bound in the United States of America

CONTENTS

Acknowledgements

I wish to acknowledge my indebtedness to Frederick A. Pottle, who by example and advice has assisted me since I attended the Boswell seminar at Yale over forty years ago; and to Marion S. Pottle, who has drawn upon her knowledge of the Boswell collection to find items of interest and who has favored me with the fruits of many other labors, among them descriptive catalog entries from her forthcoming index to the entire present collection. For translations of letters in Italian in the Boswell collection, some done before I first looked at them in 1932, I am indebted to David Patton and unnamed others connected with the Boswell enterprise. I wish particularly to thank Elise Foladare, who has translated French and Italian printed and manuscript documents beyond number; and has served to monitor my ventures in modifying structure and idiom.

I am obliged to Yale University and the Boswell Editorial Committee as well as the McGraw-Hill Book Company for permission to quote from manuscript and published material in the Boswell Papers at Yale; to the Trustees of the National Library of Scotland and Mrs. P.G.C. Somervell for letters to Sir William Forbes from Pasquale de Paoli and Euphemia Boswell; and to the William L. Clements Library for material in the Shelburne manuscript collection.

and histories *cum* biography began to appear: Renucci,
1833; Arrighi, 1843; Giamarchi, 1858; D'Oria, 1870; Bartoli, 1889; Ravenna, 1928; Rota, 1941; Thrasher, 1970.[3]
The authors' names point up the possibility of national
bias. Boswell, who dedicated his book to Paoli, did not pretend to a fine impartiality. Many of those who came later
claimed objectivity, but they cannot be said to have succeeded. Thrasher, the lone Englishman, proved no exception. Objectivity in writing of Paoli is very likely impossible.
The Southern senator who said that what was needed was
an objective history of the Civil War from the Southern
point of view delighted some in the galleries but no doubt
stirred deep responses of assent from his constituents.

Unless he were a Genoese or a Frenchman, a foreigner
visiting Paoli in 1765 would expect to find what Boswell
found—a leader whose considerable intelligence had been
informed by the great principles of the Enlightenment, a
proved skillful general, a lawmaker who dispensed im-
partial but stern justice, a legislator who sought educational opportunity for all and diminished the distance
between classes, a pious believer who nevertheless separated church from state; and finally, because he combined
all these qualities, a political master who seemed capable of
bringing his unspoiled people from a state of feudalism to
one of representative democracy in the space of one decade or at most two. In addition Boswell found in Paoli
more of the philosophical social moralist and more of the
hero; and in the people he found more simplicity, goodness, and generosity. In Boswell's discussions with Paoli
there is inevitably some Boswell, the young man trying to
find his way from melancholy and insecurity to self-con-
fidence and composure, particularly with the aid of a great
man who drew unqualified admiration; but the Corsican
Tour is primarily about Paoli and secondarily about his
people and his country. I will have frequent occasion to refer to the *Tour* as the starting point of all discussions of
Paoli's character, quoting and summarizing whatever is
necessary. Professor Pottle's *James Boswell, the Earlier Years,
1740–1769* (New York, 1966), to which the first part of this

work as it concerns Boswell is a supplement, should be readily available to the reader.[4]

Boswell published no more on Paoli than what found its way into the *Life of Johnson*.[5] During the past forty years readers of Boswell have been given a veritable cornucopia of hitherto unpublished materials—first the eighteen-volume *Private Papers of James Boswell*, 1928–1934 (index volume, 1937), and now, if publication starting in 1950 but still continuing can be so placed temporally, the trade or reading edition of Boswell's papers as well as the research edition. It should be recalled that the eighteen-volume edition of the *Private Papers* was but a selection from the Isham Collection, although it contained all of Boswell's full journals and previously unpublished letters then known. There was in the collection, also, considerable additional manuscript material relating to Paoli and Corsica. I made what use I could of it many years ago.[6] The quantity of Boswell papers at Yale now, by weight or word-count, is approximately three times what it was in the 1930s; yet the early collection was sufficiently representative to enable one to write then as Professor Pottle has written recently with the additional materials at hand: "The influence of the General of the Corsicans was perhaps more powerful for good in Boswell's life than that of any other person except his wife. Paoli advised him, admonished him, chided him, but he never once showed anger towards him."[7] Professor Pottle will have more to say about Boswell and Paoli as he proceeds with the biography. His center of attention is necessarily Boswell. My attention will be directed to Boswell's papers, published and unpublished, as primary sources for insight into the character of Paoli. What biographer of Paoli has even hinted that the General was capable of the private relationship indicated in the passage just quoted? It is because Paoli as Boswell wrote of him —Boswell's Paoli— is so completely a stranger to the person described in the extant biographies of the great Corsican that I am moved to write this work. With the permission of the Boswell Editorial Committee, Yale University, and the McGraw-Hill Book Company I will make use of over thirty as yet unpublished letters as well as several somewhat rare documents printed by Paoli in Corsica.

Boswell's published portrait enhanced through use of material in the Boswell collection is thus an immediate aim. The further aim is to show Paoli with the aid of scholars of the nineteenth and twentieth centuries. If I could I would try to accomplish the task as Boswell might have done it. That being impossible, I am left with some of his partisanship, balanced I hope by a proper modern concern for hard evidence and scrupulousness in drawing inferences.

Before the French Revolution Paoli was viewed from one end of a telescope or the other. The admirers of the forsaken hero, whether Gray, Wesley, Goethe, or the young Napoleon, admitted no qualifications; his enemies considered him an overpublicized and overrated rebel. When in 1793 Paoli turned away from France and looked to England for support his action gave rise to an entirely new set of attitudes which have persisted to the present day. One was, very simply, that he betrayed the Revolution and the ideals he had previously espoused; another—more kindly, practical, even cynical—was that he unfortunately chose the losing side. These views were opposed by those who claimed Paoli consistently worked for the maximum individual freedom and the maximum independence of his people. When he found murderous and indiscriminate terror threatening his island he made only the necessary compromises. France as a constitutional monarchy, England as a constitutional monarchy—either was tolerable. He could not have foreseen the reactionary turn England was to take. The books on Paoli take one or the other of these opposing views modified by the combinations afforded by the following national or racial assumptions:

1. The Corsicans were really Italians, and in their hearts, perhaps subconsciously, needed to renew their ancient ties with the peninsula.[8] Ravenna and Rota, both writing during the time of Mussolini's dictatorship, took this view openly; Rota's biography was one in a series of "Fifty Great Italians," beginning with Caesar, Cicero, Virgil, Tacitus, and ending, in

modern times, with Paoli, Napoleon, Garibaldi, Verdi, Marconi, and, as the culminating hero, Mussolini. (Their work should not be entirely discounted because of these circumstances.)

2. The Corsicans should never have ceased to strive for independence. Napoleon wasn't the only Corsican who at first saw the French Revolution as a means of ultimately separating Corsica from France and establishing a sovereign state. As we shall discover in the present study, Boswell consistently maintained this view even when Paoli placed Corsica under the protection of Britain.

3. In terms of power politics Corsica was unalterably a part of France. When he could no longer stomach French policy Paoli should have removed himself and spared his countrymen. Renucci took this view as did most of those in France who wrote on Corsican history.

The first extensive scholarly attempt to gather primary materials on Paoli was made by Niccolò Tommaseo, who collected the letters of Paoli which were published as Volume 11 of *Archivio Storico Italiano*, Florence, 1846. All subsequent biographers owe a considerable debt to Tommaseo; one, Giamarchi (1858), I find in many respects as satisfactory as any who have followed. Further letters by Paoli have been gathered and published in the years since, and the process is still going on.[9] The heyday of Corsican scholarship came during the period 1881–1911, when the *Bulletin, Société des Sciences Historiques et Naturelles de la Corse* flourished at Bastia, where now nothing of the kind finds sustained nourishment. Mainland Italy, and to a lesser degree France, gave signs of similar activity during approximately the same period. A flurry of Corsican scholarship, led by contributions to *Archivio Storico di Corsica* in Leghorn and Rome, began in the late 1920s and extended through the 1930s. Rota and Thrasher are the only biographers of Paoli to have been in a position to benefit from these works. I now must answer the question: Why, other than to bring to light hitherto unpublished materials in the

Boswell collection, do I find it appropriate to write an extensive revisionary work on the life of Paoli?

To put the answer simply, the early biographers are inadequate because they did not have sufficient source materials to draw upon, and the later, especially the last, are misleading when not downright inaccurate. Take Thrasher, at the basic level of factual accuracy. It is sad to see Paoli's good friend and secretary, Father Guelfucci, transformed into Gueffacci (p. 158), but he may be only one victim of the veritable plague of misprints for which these days it is unkind to blame an author. Can the same be said for substituting Chauvelin, who had all he could do to take the French legions into Corsica, for Choiseul, the crafty Prime Minister who was characterized by Chatham as being without an equal since Richelieu,[10] and who easily outmaneuvered Paoli and the British Cabinet? The substitution takes place four times on one page (p. 124) as well as on later occasions. In another place the chronology and reports of the two British agents, Stewart and Dunant, are confused (pp. 124, 135).

The errors by themselves frequently are of little moment, but in the aggregrate they suggest a pervasive laxity in the exercise of the scholarly faculty. Take the account of Paoli's attack on the fort opposite San Fiorenzo, October 1793, coordinated with an attack from the sea by the British. It ends with the statement that "Paoli had in the attack lost one of the greatest of his captains in Masseria" (p. 282). The next month Masseria, miraculously resurrected, encountered Boswell in London. Once again it is possible to follow Thrasher's trail. His claim to originality lies in the "Unpublished Primary Sources" listed in his bibliography. They are materials in the British Public Record Office and in the French Archives Nationales. Now, materials in an archive, whether in print or in manuscript form, are to be examined with the same care which should be bestowed on a raw FBI file. Who was the author? What was his purpose? Did he belong to a faction, have a special axe to grind? Thrasher was undoubtedly victimized by a story planted by

Paoli to cover the departure of Masseria to England to act as his agent.

Further, some simple facts have profound implications. When the British fleet abandoned Corsica "7,000 French *émigrés* and a little over 5,000 Corsican refugees embarked" with them, according to Thrasher (p. 325). Had Thrasher read more extensively the letters and dispatches of Sir Gilbert Elliot, on whom he appears to rely heavily for some of his narrative, he would have discovered that the entire British fleet off Toulon had been able to accommodate only some two thousand refugees when it abandoned that port, and that this number clogged the decks and passageways. As for Corsica, Nelson planned to set aside two to three ships for "600 émigrés [Corsican and French] and their effects"; the number actually carried off was probably much smaller, about one hundred of them being Corsican.[11] What the true figures require is a drastic revision in the notion of the prestige of Britain and the loyalty it commanded. So rapidly had Britain's position on the island deteriorated following Paoli's expulsion that only those closely involved with Paoli's earlier actions against France and those identified with British rule (Corsican anti-Republicans like Buttafoco and careerists like Pozzo di Borgo) felt endangered by the return of the French army, commanded by General Gentili and composed largely of Corsican exiles. Napoleon had seen to it that the extent of his amnesty was widely known. I will again attempt to follow Thrasher's unposted trail. Gentili was soon asked by Napoleon to leave Corsica to head the French expedition to the Ionian Isles. The vindictiveness of his successor, Saliceti, was curbed for a time by Napoleon's original orders. Within a year, however, the successive administrators, who were lackeys of either Saliceti or Arena, began what Paoli characterized as "horrible oppressions." As Paoli wrote to Burnaby, "My little five-year-old nephew Monticello, his little three-year-old sister, with their mother and grandmother, were exiled to Tuscany." Paoli's information indicated that the heads of at least six thousand families were exiled.[12] Perhaps somewhere in his "archives" Thrasher found numbers of this magnitude which he assumed were involved in the original British embarkation.

The mischiefs of erroneous "facts," significant as they sometimes may be, are not so disturbing as certain of Thrasher's judgements and inferences. When he says that in Boswell's writings Paoli's humanity is "emphasized by the slightly ridiculous air in which he sometimes appears as a foil to Johnson," one is curious to identify the pertinent passages. When he infers that Paoli entertained a low opinion of the English (including his being the source of Napoleon's famous characterization of the English as a "nation of shopkeepers") one recalls Paoli's many utterances, public and private, of admiration for and trust in the English. But when he writes that Paoli "was under no illusions about English politicians; he was, after all, a politician himself," one finds the implication insufferable.[13] The truth is that Thrasher does not have much confidence in the words of his "hero." He rarely gives General Pasquale de Paoli, memorably expressive in his letters, eloquent in his public speeches and printed manifestos and declarations, an opportunity to speak for himself. Thus it is that Ravenna, quoting freely from Tommaseo's collection, brings Paoli to life in her slim volume much more than does Thrasher. When allowed to speak, the man and his style fill the imagination. From reading Thrasher one cannot discover that Paoli was characteristically pithy, metaphorical, and allusive in all that he observed and said.

All this having been duly noted, it should be recognized that Thrasher gives by far the most circumstantial account of events, of the internal political struggles and physical skirmishes involving Paoli during the period 1755-69, that has so far appeared. From the time of Paoli's first exile to England to the end of his life, however, we have much better guides in Boswell and Burnaby, and in various illuminating letters, journals, and dispatches of the last part of the eighteenth century.

Some words for the biographer of Paoli are in order. What in general a biographer needs to know is what his subject thought, felt, wrote, spoke, and did. With this knowledge, added to a thorough understanding of the social and political events of the time and an ability to fuse all into an organic and coherent whole, he then takes his pen and writes. The prescription, demanding a mastery of scholarship and of art, is of course not easily filled. I shall here confine myself to the first, neglected or unknown materials of scholarship, and try to show what they signify. At the least my efforts will enable the reader of an extant biography to enhance and modify for himself; at the most they will pave the way for a proper biography of Paoli, who deserves better than he has so far received.

First, the letters. After eliminating the exchanges required merely to further private or public business, one finds much that is useful. To Mrs. Thrale, Johnson once wrote: "In a man's letters, you know, Madam, his soul lies naked, his letters are only the mirrour of his breast; whatever passes within him is shown undisguised in its natural process; nothing is inverted, nothing distorted; you see systems in their elements; you discover actions in their motives"[14] More typical was Johnson's view in the "Life of Pope": "Very few can boast of hearts which they dare lay open to themselves, and of which, by whatever accident exposed, they do not shun a distinct and continued view; and, certainly, what we hide from ourselves we do not show to our friends." Exploration of emotions and relentless self-searching were not completely beyond Paoli's capabilities, but he certainly was not given to this mode of analysis or reflection. The reader of his letters need not be on guard; he can accept what Paoli wrote to Burnaby on 13 July 1802: "It has been my inviolable custom in corresponding with my friends to speak of things as I see them, to express my opinions with simplicity and frankness." The letters to Burnaby, published in a small edition in 1804, strangely have been ignored by Paoli's biographers; they, together with the Boswell materials, provide valuable new elements in the present work.

As for what Paoli said and what he did, we can do no better than start with young Boswell. "As long as I can remember any thing," Boswell wrote in his book, "I have heard of 'The malecontents of Corsica, with Paoli at their head'" (p. 295). Paoli had headed the Corsicans for only ten years prior to Boswell's visit, and Boswell's memory was a very good one; the "malecontents," however, went back beyond recorded history. The reader of Boswell's journals knows that he did not emerge from the glooms of Holland to direct his steps toward Corsica. His was a leisurely grand tour, with many unexpected delays and side trips. One cannot presume so far as to isolate the single factor which determined an individual's action, but it is at least reasonable to conclude that Boswell would never have gone to Corsica had he not visited Rousseau at a time when, as he wrote to Temple, "The Corsicans have actually applied to him to give them a set of laws."[15]

The general interest in Corsica which had been intensified by news that Rousseau had been asked to legislate for the new nation was dampened by subsequent revisions and even denials of the story. By the time Boswell wrote in his journal that "You must see Corsica," 5 August 1765, the British newspapers had tired of the subject. As the year 1765 drew to a close the *London Chronicle* for a period of several months had not carried a single item on Corsica. Once Boswell started the pot boiling at the end of the year scarcely a single week went by without a news item or comment on Corsica, until some time after the French settled matters by force of arms in May 1769 and Paoli subsided, at least in the press's view, into the life of an exile in London.

to the French. Into exile he took with him his younger son Pasquale, now approaching his fourteenth year. Giacinto Paoli entered the military service of the Kingdom of Naples with the rank of lieutenant colonel, and early in 1741 his son enrolled as a cadet in the Royal Academy of Naples.

Very little is known of the life of Pasquale Paoli during the next fourteen years, the formative period at the end of which he emerged as a leader of men and, to the happy surprise of those who read Boswell's book, a devoted student of the classical historians and biographers. During this period, too, he apparently read, heard, or in some way familiarized himself with the lectures of Genovesi and with much of the literature of the Enlightenment.[4] One bit of information concerning this period crops up several years later in Boswell's journal: "The General said to me that if he thought at all well he owed it to *The Spectator*, which he had read when very young at Naples, and to Nicole" (2 April 1776). The thought of Addison's correct, measured style grafted upon native Corsican and Italian eloquence surprises, but upon reflection seems appropriate as a description of Paoli's own mode of expression. Boswell was pleased with the information, noting that his "own mind was first touched with elegant thinking" by *The Spectator;* but he "wondered to hear him speak highly of [Pierre] Nicole [the French Jansenist], which I supposed to be a mere casuistical, or rather scrupulous, system of morals." Practice in logic chopping, however, would have been useful to a boy deprived of extensive formal schooling. This last inference accords with the biographical facts which have been unearthed only in comparatively recent times. Paoli was, for one thing, quite poor; for another, he rose in rank slowly, not receiving a regular commission as second lieutenant until just before his twenty-seventh year. For military experience he could show only garrison duty. These facts taken with a few remarks Boswell elicited from the General portray a "singular man," an officer who had neither the means nor the inclination to be one of the boys, whether in the drawing room, bedroom, or card-room.[5]

For all this he was not the lonely outsider, gloomy and introspective; he had more important things to do. And somehow he developed the social graces which made him a desired guest in England long after novelty had worn off.

"Paoli told me that from his earliest years he had in view the important station which he now holds," wrote Boswell (*Tour,* p. 351). He was descended from a family which for hundreds of years had been conspicous in Corsica's struggle for liberty; and from early childhood he was in the company of family chiefs whose exploits were quickly turned into legend.. He did not question how circumstances would bring his talents into use. The very able Gian Pietro Gaffori was successfully leading the Corsicans during Paoli's tours of duty in Italy, and on the island the Paoli family was led by elder brother Clemente, a fanatically religious warrior who prayed for the souls of his enemies before dispatching them but was feared for all that.

In 1753, however, Genoa used its most common and successful weapon, money, and secured the assassination of Gaffori. (Less dramatic were bribes to reactivate vendettas, and awards of lands and titles to secure defections.) Genoa in the process of intensifying its efforts against the resistance had again obtained from Britain a reaffirmation of the 1736 prohibition against "correspondence with the said rebels" or "any kind of succours whatsoever" by British subjects.[6] Under the quadrumvirate which succeeded Gaffori the Corsicans continued the struggle with, as Boswell put it, "various success." Clemente Paoli performed as a member of the quadrumvirate so ably that he was offered the supreme office. Given to solitary worship when not fighting, having no inclination toward the business of administration, and perhaps believing his younger brother on every count more suited, he declined. It was now, in 1755, that Pasquale Paoli was asked to head the government of his native land as General.

In his *Account* Boswell prints in full the manifesto of 15 July 1755 by the "Supreme and General Council of the Kingdom of Corsica" which met at the convent of Sant' Antonio della Casabianca and declared to the people that

Pasquale Paoli had been elected their chief by "the general voice;" and he then proceeds to describe all that the General faced: "utmost disorder and confusion . . . no subordination, no discipline, no money, hardly any arms and ammunition . . . little union among the people" (pp. 159-60). By "persuasion and example" Paoli ignited the spirit of "all ranks" so that in a "short time the Genoese were driven to the remotest corners of the island. . . . Having thus expelled the foe . . . he had leisure to attend to the civil part of his administration," and "in a manner newmodelled the government upon the soundest principles of democratical rule, which was always his favourite idea." Having been denied legal justice, the Corsicans "had assumed the right of private revenge, and had been accustomed to assassinate each other upon the most trivial occasions." Again by persuasion and when necessary by force he established the rule of law and stamped out the vendetta. He then "proceeded to improve and civilize the manners of the Corsicans," no easy task for one who constantly reminded the people that he was dependent upon them, "elected by them, and answerable to them." He led them "of their own accord to desire the enactment of regulations of which he showed them the benefit. He established a university at Corte; and he was at great pains to have proper schools for the instruction of children in every village of the kingdom. The last step he took was to induce the Corsicans to apply themselves to agriculture, commerce, and other civil occupations. War had entirely ruined industry in the island. It had given the Corsicans a contempt for the arts of peace so that they thought nothing worthy of their attention but arms and military achievements. The great and valorous actions which many of them had performed gave them a certain pride, which disdained all meaner and more inglorious occupation. Heroes could not submit to sink down into plain peasants" (pp. 160-63).

So, simply, did Paoli lead his people. The tasks were monumental, but so were the abilities of Boswell's hero. For details one must look elsewhere. Boswell wrote the *Account* only because he realized that the intended readers of his journal and memoirs of Paoli needed to know something of the history of Corsica. For the first two chapters he used published sources. He prepared the third chapter also for the most part from materials other than those which he had collected during his travels, but some of his direct observations and much of his heart went into it. The journal and memoirs would secure respect and admiration for Paoli; however, help and even intervention from those who supplied or held power in Britain required knowledge of "The Present State of Corsica, with respect to Government, Religion, Arms, Commerce, Learning, the Genius and Character of its Inhabitants" (Chapter 3). This section of the *Account*, based largely on materials sent to Boswell by Corsican leaders and scholars including Paoli, is still valuable.[7] Bias on the part of Boswell and his informants must be allowed for. Figures for agricultural production, for example, should be discounted for being what economists call "projections," expected to be valid by the time of publication. Nevertheless, though he may shade or omit, Boswell does not hide the truth when it is necessary for essential accuracy. For example, he recognizes that "notwithstanding all that Paoli has done, the Corsicans are still indolent and averse to labour. Every year 800 or 1000 Sardinians and Luccese are employed as artificers and day-labourers in the island" (p. 244).[8]

Boswell's rather detailed description of the "compleat and well ordered democracy" of Corsica reveals it as falling short of the ideal. The General, for example, "holds office for life. He is perpetual president of the supreme council of nine. He votes in all questions; and in case of an equality he has a casting vote. He is absolute commander of the troops or militia of the island" (pp. 179–80). His attitude toward his function is that he is strengthening his people's self-reliance so that ultimately they will have no need of him. He intervenes judicially or legislatively only with reluctance, in every instance explaining why he makes a given decision and thus how the people or their representative bodies could have made the same decision on their own. Everywhere in Chapter III of the *Account* as well

as in the *Tour* one finds Paoli's acknowledgement of ultimate accountability to the people. The Corsicans' love for
Paoli "is such that although the power of the General is
properly limited, the power of Paoli knows no bounds. It is
high treason so much as to speak against or calumniate
him; a species of despotism founded, contrary to the principles of Montesquieu, on the affection of love" (p. 190).
Paoli if he wished could be styled king. The dangers in-
herent in this situation are very clear; yet prior to the attack by France no Corsican ventured to accuse Paoli of
abusing his trust.

Additionally, in Chapter 3 Boswell finds the islanders
"firmly attached to their religion" but "sworn enemies to
the temporal power of the church" (p. 192). The priests
and monks warmly support Paoli against the Genoese. The
"tyrannical bishops," who live abroad "in idleness and lux-
ury," have been deprived of their tithes, which now go to
the public treasury (pp. 196-201). Paoli relies on "a bold
and resolute militia," but they are not formally in service
except for three hundred who comprise a guard for the
General and two hundred who furnish guards for magistrates in various provinces and garrison a few small forts.
Every Corsican is subject to call and can be expected to give
a good account of himself, having been armed from birth,
as it were, "with a gun, a pistol and a stiletto" (pp. 206-10).[9]
The islanders are provided with good harbors, much "excellent timber," and are able to construct small ships.
Commerce can be expected to thrive "in oil [vegetable],
wine, honey, beeswax, salt, chestnuts, silk, rosin, boxwood,
oak, pine, porphyry, marble of various kinds, lead, iron,
copper, silver, and coral" (p. 213). The university which
Paoli established at Corte in 1764 boasts a faculty of five
who are fathers of "different religious orders." There are,
as Boswell saw for himself in 1765, "some pretty good
halls" for lectures, but no regular college buildings. The
students board in the town (p. 224).[10]

We are now very nearly ready to join Boswell in meeting
the great man. First, however, the role of Rousseau must
be clarified. Rousseau had been asked to assist the Cor-

sicans "in forming their laws" (*Tour*, p. 288) as a consequence of his having observed in the *Contrat Social* (1762):
"There is one country still capable of legislation—the
island of Corsica. The courage and constancy with which
that brave people have recovered and defended their liberty deserves the reward of having some wise man teach
them how to preserve it. I have a presentiment that this little island will one day astonish Europe." The request from
"the Corsicans" inviting Rousseau to be the "legislator" for
Corsica, and to outline "a plan for a political system," had
been signed by Matteo Buttafoco (1731–1800), a career
officer in the army of France, politically active in Corsica
and on the surface friendly with though frequently in opposition to Paoli. Rousseau, particularly after his enemies
spoke of the invitation as a hoax, sought information from
Buttafoco concerning the provisional government and the
character of Paoli. By the time Paoli issued a formal invitation to Rousseau—probably at Buttafoco's suggestion, not
upon the basis of a direct reading of Rousseau's troubled
letters to Buttafoco—the philosopher felt persecuted and
very ill (with good reason on both counts) and could think
of Corsica only as an asylum where, if his state of mind and
body permitted, he could possibly contribute by writing a
history of the Corsican people. Rousseau seriously entertained this possibility for some time, but eventually sought
asylum elsewhere.[11]

Toward the end of his tour, after he reached French-
occupied Corsica, Boswell met and "past some days" with
Buttafoco, who showed Boswell the "whole correspondence" between him and Rousseau, thus enabling Boswell
to "give a distinct account of it." Boswell's information was
neither distinct nor complete; else he would not have been
forced to copy statements concerning Paoli's intentions
from Burnaby's journal of his tour to Corsica (1766). To
take one clear example of material Buttafoco could show
neither to Paoli nor to Boswell: Rousseau, in his letter of
24 March 1765, acknowledges receipt of materials on the
Corsican provisional government and some proposals
which Buttafoco himself has made. "I have still another

reason [for abandoning the project]," he goes on, "and for
me a very cogent one. . . . The plan I would propose could
never please you [the Corsicans], yourself perhaps least of
all." As Boswell was forced to acknowledge in the third edition of *Corsica* (after Buttafoco had taken up arms against
Paoli's government), Buttafoco presented more than one
face to the world. Over twenty years later he wrote of his
approach to Rousseau as follows:

> Animated by the desire to assure the liberty of Corsica
> [against the ambition and the tyranny of Paoli], I addressed
> myself in 1764 to the celebrated citizen of Geneva for the
> purpose of engaging him to devise a political constitution.
> The philosopher received my invitation with the transports
> of a virtuous heart.[12]

In the 1760s Buttafoco gave the appearance of a loyal
Corsican in the army of France, a country anxious to shield
the Corsicans from excesses by the Genoese. During the
period of retrenchment as the Seven Years War was coming to a close, the Royal Corsican regiment had been ab-
sorbed into the Royal Italian, but better times were clearly
ahead. Early in 1762 Buttafoco proposed to the French
Prime Minister, the Duc de Choiseul, a plan whereby
France should occupy Corsica in order to stave off a possible attack by the English. Since he "is persuaded that his attachment to the service of the King is not at all incompatible
with his attachment to his country, he does not fear to offer
his services in that country. He has some right to flatter
himself that he has some influence in his nation, both with
the Chief of the Corsicans and with the principal men under him who are charged with the public administration."[13]
The war ended without threats from the English, and the
insurgents continued their success against the Genoese.
The latter secured from the British in 1763 another proclamation which prohibited the subjects of George III from
trading with the Corsicans. But as the situation of the Genoese continued to grow more desperate they concluded a
treaty with France which provided that for a period of four
years France would garrison the coastal strongholds still
held by Genoa (second treaty of Compiègne, 13 August

1764). In a letter to Buttafoco, Rousseau asked how Corsica under these circumstances could expect to form a stable government. (Buttafoco replied that France was only protecting Corsica.) To his friend Du Peyrou, Rousseau wrote: "My poor Corsicans are busy now with other matters than establishing a Utopia. . . . I still find it hard to believe that France is willing to call down on herself the censure of the world in handing over this unfortunate people to her butchers" (4 November 1764). To Alexandre Deleyre, who later showed the letter to Boswell, he expressed himself even more forcefully: "It must be owned that your countrymen, the French, are a very servile nation, a people thoroughly devoted to tyranny, exceedingly cruel and relentless in their pursuit of the unfortunate. If they knew of a free man at the other end of the world, I think they would go thither for the mere pleasure of exterminating him."[14]

Choiseul had meanwhile written to the Comte de Marbeuf, commander of the troops being sent to Corsica, acquainting him with what he was doing with Buttafoco: "In order to make the best use of his zeal I have judged it suitable to allow him to consider the reestablishment of the Royal Corsican Regiment in Corsica as depending on the efforts which he makes during his visit to the Island to recruit officers and national soldiers. . . . I have assured him that he would become the Commanding Colonel if the King has reason to be satisfied both with his political and with his military conduct during his sojourn in Corsica." Buttafoco's visit, it turned out, extended into 1768, interrupted only by trips to France "in the service of his Majesty." During this period he rose from captain to colonel, and in the summer of 1768 he was promised the rank of brigadier. What did this loyal Corsican and ambitious officer in the army of France hope to gain by asking Rousseau to become Corsica's lawgiver? Ernestine Dedeck-Héry finds the answer in Buttafoco's unsuccessful efforts to nullify the abridgements of the privileges of the nobility which were incorporated in the "Code of Paoli" —itself based upon the old Statutes of Corsica but now

modified to restrict further the powers and privileges of
both the nobility and clergy. Dedeck-Héry concludes that
Buttafoco hoped to obtain from Rousseau a "political constitution" which would favor the aristocracy.[15] It is not necessary to endow Buttafoco with such an excess of stupidity.
Anything that would weaken Paoli's irresistible authority,
that would provide a counterweight, a distraction, would
certainly have seemed desirable to him.

In the letter of introduction which Boswell printed at the
beginning of the *Tour*, Rousseau suggested that Boswell
present the letter to Buttafoco; if he were not to be found,
then directly to Paoli. Clearly Rousseau, despite clues in
Buttafoco's letters, still believed that Buttafoco had acted
from the beginning in concert with or at least with the full
knowledge of Paoli; and Boswell found no reason to think
otherwise. Later, when writing the final version of the
Tour, Boswell adopted from Burnaby the conclusion that
what Paoli "had principally in view was to employ the pen
of Rousseau in recording the heroic actions of the brave islanders" (p. 385).[16] As the years passed Boswell must have
regretted ascribing low and common practices of decep-
tion to Paoli. The subject does not arise in extant journals
and letters.

We are now ready, after nine or ten days of wearisome
travel up and down the mountain roads (*trails*, often) with
Boswell, to approach the village of Sollacarò. In Boswell's
conversations with "all sorts of people in the island" they
had represented Paoli to him "as something above humanity. . . . I almost wished yet to go back without seeing him"
(p. 314). What force could have kept Boswell from Paoli?
I shall not call attention to how Boswell the artist, author
of the *Tour*, modified his journal for publication, but like
the artist I shall try to keep the eye steadily upon the object.
Boswell presented a letter from Count Rivarola, the Corsican who was consul for Sardinia at Leghorn. "When he
had read it I showed him my letter from Rousseau. He was
polite, but very reserved. I had stood in the presence of
many a prince, but I never had such a trial as in the presence of Paoli. I have already said that he is a great physi-

ognomist. In consequence of his being in continual danger from treachery and assassination, he has formed a habit of studiously observing every new face. For ten minutes we walked backwards and forwards through the room, hardly saying a word, while he looked at me with a steadfast, keen and penetrating eye, as if he searched my very soul. This interview was for a while very severe upon me" (pp. 315–16). After an extravagant compliment comparing ancient Rome to modern Corsica, which Paoli neatly and sensibly turned aside, the General then went on to express "a high admiration of M. Rousseau, whom Signor Buttafoco had invited to Corsica to aid the nation in forming its laws" (p. 316).

The ten minutes, and more, are accounted for. Perhaps Boswell was "an espy"—the governments of Sardinia, Genoa, France, and Corsica watched his movements closely—but accommodating spies was a routine matter. The Rousseau-Buttafoco-Boswell connection, however, required examination and reflection. Boswell established an extremely important trait immediately. "A great physiognomist," possibly. What is certain from Paoli's letters and actions during this period is that he sized up people with remarkable penetration and accuracy when he observed or confronted them directly. No one in Corsica really succeeded in deceiving him. When his mind travelled outside Corsica, whether negotiating with Choiseul or interpreting the actions of the British king or parliament, it lost this critical ability. Abbé Rostini's faith expressed to Boswell, "We are not afraid that our General will deceive us, nor that he will let himself be deceived" (*Tour*, p. 338), was thus to prove warranted only in the first proposition.

These first paragraphs on Paoli reveal other aspects of Paoli's character. He knew how to keep silent, and he did not lie: he articulated no judgement on Buttafoco, whose meddling he knew he could turn to advantage through publicity should Rousseau come to the island; and for the Frenchman he expressed "high admiration," no doubt sincerely felt. The silence also conformed to a principle which Paoli during these years observed absolutely, that is, that

the Corsicans should present to the world the spectacle of
a people united in their determination to obtain freedom
and to govern themselves. Internal differences, if they
were revealed, were to be shown as completely under control within the democratic system.

Readers of Boswell's journals regret the loss of his records in Corsica, which were no doubt appropriated in the
process of "melting down" his materials into "one mass," a
process he wisely eschewed when writing the *Life of
Johnson.* The surviving outline shows that he rearranged
his journal materials freely, more to make a continuous,
unfolding presentation of Paoli's conversation than to organize individual character traits. A secondary purpose,
probably, was to give the impression of having spent more
than the actual eight or nine days in the General's company. ("Every day I felt myself happier. . . . One day I rode
out.") I shall now condense and categorize the materials,
for someone unlike Paoli frequently a life-destroying process; but the method will facilitate comparison and en-
hancement from other contemporary sources, as well as
supplementation and revision as Paoli grows older.

First, what struck the eye. "He is tall, strong, and well
made; of a fair complexion, a sensible, free, and open
countenance, and a manly and noble carriage. . . . He was
dressed in green and gold. He used to wear the common
Corsican habit, but on the arrival of the French he thought
a little external elegance might be of use to make the government appear in a more respectable light."[17] One day
Boswell rode out "mounted on Paoli's own horse with rich
furniture of crimson velvet with broad gold lace." On another occasion, after Paoli had quoted a line from Virgil
with "fine open Italian pronunciation," Boswell marked
the graceful dignity, the nobility of his manner, and
"wished to have a statue of him taken at that moment." So
should we. Boswell attempted to fill the need by sending to
Corsica in 1768 a young American artist, Henry Benbridge, to paint a portrait of Paoli. The statue Boswell had
desired, made of rubber and somewhat inflated, would appear to have been the subject of Benbridge's art. The

expressionless face (in mirror image) and top portion of the figure served the engraver for the frontispiece to the third edition of *Corsica* (May 1769). For more revealing portraits of Paoli, in words and in paint, we will have to wait for the general to become an exile in England, taking note only of young Goethe's description of Paoli when he passed through Germany: "[He was] a handsome, slender, light-complexioned man, full of grace and friendliness" (*Aus meinem Leben*).

Boswell wrote that Paoli smiled a good deal but hardly ever laughed. "I asked him how one of such elevated thoughts could submit with any degree of patience to the unmeaning ceremonies and poor discourse of genteel society, which he certainly was obliged to do while an officer at Naples. 'Oh,' said he, 'I managed it very easily. I was known to be a singular man. I talked and joked and was merry, but I never sat down to play; I went and came as I pleased. The mirth I like is what is easy and unaffected. I cannot long endure the sayers of good things.'" The smile, indicative of habitual composure and also an attitude of indulgence toward his new young friend from Scotland, could disappear in an instant. Dealing with one who had wavered in his loyalty, Paoli spoke "with the fierceness of a lion, and from the awful darkness of his brow one could see that his thoughts of vengeance were terrible. Yet when it was over he all at once resumed his usual appearance, called out 'Come along,' went to dinner, and was as cheerful and gay as if nothing had happened."

A later observation belongs here: "Though never familiar," Paoli has "the most perfect ease of behaviour." In public the General hits the proper mean between distant reserve and too easy familiarity, always with the appropriate degree of authority. "I have seen a crowd . . . with eagerness and impetuosity endeavouring to approach him, as if they would have burst into his apartment by force. In vain did the guards attempt to restrain them, but when he called to them in a tone of firmness, 'No audience now,' they were hushed at once." Boswell marvelled at his range of temperament. Though calm and fully master of himself, Paoli "is animated with an extraordinary degree of vivacity. Except when indisposed or greatly fatigued, he never sits down but at meals. He is perpetually in motion, walking briskly backwards and forwards. . . . Paoli told me that the vivacity of his mind was such that he could not study above ten minutes at a time. 'My head is like to break,' said he.[18] 'I can never write my lively ideas with my own hand. In writing, they escape from my mind. I call the Abbé Guelfucci, "Come quickly, take my thoughts," and he writes them.' "

The thoughts which teemed in Paoli's mind very likely concerned governmental, judiciary, economic, and educational matters. Readers of Boswell's earlier journals will be disposed to believe that the subjects discussed were in large part those Boswell wished to discuss, and there is no reason to believe this assumption untrue except for the fact that for the first and only time Boswell was observing closely a political leader in action, moving with already established momentum. Far from having a low opinion of politicians, Paoli believed that for him political leadership was the highest possible calling. To be sure, it is rather easy to identify some subjects as introduced by Boswell. Since Paoli was invariably courteous, patient, and obliging, the end result probably did not greatly differ from what Boswell would have secured had he been the stage manager.

First, then, Paoli's character, his basic principles and goals. "I asked him how he could possibly have a soul so superior to interest. 'It is not superior,' said he; 'my interest is to gain a name. I know well that he who does good to his country will gain that, and I expect it. I have an unspeakable pride [*una superbia indicibile*]. The approbation of my own heart is enough.' " Pride beyond the powers of expression and self-approbation the only guides—surely a sinful man; yet readers of the *Tour*, including John Wesley, found no sin in Paoli. Skipping ahead many pages, one finds an explanation. "He said the greatest happiness was not in glory but in goodness, and that Penn in his American colony where he had established a people in quiet and contentment, was happier than Alexander the Great after destroying multitudes at the conquest of Thebes." The tone persists to the last paragraph based upon the journal at Sollacarò:

> When I again asked Paoli if it was possible for me in any way to show him my great respect and attachment, he replied, "Remember that I am your friend, and write to me." I said I hoped that when he honoured me with a letter, he would write not only as a commander but as a philosopher and a man of letters. He took me by the hand and said, "As a friend." I dare not transcribe from my private notes the feelings which I had at this interview. I should perhaps appear too enthusiastic. I took leave of Paoli with regret and agitation, not without some hopes of seeing him again. From having known intimately so exalted a character, my sentiments of human nature were raised; while by a sort of contagion I felt an honest ardour to distinguish myself, and be useful as far as my situation and abilities would allow; and I was, for the rest of my life, set free from a slavish timidity in the presence of great men, for where shall I find a man greater than Paoli?

Paoli's notions of morality were "high and refined, such as become the Father of a nation. Were he a libertine his influence would soon vanish. He told me . . . he had very seldom deviated from the paths of virtue." Boswell later tried the ploy which had worked on Rousseau with unexpected results. "I ventured to reason like a libertine, that I might be confirmed in virtuous principles by so illustrious a preceptor. I made light of moral feelings. I argued that conscience was vague and uncertain, that there was hardly any vice but what men might be found who have been guilty of it without remorse. 'But,' said he, 'there is no man who has not a horror at some vice. Different vices and different virtues have the strongest impression on different men, but virtue in the abstract is the food of our hearts.'"

On religion Boswell makes Paoli appear conventional. "One day at dinner he gave us the principal arguments for the being and attributes of God." And later: "Talking of Providence, he said to me with that earnestness with which a man speaks who is anxious to be believed: 'I tell you on the word of an honest man, it is impossible for me not to be persuaded that God interposes to give freedom to Corsica. A people oppressed like the Corsicans are certainly worthy of divine assistance. When we were in the most desperate circumstances I never lost courage, trusting as I did in Providence.' I ventured to object; 'But why has not Providence interposed sooner?" He replied with a noble, serious, and devout air, ' Because His ways are unsearchable. I adore Him for what He hath done. I revere Him in what He hath not done.'" Paoli's religion will be returned to periodically. On a related subject Boswell raises a question difficult to answer. Paoli in his dreams or "visions" has "at times extraordinary impressions of distant and future events. . . . I can give you no clear explanation of it," the General tells Boswell. "I only tell you facts. Sometimes I have been mistaken, but in general these visions have proved true. I cannot say what may be the agency of invisible spirits. They certainly must know more than we do, and there is nothing absurd in supposing that God should permit them to communicate their knowledge to us." When Boswell investigated he found that this power of the General's was universally believed in Corsica. "It may be said that the General has industriously propagated this opinion in order that he might have more authority in civilizing a rude and ferocious people. . . . But I cannot allow myself to suppose that Paoli ever required the aid of pious frauds." In the absence of other comment by eighteenth-century writers and of later references in Boswell's journals, one must here let the matter rest as it concerns Paoli. Boswell's intense interest in second sight and related phenomena continued during his life.

Other views are even more clearly responses to Boswell—for example, those on sex, love, and marriage. Boswell's reasoning "like a libertine" has been related. Should the commander of a nation be married? Paoli asks now. "If he is married there is a risk that he may be distracted by private affairs and swayed too much by a concern for his family. If he is unmarried, there is a risk that not having the tender attachments of a wife and children, he may sacrifice all to his own ambition. . . . I have not the conjugal virtues. Nothing would tempt me to marry but a woman who should bring me an immense dowry, with which I might assist my country." But Paoli spoke much in praise of marriage, and Boswell was persuaded that had he been a private gentleman he would have married and proved "as good a husband and father as he does a supreme magistrate and a general. . . . He is wedded to his country, and the Corsicans are his children."

Boswell throughout his life suffered from the "Family Hypochondria," and did not exaggerate when he told the General of his "anxious speculations" which sometimes led to a kind of paralysis of the will. "All this," said Paoli, "is melancholy. I also studied metaphysics. I know the arguments for fate and free will, for the materiality and immateriality of the soul, and even the subtle arguments for and against the existence of matter. But let us leave these disputes to the idle. I hold always firm one great object. I never feel a moment of despondency."

The General, Boswell remarks, "has the best part of the classics by heart, and he has a happy talent in applying them with propriety, which is rarely to be found." In the *Tour* Boswell makes only a beginning in documenting this assertion, but in his *Life* and journal, and in various diaries and letters by those who later met Paoli in England, the General's knowledge of literature extending from Homer through Dante to Shakespeare takes on dimensions which can only be called extraordinary in view of what we now know of the limitations of his formal schooling.

Of the ancient languages Paoli apparently knew Latin but not Greek, his familiarity with such authors as Homer and Thucydides (see *Life*, II, 330–31) probably having been derived from translations into Latin or Italian. Of the modern languages Italian was his native tongue, it having been the official language of the island for some hundreds of years, as French is now. His original facility was necessarily improved while he spent his youth and early manhood as an exile in Italy. Paoli also undoubtedly had sufficient mastery of the native dialects, today called Corse. During the first hour or two of their meeting Paoli spoke

to Boswell in French (though it is difficult to believe that
Boswell didn't greet him in Italian). After dinner he spoke
Italian, in which, Boswell observed, "he is very eloquent."
The running outline, and to a lesser degree the published
Tour, show that Paoli used French whenever he felt that
Boswell could not get the full meaning of what he wished
to say in Italian. After his departure from Corsica in 1769
Paoli perforce wrote and spoke French most of the time,
although he was never fully at ease in that language. In
1790 his speech to the French National Assembly was to
bring that body to its feet wildly cheering; yet one of his last
letters in French, that to George III, 26 July 1797, is characterized by nonnative structure and idiom.[19]

When Boswell asked Paoli if he understood English, "he
immediately began and spoke it, which he did tolerably
well. When at Naples, he had known several Irish gentlemen who were officers in that service. Having a great facility in acquiring languages, he learnt English from them."
If we are to judge from Fanny Burney, in Paoli's English
accent the Italian wholly prevailed over the Hibernian.
Boswell, "diverted" by Paoli's small English library, promised to send him some English books.[20] Although he never
achieved high proficiency in speaking or writing English,
Paoli's capacity to read and to understand spoken English
permitted him to be an active observer of happenings in
England via letter and periodical, and to participate fully
in conversation when he went into exile. Of course, what
he heard in English he usually replied to in French if he
judged the listeners easily capable of understanding him.
Boswell in the *Tour* relates that he had drawn up a memorial on the advantages to Great Britain from an alliance
with Corsica, which Paoli translated into Italian "with the
greatest facility. He has since given me more proofs of his
knowledge of our tongue by his answers to the letters
which I have had the honour to write to him in English,
and in particular by a very judicious and ingenious
criticism on some of Swift's works."[21] According to Boswell,
Paoli was well acquainted with the history of Britain, had
read many of the parliamentary debates, "and had even
seen a number of the North Briton."

There now remains the task of abstracting from the *Tour* Paoli's view of his role, his ambitions for his people, and his means of achieving them. Paoli's supreme aim was to lead his nation to independence and his people to individual self-reliance. No compromise: "*There* is my object! (pointing to the summit). If I fall, I fall at least *there* (pointing a good way up)." Would he quit the island supposing a foreign power should create him Marischal and make him governor of a province? "I hope they will believe I am more honest, or more ambitious; for, to accept of the highest offices under a foreign power would be to serve. To have been a colonel, a general, or a marshal would have been sufficient for my table, for my taste in dress, for the beauty whom my rank would have entitled me to attend. But it would not have been sufficient for this spirit, for this imagination (putting his hand upon his bosom)." "We may," he said on another occasion, "have foreign powers for our friends, but they must be friends at arm's length. We may make an alliance, but we will not submit ourselves to the dominion of the greatest nation in Europe. This people who have done so much for liberty would be hewn in pieces man by man rather than allow Corsica to be sunk into the territories of another country." Boswell, whose imagination in Corsica frequently ran unchecked, mentioned the possibility of an alliance with Great Britain. "Paoli with politeness and dignity waived the subject by saying, 'The less assistance we have from allies, the greater the glory.' He seemed hurt by our treatment of his country. He mentioned the severe proclamation of the last peace, in which the brave islanders were called the rebels of Corsica. He said with a conscious pride and proper feeling, 'Rebels! I did not expect that from Great Britain.'" Paoli was well aware of the fact that history is written by the victors. Talking of the Corsican war he said, "If the event shall prove happy, we shall be called great defenders of liberty. If the event shall prove unhappy, we shall be called unfortunate rebels."

Paoli was justifiably confident in suggesting that Boswell go among the people. "This great man whom God hath sent to free our country," was what they called their General. Corsican bravery was legendary, but the reader is aware that bravery often depends upon the leader who inspires it. "If," said Paoli, "I should lead into the field an army of Corsicans against an army double their number, let me speak a few words to the Corsicans to remind them of the honour of their country and of their brave forefathers—I do not say that they would conquer, but I am sure that not a man of them would give way. The Corsicans have a steady resolution that would amaze you. I wish you could see one of them die."

Whether from zeal or calculation Paoli had developed the talent made noteworthy in this century by Postmaster-General Farley, who was said to be able to address by name every Democratic politician in the United States. "I was assured," wrote Boswell, that Paoli "knows the names of almost all the people in the Island, their characters, and their connections." As for these individual Corsicans, Paoli said "his great object was to form the Corsicans in such a manner that they might have a firm constitution, and might be able to subsist without him. 'Our state,' said he, 'is young, and still requires the leading strings. I am desirous that the Corsicans should be taught to walk of themselves. Therefore when they come to me to ask whom they should choose for the Padre del Commune or other magistrate, I tell them, "You know better than I do the able and honest men among your neighbours. Consider the consequences of your choice, not only to yourselves in particular but to the Island in general." In this manner I accustom them to feel their own importance as members of the state.'"

The democratic principles upon which Paoli founded his government were not strictly egalitarian. Those who wished to look upon the General as an advanced champion of the Enlightenment found further cause to be disturbed by the Corsican practice of using torture to extract confessions from suspected criminals. These subjects would not have found their way into the *Tour* but for Boswell's fascination with condemned criminals and, in this case, with their hangman. Not being able to find a native willing to accept the disgraceful occupation of hangman, the Corsicans often were forced merely to shoot the condemned instead of doing away with them properly. One fellow awaiting his trial had been put to the torture, Boswell noted, "by having lighted matches held between his fingers. . . . His hands were so miserably scorched that he was a piteous object." Later, after Boswell had been for some days at Sollacarò, news came that the poor wretch "had consented to accept of his life upon condition of becoming hangman. This made a great noise among the Corsicans, who were enraged at the creature and said their nation was now disgraced. Paoli did not think so. He said to me, 'I am glad of this. It will be of service. It will contribute to form us to a just subordination. We have as yet too great an equality among us. As we must have Corsican tailors and Corsican shoemakers, we must also have a Corsican Hangman.'"

After the establishment of order in Corsican society, diversified economic development and schools and the university came next (*Account,* Chap. 3). As for the arts and sciences, "we are now to our country like the prophet Elisha stretched over the dead child of the Shunamite, eye to eye, nose to nose, mouth to mouth. It begins to recover warmth and to revive. I hope it shall yet regain full health and vigour. . . . The arts and sciences are like dress and ornament. You cannot expect them from us for some time. But come back twenty or thirty years hence, and we'll show you arts and sciences, and concerts and assemblies, and fine ladies, and we'll make you fall in love among us, Sir." The last comment shows that the process of personal exploration had been proceeding in both directions.

What could Boswell do in return for all Paoli's kindness? "Only undeceive your Court. Tell them what you have seen here. They will be curious to ask you. A man from Corsica will be like a man come from the Antipodes." These words rang in Boswell's ears during the next four years. Paoli's request reflected not merely the wish that England recognize the reality of Corsica's power and self-sufficiency and thus repeal at least on technical grounds the proclamation of 1763. There is in it the expression of convictions which during the next few years were to die only after his unremitting mental and spiritual efforts failed to sustain them. Good, rational persons everywhere would respond to a people's desire to escape subjugation and establish a free society; further, England would see that even the most narrow interpretation of self-interest dictated support for Corsican independence.

So much for Boswell's portrait of Paoli in the *Tour*. Certainly Boswell is "enthusiastic." Also, there are perhaps some lines inaccurately sketched, some features and shadows omitted. What must be clear is the source of Paoli's power over his people. His were not the arts of the demagogue; he did not promise more than was attainable, did not speak out of one side or the other of his mouth as circumstance indicated. He was, on the insular level, a good political tactician and (barely suggested by Boswell) he could use tightly reasoned argument and, when necessary, withering sarcasm to make the opposition take cover. But beyond all else he appealed as a leader through sheer moral force. He was trusted, absolutely.

As for omissions, only one is of moment here, the quality of Paoli's military abilities, which Boswell for good reason barely deals with in the *Account*. Paoli's battles, whether against Genoese or unreclaimed Corsicans, had been small-scale skirmishes, usually near mountain trails or ravines, in which surprise and above all courage were the decisive elements. Brother Clemente at the head of a relatively small band more than once sent the foe scattering. Against large entrenched military forces such as the Genoese established on the coast, little was attempted. When the Genoese felt themselves in danger, as noted earlier, they called in the French. The main trials by force for Paoli were yet to come, and in them he was to prove sometimes successful, sometimes not. He was basically a textbook general, not experienced in assuming or in delegating the details of field command. For the critical defeat by the French at Ponte Nuovo, 8 May 1769, Paoli must bear the ultimate responsibility—although the factors of betrayal by subordinates through bribery by the French, never fully determined, cannot be weighed wholly against him.

CHAPTER II

STRUGGLE AGAINST FRANCE

Boswell on his return to Italy lost no time in publicizing his own special position as an authority on Corsica and in preparing the way for what was to become a campaign to enlist British support for the Corsican cause. These actions have been recounted elsewhere.[1] The propaganda campaign mounted on behalf of the Corsicans is, I believe, unparalleled in extent and effect when considered as the achievement of an individual. (Governments and large public relations firms may have done as well since.) When, in October 1768, Lord Holland exclaimed, "Foolish as we are, we cannot be so foolish as to go to war because Mr. Boswell has been to Corsica," he undoubtedly believed he was indulging in a bit of sarcastic exaggeration; but he was actually close to the true reason for the belligerent mutterings in London.

Leaving public relations and propaganda, I will concentrate on political developments as they affected Paoli. Here too Boswell enters the story briefly. Shortly after arriving in London he sought an interview with William Pitt. It was not political shrewdness which led Boswell to address Pitt rather than the Ministry. He could not have known that George III had appealed to Pitt three times since his resignation in 1761, and each time had failed to persuade him to return to office; that the Rockingham Ministry was soon to become ineffective; and that Pitt in some five months would form a ministry again. But Boswell did know that Pitt was the one public figure who in the eyes of the Corsicans (as of the Americans) could serve as champion of freedom. Moreover, Pitt had humbled France and had opposed the peace which permitted that nation fully to exercise the power which was so evident in Genoa and Corsica. Pitt answered from Hayes (16 February 1766), expressing doubts as to the propriety of receiving com-

munications from Paoli, but in a tone which certainly could
not discourage Boswell, who replied (19 February) that he
would wait upon "the prime minister of the brave" at the
first convenience.

On the morning of 22 February 1766 Boswell directed
his steps to the Duke of Grafton's house in Bond Street. He
probably did not know—for he first appeared at the door
at 9 a.m. and had to return later—that early in the morning
Pitt's carriage had been followed from the House of
Commons by mobs cheering the man who, more than anyone else, had finally accomplished the repeal of the Stamp
Act. Considering that Pitt was ill with the gout and that the
debate itself had lasted until half-past one, the old man was
in good form. He pointed out that since his resignation he
had known no more of what had been doing in the Cabinet
than the most remote man in the kingdom. "I know not
what Genoa has been able to obtain by means of France.
I—"

> BOSWELL. "Sir, that, the General—Paoli—felt severely: to be
> given into the bargain that poor Corsica should be con-
> sidered as nothing." PITT. "Mr. Boswell, I own it appears
> strange that an island of so great consequence to the
> navigation in the Mediterranean should be neglected. How
> are their harbours?" BOSWELL. "One or two excellent, with
> some expense." PITT. "Sir, that is of great consequence to a
> fleet on some grand enterprise. We have no such place in
> Italy." BOSWELL. "Sir, General de Paoli said—" PITT. "Sir,
> you'll remember my situation." BOSWELL. "Pray, Sir, may I
> ask you if you never received a letter from General de
> Paoli?" PITT. "Never, Sir," BOSWELL. "Why, then Sir, after the
> Proclamation, he wrote to you, and, as he has the highest
> admiration of your character, he was most sensibly hurt to
> be neglected by Mr. Pitt." PITT. "Sir, I never received his let-
> ter. I suppose *those next the King* have taken care it should
> not be delivered. I could not have answered it—could not
> have been in correspondence with General de Paoli, but I
> should have taken care to let him know my regard for him.
> Sir, I should be sorry that in any corner of the world, how-
> ever distant or however small, it should be suspected that I
> could ever be indifferent to the cause of liberty."

Pitt spoke of Paoli as "one of those men who are no longer
to be found but in the *Lives* of Plutarch." His question

concerning harbors and his reference to some grand enterprise were quite encouraging, granting that at some future time he would return to a position of power. Further, he demonstrated a knowledge of the realities in Corsica's situation, noting that Genoa was "not only under the protection of France but under the thumb of France."[2]

During the period following Boswell's visit Paoli continued to use "the season of tranquillity to the best purpose, in preparing for future schemes of victory, and giving perfection and stability to the civil constitution of his country" (*Account,* p. 170). The French occupation of the coastal strongholds provided obstacles which no "schemes of victory" could expect to overcome; but the Corsicans still hoped that something would happen as a consequence of the "Determinations" of October 1764, in which they particularly applied "to the powers favourable to Corsica, that they might employ their mediation with the French king, in order to preserve to the nation its rights, prerogatives, liberty and independency" (*Account,* pp. 169–70). The French for their part were fastidiously correct in their behavior.

Paoli appeared to have more confidence concerning his country's future than circumstances warranted. Certainly, if Boswell did succeed in "undeceiving" the British court with the consequent repeal of the proclamation of 1763, the stigma of "rebels" would be removed from Paoli's government and it would thus be granted a kind of legitimacy. However, though there was a good deal of bustle in the newspapers, Paoli received no official messages of encouragement from the north. Meanwhile, as the French Prime Minister, Choiseul, perceived, time was running against Paoli. That Corsica figured largely in Choiseul's schemes he did not reveal to anyone until the appropriate time arrived—and then only to the degree which served his purpose at the moment. As early as 1735 France had developed a plan for the ultimate annexation of Corsica, either by cession or purchase from Genoa, with the concurrence if not the enthusiastic support of a significant party within Corsica.[3] Choiseul possibly knew of this secret

earlier plan, but he needed neither prompting nor guid-
ance for his designs. With the passage of time the cost of
French occupation would transform Genoa from creditor
of France to debtor. The Genoese, unable to pay the debt,
would be forced to yield Corsica as security. Meanwhile, if
the Genoese should show dissatisfaction with this bargain,
Choiseul could remove French troops from appropriate
areas (as he was to do in 1767) to persuade the frightened
Genoese that they had no alternative. With nothing to lose,
Choiseul began "negotiations" with Paoli. As he saw them,
if they were successful on his terms, good; if unsuccessful,
they would on any account make the Genoese aware of
their utter dependence on France. Possibly, too, such
bogus negotiations would keep Paoli quiet and still the
spirit of independence.

Paoli's views on the French occupation, 1764–68, developed through four phases. At first, he believed that the
French would leave after the treaty term of four years, or
even earlier, exposing the coastal territories to relatively
easy conquest by the Corsicans. Diversions by Choiseul
during this period were his offers to "mediate" between
Corsica and Genoa. In the second phase, Paoli realized
that France would insist on holding some places even after
the treaty with Genoa had expired. Paoli's failure to show
flexibility during this phase would be more culpable were
it not for Choiseul's habit of adding to his demands in each
exchange, finally stating that France would choose its own
places—to be held permanently—and notifying Paoli that
he would do well to be guided completely by the wishes of
the good King. In the third phase, marked by rumors of
permanent cession to France of Genoa's rights to Corsica,
Paoli feared, correctly as it turned out, that France would
resort to assassination and bribery (money and titles) to
create confusion and subvert the Corsican government,
forming in its place one which would acknowledge
France's sovereignty. At this time Paoli asked help from
many countries—from England apparently indirectly
through Rivarola—but received assistance only from
Holland and Sardinia. He believed that though the people

would remain loyal and would resist, they needed some
tangible signs of outside support. Choiseul, when faced
with evidence of the possible success of Paoli's strategy,
embarked upon the fourth and final phase: France now
would take over all of Corsica by whatever means were
necessary. The first two phases stretched over three years;
the next two passed with unexpected acceleration.

In a letter to Paoli dated 21 May 1765 the French Prime
Minister clearly hinted that if Paoli would accede to the
wishes of the King and send an envoy to France to negotiate a peaceful settlement between Corsica and Genoa,
either he or his brother would be made colonel of the Royal Corsican regiment in the French army.[4] Choiseul saw
nothing to lose in this clumsy attempt at bribery, which
Paoli of course refused. Choiseul waited almost a year
before resuming negotiations, on this occasion notifying
Paoli (18 March 1766) that Genoa had agreed to accept the
King as mediator in the formation of a treaty. Still nothing
was done towards a settlement for yet another year—until
the spring of 1767—possibly because in the govenment of
the only country which could thwart Choiseul's plans,
England, changes had taken place which Choiseul and
Paoli alike viewed as portentous; on 29 July 1766 George
III signed a warrant creating William Pitt the Earl of
Chatham, and on the following day Chatham kissed hands
for the Privy Seal. Pitt, whose ill health would not allow
him to attend regularly in the Commons, had chosen thus
to take no office of business but as the Earl of Chatham and
Lord Privy Seal to direct his Administration from a seat in
the Lords. The acceptance of the peerage and the political
arrangement disturbed many partisans of liberty, but permitted others to find cause for rejoicing.

Paoli wrote to Burnaby (4 October 1766), asking for
copies of Pitt's speeches on the Stamp Act and of any other
speeches which he might make as Minister in the process
of setting the ship of state on course. "The fact that Mr. Pitt
has become an Earl will surely have considerably diminished the confidence of the people, but he may have
gained a proportionate amount of it in the mind of the

King, and with this equilibrium he could better and more
easily serve his country." Paoli also expressed a wish to
subscribe to English periodicals. Then in a letter to John
Dick (6 December 1766), a copy of which Dick forwarded
to Boswell, Paoli wrote:

> Now that the Earl of Chatham is in the Ministry, I venture
> to hope for good success to Mr. Boswell's generous concern
> in revoking the injurious Proclamation of 1763. That sub-
> lime genius of Great Britain, and that great spirit, will find
> in his own sentiments and in his own political views the most
> efficacious motives for causing his Court to emerge from its
> state of indifference to the affairs of Corsica.

At about the same time as the last letter, on 5 December
1766, Paoli wrote to Burnaby indicating that the hitherto
cordial relations with the French were deteriorating, and
that war with Genoa was probable when the French left in
1768. In a move of which Boswell apparently was not advised, Paoli also addressed a letter directly to Chatham
asking for English aid.[5]

As was to be expected, the incisive analysis was made by
Choiseul. "We cannot understand Lord Chatham's design
in leaving the House of Commons," he wrote to his minister in London. "All his power consisted in his remaining
within that House; he may well find himself like Samson
with his hair shorn." Nevertheless Choiseul displayed
characteristic caution. "What we must fear is that proud
and ambitious man, having lost the people's esteem, may
wish to redeem his reputation by feats of war." In the final
analysis, however, the English Ministry would not be
stronger than before. France could still count on inner
stresses and on "the ineptness of Mr. Conway, the youth
and perhaps the thoughtlessness of Lord Shelburne." Lord
Chatham, he concluded, was too heavily handicapped
within to undertake foreign ventures.[6] Despite this conclusion Choiseul suspended all activities which might
arouse his old antagonist, including the "negotiations" with
Paoli.

Boswell had not waited to be stirred into action. On 18
September 1766 he wrote a short letter to Chatham, asking

him to "befriend a noble and unfortunate little Nation."
When three months had passed without an answer he
again wrote (3 January 1767), taking pains to include a
passage from one of Paoli's letters: "Public report exalts
Mr. Pitt's talents to the stars, but the report you give me of
the conversation you had with him fills me with even
greater admiration and love for the goodness of heart of
this Pericles of Great Britain."

Boswell knew very little about Chatham's current views
or his physical condition. In the previous month Burke
had tauntingly called the Earl "an invisible deity," and soon
thereafter Chatham became invisible in fact; neither the
King nor Chatham's hapless lieutenant in the Ministry, the
Duke of Grafton, was able to communicate with him satisfactorily. Frustrations of his policies at home and abroad,
added to real infirmities (his gout at least was real), had led
to his withdrawal. By early March 1767 he was "like a man
on a death-bed," and, though few realized it at the time,
this period virtually marked the end of his Administration.
Grafton carried on—at times unwillingly—the ministry still
given Chatham's name.[7] Boswell should have considered
himself lucky when he received a note from the Earl dated
at Bath, 4 February 1767; but lucky or not he clearly found
no comfort in the message: "I see not the least ground at
present for this country to interfere with any justice in the
affairs of Corsica."

The hopes aroused by the accession of Chatham were
not unreasonable. Certainly Paoli was wise enough to recognize that France would require some nudging to get out,
and everything he knew about Chatham made appropriate
English pressure more than a likelihood. All this while
Choiseul retreated into silence, a good omen. A very bad
omen, Chatham's letter to Boswell expressing his view that
he saw "not the least ground," etc., one may be sure was not
relayed to the General. In fact, the extent of the process of
decay within the Chatham Administration was apparently
not communicated to Paoli for many months; thus, in the
period after Choiseul renewed negotiations in March 1767
Paoli resisted and made counteroffers.

The exact moment when the Corsicans actually lost their chance for independence passed some time in 1767. It is temptingly easy to say that Corsica's fate was sealed when the Bedford party finally came into the Ministry at the end of the year, but as usual searches into causes cannot be final. Perhaps the blame should fall on the Rockinghams—who might energetically have opposed the ambition of France—because they earlier had asked too high a price to enter the Ministry. But negotiations with the Rockinghams and the Bedfords would not have been necessary had Chatham not become so seriously enfeebled. The reader must look elsewhere for accounts and analyses of these matters.[8]

After marking time during the first period of Chatham's Ministry, Choiseul on 23 March 1767 wrote to Paoli that if Corsica wanted its freedom it would have to compensate Genoa, either by leaving the title of King of Corsica to Genoa, or by paying homage each year to Genoa as the King of Naples did to the Pope. If Corsica did not wish to purchase its freedom from Genoa in this way it might accept the alternative of agreeing upon a suspension of arms for ten or fifteen years. In any case, Choiseul added significantly, France would retain a place in Corsica. Soon after, Choiseul removed some of the troops from the island in order to keep the Genoese in a proper state of mind.[9] Genoa, sufficiently frightened, proposed to divide Corsica three ways, between France, Genoa, and the rebels; but Choiseul in his secret negotiations with the republic held to his plan of unconditional cession.[10]

Paoli weighed Choiseul's proposals seriously. In a memorandum dated 3 June 1767 he offered to give France Bonifacio in trust. To this Choiseul replied that France would choose its own places in Corsica and would control them outright.[11] In the next few exchanges Paoli persisted in making proposals on the assumption that France had no desire for permanent possessions in Corsica. "It is not natural," Choiseul wrote in exasperation, "for you to think that his Majesty would get involved in the affairs of Corsica without deriving an advantage; now this advantage can be

no other than that of retaining some places which are useful to the navigation of his subjects" (20 October 1767). In
vain Paoli offered to give France military custody of Bastia
and San Fiorenzo; France would have nothing less than
permanent possession of the cities of Bastia and San
Fiorenzo and the territory of Capo Corso. In a memorandum dated 28 February 1768, after assuring the French
King of his respect and attachment, Paoli wrote that it
would be impossible to continue negotiations if his Majesty
persisted in his demands, since the General Consulta at
Casinca of 1761 had solemnly sworn to accept no treaty
which did not have as its basis the liberty and independence of the entire island.

Choiseul, with characteristic cunning, continued to
move swiftly, the collapse of the negotiations with Paoli not
causing him to break his purposeful stride in the slightest.
Certainly he had been encouraged by the virtual breakdown of the Chatham ministry during the second half of
1767. In a letter to his representative in London dated
4 October 1767 he rejoiced in the troubles within the English Ministry, and expressed hope that the state of anarchy
would "last a century." At the same time he feared a return
of Grenville, not because of his views but because of his
ability to solve the financial problems of his country and
thus make it capable of waging war.[12] The entry into the
Cabinet of the Duke of Bedford, whom Choiseul had
found a sympathetic negotiator in arriving at the Peace of
Paris, was reassuring, and perhaps accounted for the increasing firmness of tone in the negotiations with Paoli.
Buttafoco, who as an intermediary had transmitted Paoli's
memorandum of 28 February 1768 to Choiseul, suggested
to the French Minister that he be satisfied with taking
Bastia and San Fiorenzo. The Corsicans, he thought,
would finally reconcile themselves to this state of affairs.[13]
Buttafoco was as innocent as Choiseul's intended victims.
The fears of the Genoese that France might abandon Corsica, and thus expose it to possible occupation by the Corsicans or even by a hostile great power, had now been
cultivated until they approached hysteria. On 4 March

1768 Sorba, the Genoese Minister at Versailles, urged Louis XV to take the island *in toto*. He repeated the request three more times in the next eight days, the last in the form of a memorial.[14]

Choiseul's frame of mind is fully revealed in the letter he now wrote to Buttafoco:

> I send you, Sir, my answer for General Paoli; his letter was nothing but an attempt to catch me in a trap; he is shrewd, but he must acquire still more cunning for us to fall so grossly into his snares; besides, in the present circumstances I believe that the best decision he can make is to remain calm and to follow in all things the wishes of France.
>
> I doubt that he will come to this decision, and in that case *I pity him*; what is certain is that he has missed the opportunity which I have so many times offered him.[15]

What Choiseul might have done had Paoli accepted his terms can only be conjectured. Paoli himself later expressed the belief that Choiseul had never been sincere, and that he negotiated with the Corsicans only to frighten the Genoese into the cessions which he finally obtained.[16] Paoli's surmise is substantiated by papers in French archives.

Well before the treaty of 1764 neared its time of expiration, then, Choiseul had reduced Genoa to the role of suppliant and Paoli to an obstacle well hemmed in. As for the British, his first very simple objective was to delay the time of revelation of French intentions until the last possible moment. Spy scares—for example, one occasioned by the report that an Englishman had taken soundings in the harbor at Ajaccio and then delivered a packet to Paoli—caused Choiseul to intensify his vigilance. He ordered Châtelet, his ambassador to England, to watch England's actions carefully, for "not only would we not suffer England to involve herself in the arrangements . . . with the Republic of Genoa, but even if it is not a question of negotiating about Corsica, it is impossible for the King to permit an English establishment at Ajaccio."[17].

British intelligence, like that of the French, was on the whole first-rate. Actions upon receipt of intelligence, however, contrasted markedly between the two countries. In

March 1768 Sir Horace Mann, British Minister to
Tuscany, sent a report from Florence warning that Genoa
was prepared to cede Corsica to France.[18] In England,
Lord Shelburne questioned Châtelet; and in France the
British Ambassador, Rochford, obtained an interview with
Choiseul. Both Frenchmen professed ignorance of any
new actions planned with respect to Corsica.[19] Shelburne
of course knew better, but up to a point he had to follow
the game's rules. On 6 May he removed the mask, summoned Châtelet and warned him that the acquisition of
Corsica by France would disturb the harmony between the
two nations. Châtelet pleaded ignorance, expressed a
strong attachment to harmony, and then went on to comment that in any case the affair was purely one between
France and Genoa. Shelburne called attention to the fact
that Article Fifteen of the Treaty of Aix-la-Chapelle guaranteed the status quo, but Châtelet replied that this applied to Italy only at the time the peace was made.
Shelburne warned that England could not view the annexation of Corsica with indifference.[20]

Choiseul now sent Châtelet a very precise plan of argument. He was to inform Shelburne that he had been ordered by the King to explain the whole affair. First, the
Treaty of Aix-la-Chapelle had no application. As to the
convention then being negotiated between France and
Genoa, it was similar to those drawn up between the republic and the Emperor, and between the republic and
France, in 1727, 1737, 1756, and 1764, to which no power
in Europe had made objections. Its purpose was simply to
keep for Genoa its places in Corsica. The *rumors* of annexation came from the stipulation in the convention that the
King was to be reimbursed for the expenses of the troops.
Rochford had meanwhile asked for authority to demand of
Choiseul a clear account of France's intentions. This authority was not immediately granted, for the Council was
too much taken up, as Shelburne put it, with a "tumultuous
spirit" which had shown itself "among the different classes
of the lower sort of people" after the Middlesex election.
Finally, on 27 May, Shelburne sent Rochford the decision

of Council, in which Rochford was authorized to state as
the opinion of his Majesty, "The extension of territory,
force or possessions of any of the great powers of Europe
cannot be a matter of indifference to their neighbors and
may consequently endanger the peace of Europe."[21]

To Choiseul, Rochford communicated the views of his
country with great firmness. The Corsican expedition, he
said, was one which "by far the greatest part of the nation"
looked upon as a violation of the Treaty of Aix-
la-Chapelle. Choiseul explained that there was no expedition, no thought of war, for which everyone knew France
was unprepared. (The British were acting upon intelligence, which embarrassed by anticipating action.)
Rochford continued by explaining that the English people
had a deep sympathy for the cause of the Corsicans. At this
point, reported Rochford, Choiseul "interrupted me, and
said he knew it; that Boswell's *Account of Corsica* had made
a great noise; that he had ordered it to be translated here,
and that it would soon be published. This by the way,"
added Rochford, "can be with no other intent than to show
the French of what importance Corsica is." Choiseul continued his explanation "in the utmost confidence." He
owned that by the terms of the treaty between Genoa and
France [15 May 1768], which he would show Rochford as
soon as it was ratified, France was to take possession of the
places in Corsica which the Genoese had formerly gar-
risoned. As soon as the Genoese repaid France for the expenses already incurred and those to be incurred, Genoa
would be presented with its former territories. Choiseul
cheerfully conceded, however, that "he believed the Genoese would not only never be able to reimburse them, but
never intended it." The Genoese "absolutely refused to
treat with Paoli, and he with them." Now France would
treat with Paoli, but with little hope of success, as appeared
from a letter Choiseul had lately received from Paoli and
from the messages and accounts he had received from
Paoli's emissary, one Buttafoco. However, France had
"assured Paoli they would not molest him in his present
possessions." Rochford asked about secret provisions in the

treaty. Choiseul replied that there were two secret articles, which at some future time he would allow Rochford to read. Had he foreseen how England would be disposed towards the affair, he added, he would never have undertaken it; but now the treaty was about to be signed and ten battalions had been sent to reinforce the garrisons. To retreat now would injure his and his country's honor.

The amiable Choiseul assured Rochford that "I might depend upon it, he would never deceive me; and that if war should ever be their design I should know it as soon as he did." As Rochford neared the end of his report he demonstrated the value of having an agent holding converse with the enemy:

> All the reflections I have to make upon this are that it is clear they mean to keep for themselves the places the Genoese have in Corsica, but if they do not come to some agreement with Paoli, which does not appear likely, the troops they send are not sufficient to get the better of the Corsican Chief. As for having any other hostile intentions, I cannot believe it; peace is certainly their present object. The very alarm the whole French nation is at this moment in, is a strong voucher how much they dread a war, and it may be added that the Duke of Choiseul is personally interested to prevent it.[22]

Shelburne of course knew better; but Choiseul had been doing his work well. One measure is the fact that Rochford's estimate of France's situation and view of its intentions exactly coincided, as we shall see, with Paoli's at the time. Shelburne's having taken the Ministry with him so far as to occasion the strong statement delivered by Rochford, however, did cause Choiseul to hesitate before taking a final step. The French Corsican policy was of his own creation, unsupported by sentiment at home. If France were to be drawn into a serious quarrel with England his enemies would take the opportunity to force his retirement and to repudiate his policies.[23] He temporized, waiting for party divisions in England to develop more fully. As he had observed in a letter to Châtelet on 23 May 1768, the English, despite their domestic strife, would probably become united by a foreign war; but, he continued with satisfaction, the Ministry was too feeble to resort to this dangerous remedy.[24]

Choiseul had been relying upon the Bedford group, whose policy was one of peace with France and Spain and of vigorous measures against the discontented elements in America and England. When, as has just been noted, the first Cabinet Council on the affairs of Corsica took an unexpectedly firm stand, Choiseul wrote to Châtelet with some anxiety:

> I must remind you how essential it is you should keep a vigilant lookout upon the movements of the English navy, in order that we may be apprised in time. Above all, you must employ all your ability to produce the impression that the King is seriously desirous of maintaining peace. . . . Say to the Duke of Bedford, we cannot possibly imagine that at a moment when he is and ought to be at the helm of English affairs he would possibly permit a miserable trifle (the affair of Corsica) to be the occasion of a rupture between two nations which have need of peace, and are indebted for it to him. If you succeed in plying him successfully upon this point, I am of opinion, provided he be not changed, that you may induce him to promise you that he will do all in his power to prevent this rupture, especially as you will be able by appealing to the knowledge which he supposes he has of my character, to banish from his mind any distrust and suspicion of me which anyone may have attempted to instil into him.[25]

Choiseul need not have troubled himself. Already Lord Weymouth, of the Bedford faction, had taken pains to express his belief that the fate of Corsica was of no consequence to England.[26] Châtelet actually conferred freely with Bedford and Weymouth and helped them construct arguments with which to oppose the policy of Shelburne, still looked upon as the policy also of Chatham.[27] Apparently some care was taken to keep the extent of the Bedford double game from public knowledge.

Châtelet left England early in July 1768 to assure Choiseul further that he could complete his plans with safety. In Paris, Lord Mansfield, for whom Chatham had never concealed his contempt, found satisfaction in declaring "that the English Ministry were too weak, and the nation too wise to support them in entering a war for the sake of Corsica."[28] Immediately Choiseul put on a bold front. "It is astonishing," wrote Rochford to Shelburne, "how since Count Châtelet's arrival the language of everybody is changed, as he has made it his particular business to set it about that we shall not engage in war on account of their expedition."[29] Chauvelin, the French commander, proceeded with his plans.

For over a year prior to the first Cabinet decision on Corsica, Shelburne, who as Secretary of State for the Southern Department had charge of the diplomatic representations to France, had been completely isolated from his colleagues amidst constant rumors that he was soon to resign. He alone followed what he believed to be the policies of Chatham, Grafton by this time having begun to drift in his own rather indiscernible direction. That the Ministry supported Shelburne's bold policy for even a short interval was surprising. While he yet held office Shelburne acted unhesitatingly. Late in May 1768 he sent to Corsica one John Stewart, a trained spy, with instructions to learn from Paoli how capable the Corsicans were of defending themselves and what help they needed. On his way Stewart was to visit certain places in France to determine the extent of that country's preparedness for war. Grafton and the other Cabinet ministers, claiming to be impatient of the delays occasioned by Stewart's itinerary, availed themselves of the opportunity to send a spy of their own choosing, a Genevese named Captain Dunant.[30]

As the two British agents were approaching Corsica, and as the Comte de Marbeuf was planning to break out of established perimeters to pave the way for Chauvelin's forces, how, one wonders, did Paoli view his country's condition? "I never feel a moment of despondency," the General had told Boswell in 1765. Truly it was not in Paoli's nature to despair, much less to permit his mind to stagnate in a state of melancholy. Yet in the unequal struggle with Choiseul, with only feeble signs of encouragement from the outside world, he indeed suffered periods of despondency. These feelings he confined to correspondence with

a few close friends, and he permitted them only a brief life.
Characteristically his resolve was firm, his attitude stubbornly, sometimes blindly optimistic. In extenuation it
must be granted that he was the victim of inadequate communication and of a lack of frankness on the part of British
officials who were in a position to interpret events at home
more clearly than they did, and to warn Paoli of likely consequences. For his own part the General too easily
embraced hopeful interpretations and proved himself a
wayward reader of portents. On the island Paoli had no
difficulty in penetrating to the hidden motives of the most
devious of his people; he usually disarmed and even fore-
stalled opposition by direct, clear statements of his views
and his reasons for holding them. The sophisticated opponent with whom he now contended operated unseen—to
the great disadvantage of the physiognomist. Choiseul
looked upon the Corsican as sometimes naive beyond belief, at other times as merely clumsy in what could only be
transparent disingenuousness.

Paoli depended heavily on informants in Tuscany and
on published "news" from England, much of it invented by
Boswell, with some items clearly suggesting that one or
more great powers would intervene whenever necessary to
save Corsica. (Was it fortunate that Paoli was never to learn
how much his young friend contributed to his unwar-
ranted confidence and intransigence, and to the complacency of British partisans of Corsica?) In Tuscany, Sir
Horace Mann, British envoy at Florence, was by far the
most experienced and informed of Paoli's sources. Paoli's
friend, Raimondo Cocchi, who held a professorship in
anatomy and also the post of antiquarian at the Uffizi, was
on good terms with Mann. Sir Horace Mann certainly
should have known enough to warn Paoli that reliance upon Chatham was ill-advised; but even prominent politicians in London fell into wild surmise when analyzing the
behavior of the King's Cabinet. What is probable is that
Mann very tardily communicated notions of differences,
weaknesses, and changes in the Ministry, and that the light
he turned upon them was necessarily unsearching. On the

coast John Dick, British consul at Leghorn, and the acting consul in Dick's absence, the Rev. Andrew Burnaby, both helped to keep the General posted. At Leghorn too was the Corsican Count Rivarola, who held the post of consul for Sardinia. When Boswell visited Rivarola in 1765 the Count's house was rapidly becoming the center of Corsican activity on the continent. According to the English spy, John Stewart, the Count's sister, who had taken the veil and was styled the Countess of Rivarola, really performed most of the business as consul and as unofficial represent-ative of Corsica.[31]

When, on 5 August 1767, Paoli predicted that Corsica would soon emerge from the shelter of peace, he must still have had in mind France's abandonment of Corsica and then his war against Genoa. Had the withdrawal of some French troops deceived him? The next month he asked, "When will the divisions within the British Ministry ever cease?" noting that such distractions prevented England from paying due attention to foreign affairs. Accounts in newspapers now certainly misled him. In England there were rumors of war. How fortunate for Mr. Pitt, Paoli wrote to Burnaby on 1 November 1767; all accounts grant him "a superior talent" for conducting war, "and I do not believe him too sick in body [to act], however much dis-gusted he may feel because of the contradictions he en-dures."[32] A complete breakdown of communication? Wilful misreading of intelligence? Escape into fantasy? All true to a degree. Certainly Paoli was under a load of mis-apprehensions. Take, for example, his comment upon learning that the Bedfords had entered the Ministry. "Now . . . the British Ministry is united . . . the English will make all powers maintain peace, and not invade other states un-der whatever pretext" (to Burnaby, 4 February 1768). Who did not know that Bedford had headed the peace-at-any-price faction during the late war, and had been on friendly terms with Choiseul during the negotiations which concluded it? Paoli's enemies years later spoke of him as suspicious, crafty, and wary, but now he appears com-pletely trusting and consequently always one move behind

his adversary. Writing on 12 May 1768, Horace Mann
maintained that Paoli had believed the promise of Choiseul

> that at the expiration of their treaty with the Republic of
> Genoa next August the French troops should evacuate the
> Island, and that the Corsicans should be at full liberty to
> take the maritime provinces not garrisoned by them; the
> reliance therefore on these repeated promises has always
> made General Paoli quite easy, not in the least suspecting
> that the Duke de Choiseul concealed the design which he
> has now manifested [that Paoli yield to France in perpetuity
> the whole province of Capo Corso]. . . . The consternation
> which all this has given Paoli is increased by the daily re-
> ports that the Genoese have made a cession of the Island
> either in part or in whole to France.[33]

Mann was here telescoping successive views of the past two
years; he had not yet been granted permission to reveal
that the British knew cession to be a certainty.

The one conviction which partly exonerates Paoli from
the charge of gross incompetence as a diplomat and political leader in time of external danger is his belief that England, even if blind to every consideration except narrow
self-interest, could not permit France to annex so strategically important and economically valuable an island as
Corsica. Writing to Rivarola on 20 June 1768, Paoli said, "I
await further your evidence on the part which the English
and their court are taking in the present affairs of Corsica,
the fate of which should not be indifferent to them. The
Duc de Choiseul has sent for Buttafoco, naturally, in order
to throw dust in the eyes of the other Corsicans and make
them think that he [Choiseul] is on my side. . . . To Buttafoco . . . he complains bitterly about my stubbornness; he
threatens that I will be lost if I do not let myself be guided
in all things by the wishes of France; that I have no other
decision to take after having missed those which he had
first proposed to me. He wishes to intimidate either me or
the others: neither fear nor flattery will make me neglect
the interest of *la patria*."[34]

Now, as if it had suddenly flooded upon his imagination,
Paoli saw that the immediate French goal was to destroy
him and replace his government—treaty negotiations were

past, and a military solution was probably in reserve. Quickly he wrote to Rivarola again:

> I am hurriedly answering you today, 26 June, because the French will succeed underhandedly in acquiring agreements. Buttafoco, despairing of our power to resist, in order not to offend France advises me to recognize its sovereignty. However, he does not have faith in the people. His reasons, although good, will be suspect since they serve him. . . . They [Corsican partisans of France] are raising hopes of marquisates, countships, pensions, until now in vain; but in the long run the people will weaken if they see no hope from without. Hurry, and we will do ourselves honor.[35]

As noted earlier, Holland and Sardinia did send money and materiel; England sent two independent agents, neither of whom had authority to make any commitments. Prior to Dunant's arrival late in July, Shelburne had written (2 July 1768) to Sir Horace Mann authorizing him to acquaint Paoli with the opinion of the English government as to the conduct of France in Corsica, and to let him know in general terms of the remonstrances made by Rochford to Choiseul.[36] However, Paoli had not been notified regarding the agents. Dunant's French manner therefore easily aroused the General's suspicions and put him on guard.[37] It is a measure of Paoli's sense of urgency that he did not hesitate personally to dictate his needs. After some preliminaries, among them the statement that he would "fight to the last gasp to defend and preserve the liberty of his homeland" and that "all who can carry arms in the whole nation are prepared to sacrifice, and have before their eyes only liberty or death," he went on to say that he needed everything: "money, small pieces of field artillery easily carried on mules, and especially small armed ships to oppose those of the French, which cruised the shores of the Island."[38]

Stewart arrived less than two weeks later, in August 1768. In the interval the French had broken their pledges by attacking the Corsicans before the treaty of 1764 had expired. To Stewart, Paoli confided "that he looked upon his nation as ruined without foreign assistance; that he was destitute of money, ammunition and provisions, and other

implements of war." The treacherous attacks had given the
French control of the "entire communication between
Bastia and San Fiorenzo, and had cut off from him the
whole province of Capo Corso, with the island of Capraja."
The Corsicans were dispirited by these losses, and needed
some "great stroke." The French were too well fortified in
their posts for him to dream of retaking them; and at this
point "a defeat would ruin him forever." However, "if he
were assisted and San Fiorenzo attacked by sea, he would
engage to keep off all succours from Bastia and would even
assault their camp behind. With the assistance of England
alone he could do every thing and it would be impossible
for the French to succeed; but as it was now he looked upon the Corsicans as doomed to destruction, with every nation in Europe wishing them well but doing nothing."[39]

In the days following the setback in the north Paoli apparently succeeded in recovering his composure—perhaps
"doomed to destruction" had been calculated to alarm
Britain into action. In any case his behavior did not prevent Stewart from characterzing him as "indeed a very
great man; his conversation was elegant, sensible, and discovered vast knowledge of men and things." Paoli surely
must have known that what he proposed for the British at
Capo Corso was nothing less than an act of war. However,
he was speaking in immediate response to Stewart's question as to why he did not retake the lost positions. The rest
of the discussion centered on what Corsica needed to continue to fight, and Paoli's other reference to England's
course was that "she had only to declare herself the protector of Corsica" for France to retreat or at least subside into
inaction. Stewart put the real situation clearly, however, in
his next dispatch:

> I am persuaded, nay positively convinced, that no assistance
> but that which cuts from the French the communication of
> the sea will be effectual to save the Corsicans—a secret sup-
> ply of arms, ammunition, etc., would be precarious, and at
> best only serve to retard their fate and to make our rivals
> pay dearer for an acquisition which in sound policy we
> ought never allow them to obtain at any price.[40]

At home, Grafton wrote to the King without waiting for Stewart's reports to be received and deciphered. "Some timely assistance prudently given," he thought, "may make very costly if it should not totally defeat [France's] purpose."[41] Some colleagues wondered if the Proclamation of 1763 should be repealed. "It was desirable to avoid that step," Grafton relates, "as it would be a publication of our intentions to send the assistance which Paoli asked for, our object being to effect it in such a manner as should least risk a breach with France." The Lord Chancellor opined that revocation was unnecessary because the change in circumstances rendered the proclamation invalid. "A moment was not lost in supplying most of the articles requested by the Corsicans; and indeed many thousand stand of arms . . . were so furnished from the stock in the Tower as to give no indication that they were sent from our government."[42]

The reports from Stewart and urgent letters from Mann changed no views in the Ministry. To the King, Grafton wrote that Paoli's "wish in regard to assistance is almost in every point already gratified except in the great measure of all, a Declaration in their favour, which if once made by his Majesty will doubtless be considered at the same time as a Declaration of War against France." George III heartily concurred: "I entirely join in opinion with you that everything that can with any degree of propriety be done for the assistance of the Corsicans has already been ordered; for I am ready to declare it to the whole world that I cannot think under the present state of debt that it can be expedient, for the sake alone of Corsica, to begin acts of hostilities against France."[43] George III was neither more timid nor more fearful of drains upon the treasury than his French counterpart. The great difference was in the Ministers, neither of whom, curiously, enjoyed extensive support among the power holders or the people. In France a strong faction wished to bring Choiseul down, incidentally aborting the Corsican operation; in England, according to the Neapolitan Minister, Marquis Caracciolo, there was a "popular clamor" amongst the London merchants, many of whom "say that war is a violent remedy but a lesser evil than the present state of the nation"—and this on 27 May 1768, when only select diplomats had any idea of the full extent of France's plans.[44] The most powerful and vocal London merchants were either in the Chatham or Rockingham camps.

Boswell's true and invented news releases, supplemented by poems, pamphlets, and letters of other origins, were suitably climaxed with the publication of his book in February 1768. Corsica seized hold of the imagination, and attachment to Corsican independence developed among a wide variety of Englishmen: (1) the idealistic and also the more practical lovers of liberty, among the former those who hoped to see the emergence of a new nation, good, virtuous, natural, with the noble Paoli at its head; (2) patriots who had gloried in the victories of Pitt and now endured humiliation from the spectacle of unopposed French expansion; and (3) practical men of trade, centered in London, many of them also sharing the views of the second group. Boswell managed dextrously to avoid offending any subgroup which might be antagonistic to another—most conspicuously he made it possible for Wilkites and anti-Wilkites to support Paoli without sharing slogans or necessarily attending the same meetings.[45] The influence, if any, of the above-mentioned types of publications, soon supplemented by long essays, could not be assessed until Parliament convened in November 1768. Meanwhile Paoli had to carry on as best he could.

The first actions in the war put Paoli the commander in a poor light. A glance at the map shows Capo Corso extending north from the eastern part of the body of Corsica like the offset head of a turtle. With command of the sea and the advantage of surprise, the French quickly pulled the noose at the base of the neck (San Fiorenzo to Bastia) and rendered the head, with nearly half of Paoli's regular troops, helpless. Every Corsican knew that the island's strong points of defense were in the mountains and their accesses. Overconfidence foolishly encouraged by the presence of British ships in surrounding waters is the most generous explanation which can be applied to the General. Stewart reached him at the bleakest moment. Within weeks, however, Paoli demonstrated his brilliance as a leader. The defections of officers like Buttafoco from the Royal Corsican regiment acted as a purge, leaving the military body essentially healthy and loyal. The Corsicans regrouped and henceforth acted bravely, daringly, on terrain of their own choosing. There were, of course, some further defections—French money for this purpose seemed inexhaustible (and who could say that money was not better spent than blood?)—but on the whole the Corsican military actions added up to a series of successes, one of them actually a very costly and humiliating defeat for the French. So discouraged was Chauvelin that he proposed a suspension of arms; Paoli agreed, provided that Chauvelin remove from his forces the Corsican "bandits," as he termed the islanders now fighting for France.[46] At the end of the year 1768 Chauvelin was recalled, to be replaced by another commander bringing with him an additional army.

In England, then, the Corsican cause was looked upon by its partisans as far from lost. Paoli knew that dangers were rapidly increasing, but outwardly displayed nothing other than extreme faith and confidence. With the knowledge that England, even if only through diplomatic channels, had firmly expressed its displeasure and opposition to Choiseul's actions, he wrote, "If the French continue to fight here Corsica will become the occasion for a general war, which France will not be able to sustain against the English." He trusted that the Sardinian king would succeed in his request for intervention.[47] To Paoli it seemed that he must hold the fort at all costs while awaiting the faint first call of the trumpet which would herald the approach of his allies. That France might eventually prove unwilling to pay the price, that fate would intervene to change that nation's policy, or that England would risk war—these were slender reeds for Paoli to lean upon. But he had no alternative, while persuading his Corsicans that

it was completely in their power to save or to lose the independence they had so painfully won. Indeed he could not
have been unresponsive to the subconscious misgiving that
he might be bootlessly wasting his people's lives. Yet something can be said for the course he took and the manner
of it. Until the Parliamentary meetings of November 1768
it was still possible for an outsider to hope for a change in
what was all too clearly the British official policy—more
remarkable reversals had taken place before. As for
France, the war against Corsica was carried on by a man
rather than by a nation, and Choiseul's enemies were setting ambushes to bring him down. The indifferent poten-
tial ally and the politically vulnerable enemy—what means
other than dramatic victories could transform them?

When "Corsica" Boswell arrived in London to luxuriate
in his new character he did not long permit himself to
forget the cause. During the writing of his book, as in all
his efforts on behalf of the islanders, Boswell had appeared
to enjoy support from friends and strangers alike, but not
from Johnson. Very early in the project Johnson wrote to
him: "I wish there were some cure, like the lover's leap, for
all heads of which some single idea has obtained an unreasonable and irregular possession. Mind your own affairs, and leave the Corsicans to theirs" (*Life*, 21 August
1766). Now, with the book out of the way, it was time for
Boswell to empty his head of Corsica, which, wrote Johnson, "I think has filled it rather too long" (*Life*, 23 March
1768). Boswell replied in a letter (26 April) which exhibits
the quality of "enthusiasm" which never ceased to charac-
terize his utterances on the subject public or private. His
publication of it in the *Life* many years later evidenced
clear satisfaction. Johnson's attitude probably was compounded as usual of many factors. He certainly had not
lost his place in Boswell's esteem, but he would have been
dense indeed not to sense that he now shared his role as
moral authority. In Boswell's private papers and letters
"This is unworthy of Paoli's friend" was now as likely to oc-
cur as "This is unworthy of the friend of the Rambler."
Perhaps, though, Johnson's distrust of "enthusiasm" in any

form, certainly when coupled with catch phrases about liberty, primarily accounts for his unsympathetic, even scornful comments on the Corsicans right up to the time of his meeting with Paoli, when all criticism dissolved.

Boswell knew that the battle remained to be won. His activities now as always helped to feed his vanity, but this factor I will not attempt to isolate or weigh. He continued to submit "inventions," not always helpful, as well as official "Corsican Intelligence." He no longer had to provide the main spark. By the summer of 1768 letters from many sources began to flood the newspapers, as well as sizeable essays, most of them stressing the commercial advantages of trade with Corsica, the threat to the balance of power in Europe resulting from French occupation of Corsica, and the consequent danger to all British commerce in the Mediterranean. Occasionally assistance to Corsica was praised as being in the general interest of humanity and civilization.

As the time for the opening of Parliament approached it was widely believed that the government would come under heavy attack for its actions vis-à-vis France. Information on Corsica's value had reached the remotest province; and the pusillanimous behavior of the King and his Ministry, particularly now that Chatham and Shelburne had been maneuvered out of office, could no longer be easily concealed.

Choiseul, never one to leave a resource incompletely exploited, now wrote to the Duke of Bedford, noting with concern that "the present peace, which is, I dare say, our common child, is in danger." The French King desires peace and repose above all, and his Minister, "by duty and by conscience" thinks exactly as he does. We fear, he goes on, "that a spirit of faction, popular ardor, or ministerial interest" might "plunge us into the misfortune which we wish to avoid." Of course, France has been forced to put on a bold front precisely because of its previous misfortunes. With respect to England, because that country's frequent changes of leadership have made a relationship of trust and confidence impossible, France has been forced to proceed alone in pursuit of just and proper national self-interest. "I do not speak to you of Corsica, my Lord; one cannot dispute the fact that neither our treaty with Genoa nor the possession of Corsica by France can justly concern England; we have sent you a copy of the treaty, and you may well feel that if we had dealt with the [English] Ministry which had made the peace [of Paris] the treaty would have been made with it before being made with Genoa. Would you have advised me to place this confidence in my Lord Shelburne, who I am informed each week has been discharged?" It was in France's interest to occupy Corsica; a method of doing so had been found which was honorable and not prejudicial to the interest of England. "We as well as our allies fear war; we will do our utmost to avoid it reasonably and without dishonor." M. de Châtelet, who will be leaving for London in a few days, is authorized to speak to you in full confidence, and "you can without fear open yourself to him; he will speak to you, my Lord, of my affection for you." Bedford's reply, which he found reason to delay until well after the parliamentary debate, ends with a question which can most kindly be called curious: "Will there not be a means, my dear Duke, of smoothing over this difficulty by finding some honourable pretext for withdrawing your troops from the island of Corsica?"[48]

The Administration by the end of October 1768 had fully consolidated its position, and on all major issues could speak with one voice. The speaker officially was Grafton, but the words, particularly on foreign policy and America, were those of the Bedfords. The Duke of Bedford's brother-in-law, Lord Gower, was Lord President of the Council; Viscount Weymouth was in Shelburne's previous office as Secretary of State for the Southern Department; Lord North was about to become Chancellor of the Exchequer; and Richard Rigby, Bedford's political man of business, had just moved from the post of joint Vice-Treasurer of Ireland to that of Paymaster of the Forces. North had been earning respect and esteem since January 1768, when he became the Administration leader in the House of Commons; Rigby, as the foremost spokesman for the Bedfords,

invariably indulged in expressions considerably less restrained.

The chief problems as the government viewed them at
this time were "discontents"—discontents in America and
discontents in England, the latter, no matter how their
management was attempted, invariably focusing on the
case of Wilkes. Relations with nations on the Continent the
government now considered of lesser import. Histories of
the period, particularly those written in this century, very
rarely take note of Paoli and his struggle. It is nevertheless
true that as of November 1768 the question of Corsica
loomed as large in the popular mind as many which have
survived conspicuously in works of scholarship. Further,
many an experienced English politician saw the Corsican
expedition as Paoli saw it, an action demanding response
from every great nation concerned with maintaining the
balance of power in Europe.

The King's speech to both Houses on 8 November 1768
was not received passively. Dowdeswell expressed especially bitter criticism of the Administration's conduct
towards America; Burke went on to direct attention to
France and Corsica:

> Is the world of opinion, is all mankind of opinion, that Cor-
> sica will not be an advantage to France? Corsica naked I do
> not dread; but Corsica a province of France is terrible to
> me. . . . There never was a time when the balance of power
> in Europe required more watchful attention.[49]

George Grenville, his following having dwindled to the
point where at best he could be called a wise senior statesman, at worst a mischief-maker intent on showing how his
successors were bungling a job he had done so well, wondered whether "any remonstrance has been made to
France by any court in consequence of the cession of Corsica. The proclamation [of 1763—nominally the work of
his administration] . . . relative to Corsica was a bad measure." Lord North defended the Administration: "With regard to Corsica, Great Britain is but one of eight
contracting parties to the treaty of Aix-la-Chapelle. None
of the other seven have thought it necessary to declare war

in consequence of the cession of that island to France. Is,
Sir, the affair of Corsica a matter for which we ought to go
to war?" Two admirals, Saunders and Hawke, also had
their say, Saunders commenting that "I have no objection
to treating with France on the question of Corsica, but I
would have a fleet there at the same time"; while Hawke
belittled the importance of Corsica to France, saying of
their ports that "they are rather gulphs . . . in which I
would engage to burn all their ships." At length the members thanked the King and adjourned.

The timing of the debate on Corsica, when it did take
place in the Commons on 17 November 1768, caught
many members by surprise; and the terms of the issue
puzzled all but the Grenville group, who were responsible,
at the odd hour of 3:30 p.m., for bringing it before the
House in a motion by Henry Seymour requesting

> that there be laid before the House copies of all correspon-
> dence between either of his Majesty's principal Secretaries
> of State and any of his Majesty's Ministers residing in for-
> eign courts relative to the affairs of Corsica, since the first
> of January 1767 to the present time; and also copies of all
> instructions to any of the said Ministers, and of all
> memorials and representations to or from any foreign pow-
> er, with the several answers thereunto relative to the said
> affairs of Corsica, from the said first of January 1767 to the
> present time.[50]

Nine days earlier North had twitted Seymour's chief,
Grenville: "Gentlemen should not throw out insinuations,
since they cannot form a correct judgement, not having
seen the memorials." Here was the response, and while it
may have satisfied Grenville it doomed to defeat any attempt to influence British policy on Corsica. The concern
was supposedly whether England had acted effectively in
attempting to forestall France's takeover of Corsica; but the
question, no matter how the arguments strayed, was on the
propriety of producing in the House of Commons all papers—confidential or otherwise—in a specific series of
diplomatic negotiations with a foreign power.[51] On that
question the House was not finally brought to vote until
10:00 p.m., having for at least ninety percent of the time (if

we are to trust Cavendish) argued for or against taking stronger measures against France. All possible notes were struck, more than once. Dowdeswell commented "that whilst foreign nations were sending armies into the field we were sending ambassadors." North replied, "Let France continue in possession of Corsica: notwithstanding that, Sir, we shall be just as able to go to sea as we ever were." Admirals Saunders and Hawke exchanged contradictory assessments of the strategic and mercantile value of Corsica. Barré took over: "The honourable mover has termed Corsica a sentinel to all the seaports in the Mediterranean. A very little, Sir, would make her a citadel." The Colonel went on to speak of Corsica's ports, timber, and manpower, exhibiting knowledge generally unavailable to Englishmen prior to the publication of Boswell's book. He left no doubt concerning the Chathamite attitude: "In taking possession of Corsica [France] has shown a disposition to go to war with you; and it is your duty by all proper means to resist immediately." A short time later Burke made the Rockingham position equally forceful: "Corsica is under the protection of Great Britain; we should have consecrated it by that word." Rigby gave the Ministry's game away with a contemptuous observation, made valid simply by the utterance: "Choiseul is not to be terrified by representations of this House, though backed by the oratory of the honourable gentleman." As Walpole noted in a letter to Sir Horace Mann, the proposal would have required "a very opponent stomach to digest. . . . It was a great day for the Administration, a better for the Duke of Choiseul, a bad one for this country; for, whatever the Ministry may incline or wish to do, France will look on this vote as a decision not to quarrel for Corsica."[52]

The French understood clearly enough that England had washed its hands of the Corsican problem. Châtelet the next day wrote to Choiseul on the desirability of taking part in the struggle between Britain and its colonies, a proposal which Choiseul looked upon with favor.[53] The actions in London carried the unmistakable message to Paoli: support for the Corsicans from the British government could no longer be expected even at the diplomatic level. The General's comments to Burnaby on hearing of the debate were remarkably restrained:

> The response of the House of Commons seems to me a little cold; yet the acquisition of Corsica would in time greatly strengthen the French navy and shift the balance of power in the Mediterranean. . . . The French no longer conceal their intentions, because they believe that this British Ministry is too occupied with the dissensions in America.[54]

Burnaby, sympathetic though he was, nevertheless officially represented the British government. Writing to Raimondo Cocchi the General went further, expressing a conviction he simply could not yet shake off, namely that the British in an affair of such importance would not "leave the Corsicans to act alone."[55]

That Paoli was somehow perversely dull-witted in appraising the British is too simple a conclusion. No nation, he believed, could blind itself indefinitely to the realities of power. In the politics of power, history had demonstrated to him that cycles were inevitable, that the wheel must turn, and that thus it was primarily a question of time before the British people and the eminent leaders of the opposition would cause a change in that country's policy. By early 1769 he became aware that no such change could come in time to assist him if France should field overwhelming forces like those which had nearly destroyed Corsica when he was a child. While Paoli continued to encourage all who favored Corsica, to acknowledge every private gift of money or supplies from England, he recognized the urgent need now for quick victories which might reverse France's stand, even drive Choiseul to ruin. Before examining the events which were to end in the tragic spasm of defeat, we may profitably return to England to throw more light on Paoli's attitude towards that country during the critical last year of the Corsican nation, and on the reasons for his becoming an "Englishman" for over thirty years.

In England the general torrent of letters, short articles, and even sizeable essays in favor of the Corsicans, which

began even before the publication of Boswell's book, provided sustenance of a kind dearly needed by the General
and his people. Paoli subscribed to at least one English periodical, and it is safe to assume that Boswell and other
friends forwarded copies of items which might not otherwise have reached the island.[56] After rumors of France's
intention to seize all of Corsica became generally known,
the writings grew more strident in tone and specific in ad-
vocating British intervention of some kind. If the government was too timid to act, the people could do so by means
of voluntary subscriptions, exclaimed "An Englishman" in
a letter to the *Public Advertiser*, 1 June 1768. Boswell
himself acted on the suggestion quickly, adding, in a letter
signed "O.P." in the *Public Advertiser* for 6 July 1768, concrete suggestions on how the public-spirited merchants of
London could forward the scheme. In Scotland, Boswell
was active in soliciting seven hundred pounds to acquire "a
tollerable train of artillery" for shipment to Corsica. Upon
hearing that it had been sent Paoli wrote: "Princes give
succours from political views and interests. This is the sub-
sidy of virtue and humanity."[57]

Several weeks after the critical debate in Parliament,
Boswell brought out a collection of *British Essays in Favour
of the Brave Corsicans*. Most of the *British Essays* had appeared in newspapers during that period in 1768 when in-
fluencing Crown and Parliament seemed the most
promising means of aiding the islanders; during the same
period several essays so long as to require publication in
pamphlet form also appeared, and these Boswell did not
reprint. Of the twenty *British Essays*, Boswell, who wrote
seven, was ignorant of the source of eight; neither, apparently, did he know the authors of the long pamphlets,
which he mentioned in his preface.[58] Though the book
came out too late to accomplish its original purpose, it reinforced the sympathies of the partisans of the Corsican
cause, for whom no recourse remained other than the use
of their purses. Apparently with the knowledge and approval of London merchants like Vaughan, Beckford, and
Trecothick, Boswell now in the *London Chronicle* for 10 De-

cember 1768 printed a signed "Memorial for a Contribution in Behalf of the Brave Corsicans," which based its appeal not only on the grounds of national interest but on considerations of humanity and generosity toward a distressed people. Contributions, Boswell concluded, would be received by named bankers in London and Edinburgh. At least three periodicals reprinted the entire memorial, and the *London Chronicle* at frequent intervals printed shorter advertisements for contributions.[59] Upon receiving a copy of the memorial Paoli informed Burnaby that he had ordered it translated, "that our people may take courage, and that their zeal may be reanimated with new fire at the sight of what is being done for their liberty by the virtuous men of the first nation of Europe."[60]

The income from benefits, subscriptions, individual contributions from all sections of the British Isles and even from Englishmen abroad amounted to over fourteen thousand pounds if one accepts all the published accounts.[61] Paoli made sure that his people's gratitude became known. In a letter which appeared in the *London Chronicle* for 25 April 1769, acknowledging the efforts of William Beckford, Barlow Trecothick, and Samuel Vaughan, who by May were to raise their total of collections to three thousand pounds, Paoli wrote: "I have applied this collection to the support of the families of those patriots who, abhorring a foreign yoke, have abandoned their houses and estates in that part of the country held by the enemy, and have retired to join the army." Possibly the sums received exceeded those reported; even so, they were significant only as they strengthened Corsican morale. More was needed; before he finished the above-mentioned letter to Burnaby on the circulation of Boswell's memorial Paoli went on to make an observation which he would have occasion to repeat—not often publicly—during the next decade: "I cannot wish evil upon the Americans, but I do wish that they would become calm. Their actions are of great significance to our enemies."

Outside Corsica the military position of the islanders appeared hopeless, with the only chance to save them resting upon the charms of the Comtesse Du Barry and her supporters, irreconcilable enemies of Choiseul. It was generally believed that her rise in royal favor would bring down Choiseul and reverse his Corsican policy, which was becoming increasingly unpopular. At the beginning of the year 1769 only a court presentation, which would give her the right to share in the personal life of the King, was required to make the ascendency of Du Barry and her party complete. But accidents and intrigues delayed the event from 25 January to 22 April. Walpole and Mann "prayed" that the presentation would come soon enough to save Paoli.[62] The General, who undoubtedly knew of the intrigues at the French court and their supposed significance, counted not upon them but upon his army. A series of actions designed to pave the way for a decisive blow for the most part went well enough, but the unexpected climax at Ponte Nuovo on 8 May 1769 proved to be a disaster. There were as many versions of that battle as there were individuals who chose to write of it. What is clear is that in the confusion before the battle was over Corsican fired upon Corsican—or upon allied foreign mercenary or volunteer—with heavy loss of life amidst cries of treachery, the latter very likely justified. That Paoli did not blame his commanders he showed by taking one of them, Count Gentili, with him to England as his companion.

Despite the demoralization and the enormous weakening of the Corsican military position, continued resistance was possible, and for some days Paoli and his chiefs weighed various plans. In the version followed by Burnaby (p. 67n) the chiefs finally "unanimously resolved that, as there was no hope of receiving foreign succour . . . nor any probability of opposing the enemy with success," they would expose "their lives and fortunes to preserve that man who alone on some future occasion" might be able to rescue their country. It was in character for Paoli to accept their decision. Guerrilla warfare was still possible—some bands of resisters were to continue forays for years—but the cost to the people and to all that they had painfully grown and built would not be justified. No, it was better for Corsica to maintain its character as a nation, unified though defeated and occupied, in anticipation of a happier day when it would be freed of the foreign yoke. An English vessel picked up Paoli and a group of his followers at Porto Vecchio on 13 June 1769. Among those who elected to stay behind was Paoli's former adjutant, Carlo Buonaparte. He and his wife retreated through the mountains, and when the French offered pardon they returned to Ajaccio. There, two months later, was born their son Napoleone.

Paoli disembarked at Leghorn. Everywhere the General was welcomed by admiring crowds who made his appearances triumphal processions. His likeness, bordered with the colors of Corsica, was printed on handkerchiefs which sold in large numbers. Sometimes he found it necessary to remain locked at home to avoid the crowds.[63] The spontaneous adulation of the common people, which Paoli did nothing at this time to cultivate, displayed itself wherever he went—across Europe to Holland and then to England, and two years later, just as prominently when he journeyed to Scotland. Paoli apparently was seen as more than a gallant political leader who had sought to bring his people independence. There was something in his leadership and in the mode of living of his Corsicans that appealed to yearnings which were to express themselves violently twenty years later. Not revolutionary Americans but Pasquale Paoli presaged the coming of the French Revolution. Vittorio Alfieri in 1788, riding a wave of Italian nationalism, dedicated *Timoleone* to the Corsican hero.

The French lost no time in beginning the formal pacification of Corsica. Even before they were able to defeat him they disparaged Paoli's qualities as a soldier; now they sought also to destroy his reputation as a national leader. The victory undoubtedly extended Choiseul's period of office; despite almost daily predictions that "the Choiseul party must fall,"[64] he held on until the end of 1770.

Paoli's immediate concern was to keep alive a spirit of independence on the island and, at a secure base elsewhere, establish a nucleus for a government in exile—not his phrase, and more pretentious than warranted by a party consisting of himself, Count Gentili, Father Guelfucci, and one or two servants. For this purpose Tuscany and Sardinia though friendly were not sufficiently powerful. Paoli took pains to assist in arranging the disposition of fellow exiles. The Grand Duke of Tuscany helped by assigning lands to Corsicans who settled in his dominions. Other exiles entered the service of Sardinia, and some went to Minorca. Clemente Paoli, after a brief period of wandering, settled among the monks at Vallombrosa. Ultimately England was to make provision for Pasquale Paoli and his retinue to live in London, and to subsidize other Corsicans who lived in Tuscany;[65] but when Paoli finally set off for Holland he apparently did not know whether he would continue on to England.

As Paoli began his wanderings Choiseul wrote to Louis XV of his achievement in obtaining a means of "dominating all the coasts of Italy."

> The English saw, just as I did, Sire, the advantages of [controlling] Corsica; they did not oppose [the expedition]; they only showed displeasure, powerless because they lacked political unity. Corsica was under your Majesty's domination before they had had the time to formulate a means of opposing it. . . . So we have reached our goal, at the cost of only a sense of disapprobation in France.[66]

The verdict of history, as written by British naval commanders twenty-five years later and by Admiral Mahan a century after that, generally supports Boswell and the Opposition. The port of San Fiorenzo proved of great value as a base for the British navy in 1794–96, and the island helped in provisioning. Essentially, the French national interest required only that Corsica not be available for use by a strong foreign power. Independent and neutral, the island posed no threat to France; and France did not greatly need its facilities. The kernel of truth in Choiseul's estimate, then, is only that by taking Corsica, France removed the possiblility of others taking it.

Paoli's own judgment as well as that of his advisors had indicated England as the most desirable place of exile; but

CHAPTER III

PAOLI IN ENGLAND, 1769–1790

Boswell's reunion with the General, related in the journal first printed over forty years ago, suggests an experience quite as memorable as the first meeting with Johnson. The footman made difficulties; the valet, when he heard "My name is Boswell," gave a jump, "catched hold of my hand and kissed it. . . . opening the door of the General's bedchamber, [he] called out, 'Mr. Boswell.' I heard the General give a shout before I saw him. When I entered he was in his night-gown and nightcap. He ran to me, took me all in his arms, and held me there for some time. I cannot describe my feelings on meeting him again" (22 September). Before he parted Boswell reflected: "As I hardly hoped to meet Paoli in this world again, I had a curious imagination as if I had passed through death, and was really in Elysium. . . . I was filled with admiration whenever the General spoke. I said that after every sentence spoken by him I felt an inclination to sing *Te Deum.* Indeed, when he speaks it is a triumph to human Nature, and to my friendship."

Crowds milled in front of the General's house and followed him whenever he left it; his every movement was reported in the papers.[1] They expected to find the hero of Boswell's book, enhanced in stature by events following the publication of that work. The book's hero should have been enough. The poet Gray had written to Walpole that he had been pleased and strangely moved by Boswell's portrait: Paoli was "a man born two thousand years after his time." John Wesley's impression had been uncommon in its eloquence but not in its view that Paoli was as great a lover of his country as Epaminondas, and as great a general as Hannibal.[2]

Paoli's first formal acts were to visit the Duke of Grafton
(21 September) and then, after George III had returned to
London, to present himself at Court (27 September).
Members of the Opposition, who had fought for Paoli in
the press and in Parliament, and who, when all else failed,
had sent him money, felt slighted, even grievously offended. Paoli sought to mollify them, indeed took immediate steps to meet with and to thank them once he had
discharged his formal duties; but for many nothing short
of joining their ranks would do.[3] From Paoli's point of
view, quite apart from the demands of protocol, nothing
was more clearly in the interest of the independence of
Corsica than paying court to the Ministers and the King
who had supported him, albeit inadequately, whose ships
had rescued him and his faithful followers, and whose
ships alone could reinstate him. When he thought about
the policies of England he concentrated on the use of the
nation's power in Europe rather than on the disturbing
divisions within. Many members of the Opposition viewed
matters in a different light. Boswell in the introduction and
body of *Corsica* had undoubtedly intensified an already
eager desire among many reformers on both sides of the
Atlantic to look upon Paoli as one of their champions, at
the time unhappily confined to affairs in the mountains of
Corsica. They were not completely wrong, but Paoli in
England as a political being was driven by one consideration only, the freeing of his people.

During the period from about 1766 to 1770 Paoli was for
the colonists a hero second only to men like William Pitt
and John Wilkes. John Hancock named one of his
merchant vessels "Paoli," and several patriot families in
Boston named their sons "Paoli" or "Pascal Paoli."[4] In England, Paoli's period of political popularity coincided with
that in the colonies, and for related reasons. Do what he
could personally to express gratitude for the generosity of
the individuals who assisted his country, he could not
placate all of them. In the eyes of the most extreme he had
betrayed his country by selling himself to the King and his
ministers. Samuel Vaughan accused him of having used

money paid him by the English Ministry to purchase an estate in Switzerland; he had deserted the "noble cause of liberty." Vaughan implied even more in the statement (which happened to be true) that Paoli's "estate in Corsica had not been molested by the French."[5] Indicative of the general feeling was the *Critical Review's* comment that Vaughan "passes too severe a censure on the much admired Corsican hero"; and on an earlier occasion the same magazine's observation that "the best service that can be done to the Corsican Chief is to let him, his actions, and character rest in quiet."[6] The people did not quickly abandon their loyalty, and for some years were to follow and to cheer him.

Indeed, except for Horace Walpole, who at Court took him for merely "an English, or at least a Scottish, officer" whose simplicity of appearance and quite ordinary behavior provoked not "the slightest suspicion of anything remarkable about him,"[7] any reference to Paoli was for many years likely to be prefixed by a word such as "illustrious." John Wesley recorded in his *Journal* that on a visit to Portsmouth, 13 October 1769, he "very narrowly missed meeting the great Pascal Paoli. . . . Surely He who hath been with him from his youth up hath not sent him into England for nothing. Lord, show him what is Thy will concerning him, and give him a kingdom that cannot be moved!"[8] The expectations of those who missed him were invariably satisfied when later they met. Wesley's visits with Paoli many years later will be related in their appropriate place.

Bringing England to its senses might take time, Paoli thought, but he had the tact and the patience to do it. The continual dampening of Paoli's large hopes, the diminution of his practical expectations, is sad to relate. Boswell spares us; Paoli himself gives rare clues. An immediate shock was the violence of domestic dissension. "I am come here to a northern country," he told Boswell, "and I find the newspapers all on fire" (Journal, 22 September). As he waited for the King to return to London he recognized that he had underestimated the problem. Writing to Rivarola he said: "If the English were not so strongly engaged by the problems of America and Wilkes, some bold protest [regarding France's seizure of Corsica] would be inevitable; but they are divided beyond belief, and the spirit of faction agitates the people against the Ministry."[9] George III's welcome, however, was heartening. "The King spoke to me strongly about the cause; on my private concern he overwhelmed me with kindness." Again: "I was in private conference with the King; he detained me an hour and a half in *tête-à-tête*, and was not silent in the good cause."[10]

Shortly after he arrived in London, Paoli wrote, "I have not slept, and do not sleep."[11] Unhappily, with regard to Corsica the British were soon put to sleep. The Wilkes affair dominated the scene in 1769–70, embittering and distracting the minds of all in public life. With the resignation of Grafton and his replacement by North early in 1770 the tone in Parliament became more calm, and, without serious confrontations or obvious reversals of principle, the Wilkes problem gradually began to occasion less concern, although the date for its final solution can not be placed earlier than 1774, when Wilkes was allowed to sit unmolested as M.P. for Middlesex. Under North no really basic changes developed in the Ministry's attitudes toward European involvement and American obstreperousness. The Bedfords were still in the Administration. With the death of George Grenville in 1770 North was able to bring back into office important Grenvillites, and in June 1771 to persuade Grafton to resume a place in the Cabinet. Indeed, so extensive was the base of North's support that even after the dispute with Spain over the Falkland Islands (1770–71) had revealed Britain's weakness, particularly that of its navy, North was able to weather criticism. After all, his compromise had kept the peace and clearly saved money. Thus, despite the building up of dangerous pressures in America and the fact that military and diplomatic weaknesses were not being corrected, the first years of North's Ministry seemed to many in England relatively quiet, even promising.

To Paoli the government's mood seemed one of indifference. Worse, outside the Administration Paoli perceived no leaders who offered comfort. Burke in his *Thoughts on the Cause of the Present Discontents* (1770), which had been brewing through 1769, expressed the view that there existed "a cabal of the closet and back-stairs" which was the real power behind the Cabinet, that supporting the cabal in Parliament was a Court party—the "King's Friends." Paoli, who wished to see Britain united and strong, could only wring his hands when confronted with Burke's fantasy. It was in his actual analysis of the way in which British power had decayed that Burke revealed how fully the English friends of Corsica had placed Paoli's defeat in the remote and irremediable past. In Burke's view the "interior ministry"—the secret cabinet which really controls decisions—realized

> that war is a situation which sets in its full light the value of the hearts of a people; and they well know that the beginning of the importance of the people must be the end of theirs. For this reason they discover upon all occasions the utmost fear of everything which by possiblility may lead to such an event. . . . Foreign powers, confident in the knowledge of their character, have not scrupled to violate the most solemn treaties; and, in defiance of them, to make conquests in the midst of a general peace, and in the heart of Europe. Such was the conquest of Corsica by the professed enemies of the freedom of mankind, in defiance of those who were formerly its professed defenders.

The Earl of Chatham, who recovered from his malady or maladies in the summer of 1769, also had been brooding on the state of his country. His thoughts did not issue forth in a pamphlet but in a ringing speech in the House of Lords on 10 January 1770, in which he was reported to have observed with sorrow that he found England, baffled on Corsica, standing "on the slippery edge of a new war —without allies abroad, and without unanimity at home." He went on:

> The situation of our foreign affairs was undoubtedly a matter of moment, and highly worthy their lordships' consideration; but . . . he declared with grief [that] there were other matters still more important and more urgently

demanding their attention. He meant the distractions and
divisions which prevailed in every part of the empire. He
lamented the unhappy measures which had divided the colonies from the mother country, and which he feared had
drawn them into excesses which he could not justify. He
owned his natural partiality to America, and was inclined to
make allowance even for those excesses. . . . they ought to
be treated with tenderness.[12]

However different their views on the responsibility for the
current state of affairs, then, Opposition and Administration were in agreement on priorities.

   With the abandonment of the search for a British role in
Europe by its ablest and most eloquent exponent, Paoli
perforce put aside any hope for early actions which might
affect Corsica's position. He followed debates in Parliament
very closely, read all important political writings, and neglected no one whose thoughts or achievements were worthy of attention, whose influence however slight might
weigh in favor of Corsica. What little we can learn from his
correspondence indicates that he adjusted to the position
of bystander, while at the same time he did not remit his
efforts to keep the Ministry aware of the importance of
Corsica and his own usefulness in a struggle with France.
A stream of visitors kept him in touch with affairs in Italy
and France. Direct letters to or from the continent, easily
intercepted, were out of the question. On 4 March 1770
Paoli reached the conclusion that despite the hostile preparations of the house of Bourbon, "in the ordinary course
of things this year there is little or nothing to hope for
[from the British]. The French will profit from this indifference to beat down the spirit of my countrymen and to
persuade them to look upon liberty as lost forever; and
consequently to make them not only accept domination
but, by zealously distributing favors, yield their affection."
Paoli's pessimistic mood must be assumed to have deepened during the ensuing years. It was not long before he
began to sense "an intolerable coldness" at court, which
moved him to reduce the frequency of his visits.[13] On 12
June 1772 Lord North informed him that the payments to

the exiles in Tuscany would be terminated in June of the following year.[14]

Leaving the General as lobbyist and insistently palpable symbol of Britain's obligation to Corsica, we may turn to the generally pleasant story of Paoli's stay among his English friends. Continuous chronological narrative, which cannot be written satisfactorily on the basis of available evidence, will give way frequently to efforts to fill out, alter, or supplement qualities of character set forth by Boswell in *Corsica.*

Immediately after Paoli's arrival in London, Boswell in his excitement brought the General visitors whom he did not greatly need. The Duke of Queensberry "seemed much struck;" Sheridan, a commoner for whose visit Boswell was careful to obtain leave, was also "exceedingly struck." In the midst of all the busy exhilarating activity only two subjects claimed possession of Boswell's mind. His problems with his father probably began beyond the reach of his conscious memory. Now Lord Auchinleck's plans for remarrying agitated his son. Paoli like most sons had had difficulties with his father, but he did not allow his own experience or his developing sympathies for Boswell to permit hasty judgment. "In a cursory way, he seemed to approve my warm resentment of my father's conduct." It was an entirely different matter when they passed to the "beautiful subject of Miss Montgomerie. I took out her *most valuable letter* [22 July 1769]. Paoli read it, and translated it with elegant spirit into Italian." One passage he read "over again and again, saying 'Questo è sublime' (this is sublime)." Such were the beginnings of a deeply affectionate friendship that was to envelop Peggie and her offspring until the end of the General's days.[15]

On 27 September Boswell waited impatiently at Court to see the presentation of the General to the King of Britain. From one who spoke to the King, Boswell learned that his Majesty said Paoli had a "most sensible and spirited countenance." Paoli himself related to Boswell the King's comment: "I have read Boswell's book, which is well written (*scritto con spirito*). May I depend upon it as an authentick account?" The General answered, "Your Majesty may be assured that every thing in that book is true, except the compliments which Mr. Boswell has been pleased to pay to his friend."[16]

On 31 October the meeting between two "illustrious men such as humanity produces a few times in the revolution of many ages" took place. On the same page of the *Tour* (p. 356) from which the above is quoted Boswell continues: "What an idea may we not form of an interview between such a scholar and philosopher as Mr. Johnson and such a legislator and general as Paoli!"[17] Boswell's record conveys nothing earthshaking; but the meeting was satisfactory enough for any admirer of Johnson or Paoli. "They met with a manly ease, mutually conscious of their own abilities and of the abilities one of each other. The General spoke Italian and Dr. Johnson English, and understood one another very well with a little aid of interpretation from me, in which I compared myself to an isthmus which joins two great continents." Paoli, as might have been expected, paid the first gracious compliment, but Johnson lagged scarcely a breath behind. Paoli introduced the subjects for discussion. The first naturally arose from Johnson's reputation as a lexicographer. The second had been set up by Boswell four years earlier in Corsica (*Tour*, pp. 356–57). On the General's observations concerning language Johnson commented, "Sir, you talk of language as if you had never done anything else but study it, instead of governing a nation." After an exchange of compliments the General "asked him what he thought of the spirit of infidelity which was so prevalent." Paoli now as always showed himself a pious man—no trouble with Johnson here. Johnson then returned to language, finding after a moment that he needed pen, ink, and paper to phrase his question (in French) as he wished. It concerned something Johnson had read in the geography of Lucas de Linda, who wrote that in both Corsica and Sardinia there existed a language different from Italian and from all others which derived from Latin. "The General immediately informed

him that the *lingua rustica* was only in Sardinia." The reader as usual accepts Boswell's report as accurate. Why did
Paoli deny the existence in Corsica of the dialect or family
of dialects now called Corse—which neither the Genoese
nor the French succeeded in eradicating, and which in
these days of ethnic consciousness is to be found in printed
pamphlets and papers?[18] Paoli undoubtedly recognized
that a dialect without a legitimate ancestry and printed literature was believed to stamp its speakers as wild and un-
cultivated. His deep conviction that the Corsicans were
ready for the most advanced form of government in Europe led him, for what was not to be the last time, to compromise his ideal of absolute honesty. The fact that his
people also spoke Italian and could thus lay claim to a distinguished literary heritage would not, Paoli perceived, affect the popular view. Johnson went home with Boswell
and drank tea till late in the night. He said "General Paoli
had the loftiest port of any man he had ever seen."

Thus met the surrogate fathers of Boswell. It seemed an
ill-suited pairing. Boswell was fully aware of the disparities
in character between the scholar-philosopher and the leg-
islator-general. Paoli could no more be imagined as writing
parliamentary debates or drudging at a dictionary than
Johnson as exhorting the "wild" Corsicans into battle or
bringing the French Assembly to its feet with impassioned
oratory. Paoli lived like a high-ranking officer or fine gentleman, with servants and a coach—no need for anyone to
clap a clean wig on his head before dinner—and moved
easily in high society. Johnson, although by this time he
was welcomed in many a noble and genteel home, probably never looked as if he belonged there. (Though, as Boswell noted, all consciousness of his appearance vanished
when he began to speak.) The deep complexity of Johnson's character contributes to the bulk of many journals
and occasions many books. Paoli appears to us much sim-
pler, and probably was, although he certainly was not as
simple as his biographers or their versions of him.

What does call for comment is the case for similarity and
congeniality, quite apart from Paoli's and Johnson's func-

tions in Boswell's life. Like Johnson, Paoli could make himself at home in any company and speak logically and interestingly on any subject, not, however, with Johnson's sense of having weighed the evidence and determined the course of argument long before, so that now all came out beautifully composed and irresistible. An exception was Paoli's own mastery and certainty concerning matters of conduct, whether of the individual or of society, and of ideal government. Here Paoli could speak forcefully, although for various reasons he did not choose to be a stubborn adversary. Commentators thought it amusing that the avowed Tory and enlightened champion of liberty should be joined by Boswell, but again the differences were exaggerated. Johnson would never have said of Paoli what he wrote of Akenside, that he had "an unnecessary and outrageous zeal for what he called and thought liberty; a zeal which sometimes disguises from the world, and not rarely from the mind which it possesses, an envious desire of plundering wealth or degrading greatness, and of which the immediate tendency is innovation and anarchy, an impetuous eagerness to subvert and confound, with very little care what shall be established." Johnson was of course thinking of England. In practice he displayed a love of the poor which worried Mrs. Thrale and Sir John Hawkins. What to do about them was beyond Johnson's power, but he knew that granting "liberty" would not help. Paoli had shown himself quite eager to break with tradition and establish new ways of organizing man in society and government. He easily avoided the subject in conversations with Johnson, and apparently considered English reformers that country's problem. Had he been asked by George III to form a government (and endowed magically with perfect command of the English language), he would have thrown up his hands in horror. The multiplicity of English religious and political sects dismayed him, as did the great discrepancies in wealth and power. In Corsica, although he maintained a respectable station, he could speak with the lowest peasant; moreover, that peasant would know that he was being listened to, had control in some measure of his own political and economic destiny, and would not lack for food or shelter as long as any was to be had. (It was difficult to find a Corsican who couldn't lay claim to a piece of land.)

On one important aspect of the Enlightenment, its emphasis on the powers of rational thought, Johnson and Paoli were not far apart. Johnson did indeed distrust innovation, but the difference between the two for the most part was confined to the subject of government. On religion, for example, Paoli was not the radical depicted by some, and in the general realm of ideas he was not unlike Johnson in being eager to explore and to understand. It takes little from Paoli, relative to his contemporaries, to say that Johnson's mind was more comprehensive, his curiosity more devouring.

Boswell needed them both. If Johnson kept the drowning Boswell afloat, Paoli gave him the power to swim. In his oft-quoted statement to the General, Boswell did not exaggerate: "It was wonderful how much Corsica had done for me, how far I had got in the world by having been there. I had got upon a rock in Corsica and jumped into the middle of life."[19] Wherever he went after his visit to Corsica—Italy, France, England, Scotland, Ireland—he was given a sense of importance as the adventurer who had sought out and become the friend of the great Paoli. Even in far-off America the Sons of Liberty did not forget to give a toast to Boswell when they met to celebrate Paoli's birthday.[20] Johnson and Paoli together could not effect a complete cure; but the friendship with Paoli was for a long time among Boswell's chief means of cheering himself up: "It is amazing how much and how universally I have made myself admired. This is an absolute fact. I am certain of it; and with an honest pride I will rejoice in it" (Journal, 31 August 1769).

Boswell continually sought advice from Johnson and Paoli. As the *Life* demonstrates, Boswell recognized that on matters of law Johnson was expert. To Johnson also Boswell was accustomed to turn with problems concerning Lord Auchinleck, and was no doubt comforted by John-

son's early sad observation that "there must always be a
struggle between a father and son."[21] On practical matters
concerning his personal and professional life Boswell usually turned to Paoli, who was more fully acquainted with
Boswell's lapses (having many times seen their consequences), had a greater familiarity with the laws and cus-
toms governing Boswell's world, and was apt to treat
Boswell more kindly. It was Paoli who received Boswell's
oaths of sobriety and who ultimately had to forgive their
violation. Boswell would not have occasion for resentment
or dissatisfaction after an encounter with the General such
as he records after a session with Johnson: "I recollected
also how roughly he discouraged me from my exertions in
favour of the Corsicans, by which, as I myself foresaw, I
raised myself twenty degrees higher in fame and in general
advantage as a social man than I should have been had he
been successful in repressing my generous ardour." This
reflection on Johnson, coming at a time when the "fretfulness of his disease" deserved indulgence, at a time also
when Boswell was taxing the patience of all his friends with
irrepressible personal preoccupations, was not primary
among the thoughts he habitually entertained of his great
friend. The journal of that day (23 March 1783) does indicate, however, that Boswell had been troubled before by
the absence in Johnson of a quality which Paoli possessed
in abundance: "amidst all my admiration of his great talents, I recollected how Sir John Pringle objected that he
had not wisdom for giving counsel."

At heart no one could be more compassionate than
Johnson; the problem was that he tended to hold his friend
to his own standards and principles. But enough of com-
parisons and differentiations. What the two men had in
common most of all was a massive integrity, not only in the
usual sense but in the radical—each was of a piece, an organic whole. How important this was is illustrated by a
comment Burke made late in Boswell's life: "[You have
the] art of reconciling contradictions beyond any man."[22]
Boswell did not so much reconcile contradictions as live
with them, like most of us.

Boswell certainly hoped that Johnson and Paoli would become fast friends. It is fair to say that they became friends—no easy achievement in the eyes of the Rambler—and that over the years they met many times without the intervention of Boswell. There is no evidence that either invited the other to a private dinner or meeting, but there are many references to Johnson's being one of a dinner party at the General's where, as he put it in a letter to Mrs. Thrale, he loved to dine. Unless he was with Boswell, Johnson apparently needed a specific invitation. As late as Easter Sunday, 1772, when Boswell and the General visited Johnson, Paoli found it necessary to press "Mr. Johnson to come often to see him, without waiting for an invitation. Mr. Johnson said, 'I will come with my friend Boswell, and so I'll get a habit of coming.'" To come only with Boswell was of course to come only during the periods of Boswell's stay in London—unless, with more than two years already having passed, the "habit" was expected suddenly to develop. Sometimes Paoli's and Johnson's different social orbits intersected by accident; however they met they were on an amiable footing. On occasion they must have sought privacy to discuss their young friend's problems, as when "General Paoli spoke to him [Johnson] with much concern of my drinking; that it would make me go mad, for madness was in my family" (Journal, 19 September 1777).

Paoli fully appreciated Johnson's abilities. In one passage recorded by Boswell he coined a characteristically lively phrase: "When a new subject is started Johnson bends himself like a bow" (Journal, 13 April 1779). Johnson could reciprocate; in a letter to Mrs. Thrale he quoted appreciatively Paoli's saying that "A man must see Wales to enjoy England."[23] To be sure, there were qualifications. Paoli like most men must have been susceptible to flattery, but if so he made no obvious display. On Johnson's behavior toward Lord Newhaven, related by Boswell in the *Life* (12 October 1779)—"He bowed his head almost as low as the table, to a complimenting nobleman"—Paoli enhanced mere description by noting that Johnson "held down his head to have the full pail of flattery poured on." Paoli had other things to say of Johnson which Boswell omitted from the *Life*. Although they were not said on occasions reported in that work, they were appropriate in discussions of Johnson's mind and character. Boswell was no doubt pleased when the General remarked of Johnson that he "was too apt to take personal qualities of some [of] those whom he met in Scotland for natural ones." Two other comments dealt with Johnson's imperiousness and inflexibility. "Johnson is like a God who is either damning you or giving his orders with awe. He is not like Jupiter, who lets Thetis sit on his knee and play with his chin." Again: "What is upright is good for supporting a building but does not ply to other uses."[24]

In the *Life* more than once Johnson rejected or corrected an assertion by Paoli, with the General making little or no response. One class of topics involved taste, a fundamental or unquestioned belief, or what is today usually called a value. In these instances, if the General uttered his view and Johnson contradicted, the General knew that nothing was to be accomplished other than to allow Johnson the last word. Such was Paoli's assertion that there was no beauty independent of utility, and Johnson's contradiction accompanied by the display of a beautifully painted coffee cup. (31 March 1772). The second class involved truly debatable but not provable propositions. Paoli rested after he made his view clear. An instance occurred just prior to the coffee cup episode. Here Paoli maintained that the state of marriage was natural to man. Johnson replied that it was so far from natural for a man and woman to live together in a state of marriage that "the restraints which civilized society imposes to prevent separation are hardly sufficient to keep them together." Paoli ventured to speak a second time, giving reasons for the greater strength of the bond between man and woman "in a state of nature." Johnson began the job of demolition instantly, culminating with, "Besides, Sir, a savage man and a savage woman meet by chance; and when the man sees another woman that pleases him better, he will leave the first."

An interesting exception, if it may be so called, occurred when Boswell, Johnson, and Goldsmith dined at Paoli's, where there was also present Vincenzio Martinelli, an Italian whose history of England had been published by a London printer (*Life*, 15 April 1773). Johnson made a pointed reference to Martinelli: "A foreigner who attaches himself to a political party in this country is in the worst state that can be imagined: he is looked upon as a mere intermeddler. A native may do it from interest." Paoli did not enter the discussion. By a circuitous route Johnson was brought to quote Dryden:

> For colleges on bounteous Kings depend,
> And never rebel was to arts a friend.

"General Paoli observed that successful rebels might. MARTINELLI. 'Happy rebellions.' GOLDSMITH. 'We have no such phrase.' GENERAL PAOLI. 'But have you not the *thing*?' GOLDSMITH. 'Yes; all our *happy* revolutions. They have hurt our constitution, and will hurt it, till we mend it by another HAPPY REVOLUTION.'" If anything further was said on the subject Boswell did not publish it. Johnson, who never gave the Americans any quarter, by his silence paid tribute to Paoli and signified approval of the Corsicans' revolution.

One must take a special factor into account when reading of Paoli's encounters with Johnson. Early in the journal entry from which he took the passages on beauty and utility and on marriage in nature for the published *Life*, Boswell wrote; "It was no small disadvantage that the General did not well understand Mr. Johnson and could not well answer him. However, by my aid as an interpreter, things did pretty well." Shortly before Johnson and Boswell ended their visit, the latter noted in his journal that Paoli "spoke English much better than I imagined he could do. 'Sir,' said Mr. Johnson, 'you must speak it before your friends, with whom you need not care though you spoil a thought.'" Paoli took the meaning intended and ignored Johnson's unconscious patronizing, which he surely felt. Indeed it was less than three weeks later that he pressed

Johnson to visit him often without waiting for an invitation.
The problem remained despite Paoli's increasing mastery
of English. Six years later, "disputing one morning as to
something Johnson had maintained, [Paoli] said, 'That
damned dictionary-making. He is all definitions'" (22
April 1778). Paoli also valued making the precise dis-
crimination, using the exact word. How would the two
have done if Paoli had been permitted to speak Italian and
Johnson forced to answer in the same tongue? In his Welsh
diary of 1774 Johnson was still spelling Paoli's name incorrectly.

On the whole the two men did well enough, the friendship becoming closer as Johnson approached his last
years.[25] Johnson's health, always bad, began to occasion
particular concern among his friends late in 1781. Boswell,
unable to make his trip south in the spring of 1782, hoped
to meet Johnson by summer. The death of Lord
Auchinleck on 30 August did not deter Boswell from planning to visit his friends in London and to seek their advice
on proposals to further his political career. Johnson advised him to stay at home, mind his own affairs, and above
all to do everything he could to preserve the health of Mrs.
Boswell. Paoli in the spring had urged Boswell to come to
London to "fish in these troubled waters," but by
September he too might have written to the same effect.[26]
The General made it his business to give Boswell news of
Johnson's health. In a letter dated 26 April 1782 (C 2157)
Paoli had noted that Johnson seemed perfectly well again,
"florid" (without the English connotation of feverishness);
the truth appears to be that Johnson, now never really well,
did give the appearance of normal well-being in society except when his illnesses were absolutely unbearable. As he
wrote to Boswell on 7 December 1782, he had passed
"almost this whole year in a succession of disorders," but
was "now reasonably easy though at a great distance from
health." Fanny Burney found him at this time "in most excellent good humour and spirits"; on 22 August of the
same year Mrs. Thrale indeed had believed Johnson sufficiently recovered from a dangerous illness to tell him of

her plans to leave Streatham and go abroad.[27] Johnson's diary indicates that perhaps as early as 11 December his health began to fail again, but he was able to dine out and pursue some of his usual activities. On the afternoon of Christmas Day, after attending church and dining with friends he was, as he wrote to Mrs. Thrale, "seized with a fit of convulsive breathlessness such as I think you have never seen." A few days later he was well enough to return home from Mrs. Thrale's and resume limited activities. To Boswell, Paoli wrote on 24 January 1783 (C 2158) that Johnson was now recovered sufficiently for the General to venture the "hope that he will have oil in his lamp for many years more."

Boswell arrived in London on 20 March 1783. Johnson spoke of himself as ill, but Boswell, although he quickly noted the truth of Johnson's statement, was able as usual to set conversation going. Aside from signs of fretfulness and impatience, and his occasional early retirement from company, the record shows Johnson's talk as lively and pithy as ever. On 29 May, the day before he was to set out for Scotland, Boswell spent "a part of the day with him in more than usual earnestness, as his health was in a more precarious state than at any time when I had parted from him. . . . I walked from his door today with a fearful apprehension of what might happen before I returned" (*Life*).

Paoli resumed his role as Boswell's informant. Others, including Boswell's brother, also kept what now could be called a vigil. On 16 June Johnson suffered the paralytic stroke described in the well-known letter to Mrs. Thrale. Paoli was alarmed, made inquiries, and was sufficiently reassured to inform Boswell that Johnson was recovering. In answer to an inquiry concerning portraits of Johnson the General, who knew and admired Sir Joshua, judged that the finest was that by Barry, in which the head is like that of "Jove meditating" (28 June 1783: C 2160). Boswell looked upon the news of Johnson as an "awfull prognostick" (8 August 1783: L 1016). Before Boswell could rouse himself from a state of "heavy dejection" Johnson was al-

ready on the move, spending nearly a fortnight with
Langton at Rochester and making "little excursions as easily as at any time of his life" (*Life*, IV, 233). In late August
he went as far as Heale, near Salisbury, "no more wearied
with the journey, though it was a high-hung rough coach,
than I should have been forty years ago" (Letter to Dr.
Brocklesby, 29 August 1783); and on 11 September he visited Stonehenge. All this following a stroke, while suffering
the pains of gout, and anticipating the possibility of
surgery for a sarcocele. Johnson chided Boswell for writing
so rarely when he knew the "uniform state of my health"
(30 September). With the onset of cold weather in December Johnson's asthma (perhaps more correctly described
today as emphysema) afflicted him with great pain, and
within a few days he began to be troubled with dropsy,
which Boswell singled out as a "fatal disease."

On 20 February 1784 Paoli wrote to Boswell that Dr.
Johnson this year had done well to escape with his life.
During the period of greatest danger Paoli himself went to
inquire about Johnson's health. "If he could spend a year
in the gentle climate of Italy he would be restored to
health, and his friends would have a more reasonable hope
of enjoying for many more years the conversation of a man
who never utters an untrue or unwise thing, or anything
which fails to lend lustre to virtue and discomfiture to vice"
(C 2161). Hawkins and Boswell agree that the scheme of
providing Johnson the means to escape the rigors of a
British winter was the work of Johnson's "friends."
Hawkins names Sir Joshua as the prime mover; in Boswell's account Sir Joshua is an active participant, but Boswell writes the letter to Lord Thurlow. The scheme was
"brought to a serious resolution at General Paoli's, where
I had often talked of it" (*Life*, 22 June 1784). Paoli's letter
several months earlier shows that he had actively pro-
moted the trip to Italy; undoubtedly he had made concrete
suggestions for the most salubrious places of residence.

The anxious Boswell at last arrived in London on 5 May,
and the next morning "had the pleasure to find Dr. John-

son greatly recovered." Paoli does not figure in the *Life* during Boswell's eight-week stay except for the time, on Friday, 25 June, when Boswell and Johnson dined with him.

> There was a variety of dishes much to his taste, of all which he seemed to me to eat so much that I was afraid he might be hurt by it; and I whispered to the General my fear, and begged he might not press him. "Alas! (said the General) see how very ill he looks; he can live but a very short time. Would you refuse any slight gratifications to a man under sentence of death? There is a humane custom in Italy, by which persons in that melancholy situation are indulged with having whatever they like best to eat and drink, even with expensive delicacies."

On both sides esteem, good will, easy familiarity, but not intimacy. Of Johnson's and Paoli's small number of truly intimate friends, Boswell was the only one they shared.

Johnson's "Sick Man's Journal," from 6 July to 8 December 1784, demonstrates for the modern reader the unhappy truth of Paoli's perceptions. Writing to Boswell on 27 July 1784 Paoli says that Johnson is in the country at Dr. Taylor's [Ashbourne], but that the change will not cure him of the great malady of being seventy-five years old (C 2163). A month later Antonio Gentili at the behest of the General, who was now disabled, once again brought up the subject of providing for Johnson's trip to Italy. "The Lord Chancellor has not yet given his reply to your proposal to send Dr. Johnson to Italy for the winter. He surely must have forgotten about it, and no one here is bold enough to remind him of it. If you do not hasten this matter to a conclusion, and very soon, you will be too late, for the season is already far advanced. Write yourself to the Lord Chancellor, or arrange for some friend to talk strongly to the point." Apparently Paoli feared that Reynolds was not persevering energetically in the negotiations with Lord Thurlow. In a few days, however, without any further intervention by Boswell, arrangements were settled after a fashion.[28] If the story of the Johnson-Paoli friendship needs an epilogue, let it be noted that Paoli was among the select group of mourners at the great man's funeral, and that he steadily encouraged Boswell in his projected writings on Johnson.

When Johnson died Paoli was in his sixteenth year of exile. It is time to return to the beginning and observe him through a lens with a properly wide angle of view. The question of his pension makes a good start. The newspapers had Paoli settled with a comfortable pension within days of his arrival in London. Actually, five months later he found it necessary to write to Burnaby that the promise of a pension was well and good, but that he had need of the real thing; otherwise he would be forced, much against his will, to consider other expedients. One of the expedients, Burnaby explained years later, involved the offer of Tsarina Catherine of an "honourable retreat" in St. Petersburg with a pension of six thousand rubles and the added hope that Russia would someday reinstate Paoli in Corsica.[29] Having thrust aside the obstacles presented by the Ottoman Empire and moved large units of its fleet to the western Mediterranean, Russia was hunting for appropriate bases, and possibly had its agents sound out Paoli while he was still in Europe. More than his usual alert consideration of international affairs might have been behind Paoli's comment to Boswell on their very first day in London that "the Russian fleet was moving up the Mediterranean like the mother of Proserpine, with a torch in each hand to kindle a fire all the way she advanced." When Paoli's situation was brought to the attention of the proper authorities he was immediately made solvent, with assurances that he would remain so for the rest of his stay in England.

Burnaby had procured for the General lodgings on Old Bond Street, "the most magnificent," Boswell supposed, "to be hired in all London." Paoli lived in appropriate style during his exile, enjoyed the privileges of coach, footman, servants, secretary, and the pleasures of inviting a rather large company to dinners which answered even to Johnson's taste. But adequate rather than elegant lodgings —always with a room for Boswell unless there was an impermanent guest—were more suitable to his state. Over the years he moved to lodgings in Albemarle Street, Jermyn Street (St. James), Hill Street (Berkeley Square), South Audley Street, and Portman Square.[30]

As noted earlier, it soon became clear to Paoli that Britain was not likely to take action with respect to Corsica until it had solved its immediate domestic problems as well as those with America, and even then not unless some unforeseeable drastic change took place in the balance of power in Europe. Paoli moved as inconspicuously as possible in the political background, never forgetting the kindness of the King and his Administration while at the same time developing his acquaintance among the Opposition only to a degree that was inoffensively correct. Not that he concealed his feelings entirely. Lord North's calmness, his distracting pleasantries—faint masks for unconcern—once moved the General to an impatient characterization in imitation of Horace: "If the vault of heaven were to break and fall, the ruins, though they struck him, would not rouse him from indifference. . . . Great men have never been dispensers of fine phrases. Cicero was, but never Caesar, never Augustus."[31]

As Paoli appeared to drift into the life of an English gentleman interested in letters, art, good conversation, and pleasant rounds of tours and visits, his hosts and companions did not suspect that the continued degradation of his people, enough of whom continued to fight by whatever means they found, caused him great anguish. He did not want the Corsicans to believe he had abandoned them; yet he was too wise to encourage foredoomed attempts at rebellion, such as those which took place in 1774 as a consequence of the hardships imposed by the French, not only in continued inflation and high taxes but in cruel reprisals against the relatives of those who resisted.[32] When abortive Corsican attacks on the French did take place Paoli could be as sure of English criticism as of French blame. In "The Country Justice" (1774) John Langhorne wrote of the brave struggle for freedom of the ancient British. Are thoughts of freedom and liberty now dead?

> Ask on their Mountains yon deserted Band,
> That point to Paoli with no plausive [applauding] Hand;
> Despising still, their freeborn Souls unbroke,
> Alike the *Gallic* and *Ligurian* Yoke!
>
> (I, 21-24)

The criticisms of a few Englishmen were not what seriously affected Paoli's state of mind. In the following pages, as Paoli will appear to have "adjusted" remarkably to his extended life in exile, the reader should be mindful of a late outburst which reveals feelings Boswell was never fully permitted to sense and record:

> They are wrong, those who have complained of me; while in order to serve them well God knows to what danger I have exposed myself and what life I lead; when, if it were not for them I would truly be able to compensate myself for the lonely life, or to say it better, the slave life I have led for so many years.[33]

Boswell's fully written journal for his stay in London in 1769 ends on 25 September, but he did not depart for Scotland until 10 November. Surviving notes and fragments, letters, and passages from the manuscript for *The Life of Johnson* help to fill the gap. For Paoli we must also accept the assistance of the *London Chronicle*, accurate for at most half the time, and other correspondence. Boswell spent much time with the General, but both even from the first days in London were busy with other engagements. The *Chronicle* had Paoli visit the Earl of Rochford on 21 September—probably true, since it is certain that he saw Grafton that day; and also on the same day the General was reported to have visited the Marquis of Rockingham —possible, but not very likely.[34] On Sunday, 1 October, Burnaby, Boswell, and the General visited St. George's Church, walked by the side of Serpentine River, and through Kensington Gardens. The same group with other friends went a week later to view St. Paul's Church, the Bank, and the Tower; and a few days later Boswell took the General and some other gentlemen to see the palaces and gardens at Richmond and Hampton Court. This kind of activity must be assumed to have continued but with less frequency. On the 22 or 23 October, according to the newspapers, "the Countess of Pembroke gave a very elegant entertainment to General Paoli and many of the nobility at her house in Privy Garden, Whitehall."[35]

Without Boswell, Paoli made other forays outside London, perhaps to escape the crowds which everywhere surrounded him, perhaps to keep himself busy in circumstances which he increasingly came to realize would frustrate attempts to fulfill his life's mission. A trip to Portsmouth, according to the *Chronicle,* took place on 11 October, with Paoli accompanied by Lord Palmerston and Mr. [Hans] Stanley. Writing on 6 November to Sir Horace Mann, Walpole told of Paoli's tour of Oxford and of Bath. Everywhere he was "received with much distinction," and at Bath he made part of a very brilliant assembly.[36] Boswell hoped that the General would come to Scotland to attend his marriage ceremonies, but he had to be content with Pasquale de Paoli's signature as a witness to the marriage contract. Paoli did hope to come to Scotland the following spring.[37]

The General finally set out for Scotland on 26 August 1771, accompanied by the Polish Ambassador, Count Burzynski. He had in the meantime already made the acquaintance of Mrs. Elizabeth Montagu, Queen of the Blues, whom he was to see again during his stop at Hagley, the estate of Lord Lyttelton, on the way to Scotland.[38] Two quotations from Mrs. Montagu's letters testify to Paoli's charm, complaisance, general good nature, and to a few of the rigors of the "slave life" to which he was already reduced.

> By the by I fell in love with General Paoli the other day at Court. I heard him talk a great while; there is an ease in his conversation that charms one. Some persons said the ladies here often meddled in politics; with a smile of cautious finesse he answered that it was *pour mettre de la douceur.* I felt a great deal of pity for this noble patriot reduced to beg an alms for Liberty of those who think Tyranny a greater Goddess.

Speaking of the house party at Hagley, Mrs. Montagu wrote:

> I was then much taken up in coquetting with the great Paoli; it is not the least of his heroism to coquette with an old woman, so I mention this circumstance for his glory as much as my own. . . . my hero was gone to visit his old sweet heart the Mountain Nymph sweet Liberty on the Moors of Scotland.

There was to be no end to punishment of this kind. Mrs. Delany wrote in 1779 that "the Duchess Dowager of Portland is charming well; and at this moment *charming* with her peculiar address General Paoli." Hannah More in 1782 exclaimed that "Paoli is my chief beau and flirt this winter—we talk whole hours." Paoli apparently did not escape any of the eminent bluestockings—Mrs. Vesey, Mrs. Boscawen, Miss Monckton, and if one stretches the term, Mrs. Thrale.[39]

Boswell noted that "General Paoli described a bluestocking meeting very well: 'Here, four or five old ladies talking formally, and a priest (Dr. Barnard, Provost of Eton), with a wig like a globe, sitting in the *middle*, as if he were confessing them.'"[40] Why, then, after the first initiations, did Paoli continue to accept invitations? First, it may be observed that Paoli, who in Corsica could be as abrupt and brutal as Johnson, in England was a pensioned guest very careful not to offend unnecessarily. Second, after all had been said against these fine ladies, it was incontestable that they brought together many interesting people, some of whom had political connections. Third, although Paoli more than once found his immediate social situation tedious, on the whole the meetings served, as Johnson would be the first to point out, to fill a man's time. Paoli read intensively, both in the classics and in some of the more modern authors, and he did much sightseeing, but cut off from what he could do best he perforce became a familiar figure at social gatherings.

To return to the journey to Scotland. The Count and Paoli arrived incognito at Edinburgh on 3 September. Information on the visit derives from a few surviving disjointed notes by Boswell, his letter to Garrick of 18 September, and, primarily, from Boswell's enthusiastic unsigned account in the *London Magazine* (XL, [September 1771], 433-34). In Edinburgh the Count and General were treated to the usual sights and introduced to Boswell's eminent friends. Dr. John Gregory, to whom Mrs. Montagu had given Paoli a letter of introduction, informed that lady, "I think General Paoli one of the first men I have ever seen, while I revere him as a hero and a genuine patriot." He went on to say that Hume, Robertson, and Blair among others were all charmed with the two visitors. Leaving Edinburgh for the west, the tourists went to the Carron Iron Works which produced the "warlike stores" sent to Paoli. "They were elegantly entertained at dinner by Charles Gascoigne, Esq; of the Carron company, and while they sat at table all the vessels at Carron-shore, which were just in their view, had their flags displayed, a circumstance which led the general to speak with his usual esteem of the British *hearts of oak*." That evening they went to Glasgow, and for a time the next day were able to tour the city without being known. But soon reports circulated that General Paoli was in town, and "every body was in motion, crowding to see him." The university, though not "sitting," was able to produce enough eminent professors to show the institution to good advantage. The professors were rivalled in hospitality by the magistrates of Glasgow. Paoli, who was instrumental in bringing the first printing press to Corsica, was especially pleased to visit the Foulis brothers, whose press had produced the "beautiful editions" of the Greek and Roman classics of which a few had been sent to Corsica by Boswell (*Tour*, p. 322n).[41] From Glasgow "Mr. Boswell conducted their excellencies . . . to Auchinleck, the seat of his father, who was extremely happy to receive such guests." It is difficult to believe that Paoli didn't manage to get along with Lord Auchinleck, to whom Sir Walter Scott later attributed the characterization, "landlouping scoundrel of a Corsican." To Garrick, Boswell wrote, "you may figure the joy of my worthy father and me at seeing the Corsican Hero in our romantic groves." After two nights at

Auchinleck the party toured to Treesbank and then, after another night at Glasgow, make the obligatory but nonetheless pleasurable visit to Loch Lomond. By Wednesday noon, 11 September, the group were back at Edinburgh. The General "slept under the roof of his ever grateful friend." The next day the party departed for London.

This was to be Paoli's only visit to Scotland, although Peggie and her husband were often to beg the General to return, and he more than once really expected to do so. Boswell's short journal notes are puzzling, but one comment by Paoli is clear and intense enough to deserve printing. The mountainous terrain of Scotland reminded Paoli of his native land. "Ah," he said, "que cela me fait souvenir que je ne vaut plus rien" [Ah, how this makes me recall that I am no longer of any value].[42]

When Paoli arrived at his lodgings in London he found little changed. About this time his secretary, Father Guelfucci, left for Tuscany because the English climate was finally proving too unbearable, but his place was soon taken by Father Andrei.[43] Count Gentili, self-sufficient with a British pension of two hundred pounds, was rooming in London with two Scots ladies, but he no doubt frequently favored Paoli with his company. By the next spring the Count was back as a permanent lodger, "very troublesome to the General, who is very good to him," but due to remain another four years before embarking on the voyage which took him to an unknown fate in Surinam.[44] The General did not simply sit at home awaiting visitors nor only bestir himself to return visits, although activities of this kind were enough to contribute increasingly to his social life. After some time he established the custom of a Sunday dinner with many distinguished guests from the continent. Boswell had introduced the General to all his distinguished friends in London, but continued reciprocal movement did not necessarily take place. Garrick, for example, was asked by Boswell in his letter of 18 September 1771, "Why have you not called on General Paoli, since I had the pleasure of presenting you to him in your morning dress, *comme un Roi déguisé*, and he paid you so handsome a compliment, which, I dare say, you have added to your cabinet of jewels?"[45] It nevertheless may be assumed that during the early years Paoli had more invitations—out of curiosity, perhaps—than he wished to accept, and that during the later years he was cultivated by politicians and bluestockings to a degree which kept him busy. His own taste ran also to artists, historians and antiquarians, scientists, and explorers; his election to the Royal Society must have given him considerable satisfaction.[46]

An account of all Paoli's acquaintances in England —even those mentioned in Boswell's papers, which after all present only a kind of accidental sampling—would be inappropriately long except in a multi-volumed biography.[47] Selected illustrative examples, mainly from Boswell, will serve the present purpose. The first half dozen years or so, until 1776, could be described as the initial period of adjusting, of settling down. Boswell's visits to London of 1772, 1773, 1775, and 1776 reveal what may be typical of the period. Paoli had as frequent guests two portrait painters, Richard Brompton, who had studied in Italy, and Antonio Poggi, the son of a Corsican, "of distinguished talents but little application." Boswell's judgment no doubt came from Paoli, who nevertheless ultimately had Poggi paint his portrait.[48] It is of interest that among Italian-speaking Londoners Paoli cultivated painters, historians, and scientists, but not until very late the most common variety, musicians. Visitors mentioned in Boswell's journal are almost equally divided between friends of Boswell, like his fellow advocate Andrew Crosbie and Sir William Forbes, the prominent banker who was to be the executor of Boswell's estate, and acquaintances of Paoli, like Captain Dunant, the Genevese who had visited Paoli in Corsica as a British agent, and Count de Neny, "one of the Council of Six in the Low Countries, and a great favorite at the Imperial Court." Neny, Boswell continues, "had visited Corsica the year after I was there, and had procured for General Paoli the kindness and esteem of the Emperor and [the] Great Duke of Tuscany. He was a very polite man, and had read a great deal."[49] To these should be added total strangers who over the years sought out the great man depicted in Boswell's *Corsica*. On a given day these could range from someone like a nephew of Alexander Pope to Baron Nolcken, Swedish Ambassador to England.

Just as Boswell brought Paoli into contact with the Johnson circle, in the early years the General did his part by introducing Boswell to a variety of celebrated people. The adjective is Boswell's: when he drove to the "celebrated Mrs. Montagu's" it was because she had sent him a card to meet the General with her at dinner. Among those present were his old friend Lord Lyttelton, the Archbishop of York (Robert Hay Drummond), and Thomas Anson, elder brother of the great Admiral. Boswell and Paoli shared responsibility for their connection with Henry Herbert, tenth Earl of Pembroke; Boswell for making a visit to Corsica an irresistible adventure for several English readers of his book, and Paoli for measuring up to Boswell's portrait when observed in the flesh. Boswell had given Pembroke a letter of introduction to Paoli; the Earl, accompanied by Captain Charles Medows, later first Earl of Manvers, then visited Paoli on the island. [50] When Pembroke was in Edinburgh, August 1774, Boswell invited him to dinner. "He agreed to come any day I pleased. . . . I said 'We Corsicans should meet.'" The dinner on 11 August was a huge success. The Earl called on Boswell on 18 August and said, "I set out tonight, and am come to ask Mrs. Boswell's commands for London." Boswell's bass fiddle was standing in a corner. "What!" said Lord Pembroke, "are we brother bassers as well as brother Corsicans?" An invitation for Boswell and Paoli to visit Wilton, when it came to them the next year, was readily accepted.

Pembroke, a very fashionable nobleman whose chief interests were women and horses, was quite a favorite at Court, and three years later was to entertain George III and Queen Charlotte where now he received Paoli and Boswell. Among the distinguished company were Captain Medows, Brompton the painter, the Rt. Rev. Dr. Richard Marlay, later Bishop of Waterford, Mrs. Fulke Greville, her daughter the beautiful Mrs. Crewe, and the Honorable Miss Monckton. Like Mrs. Montagu and Mrs. Vesey, who were to take more of Paoli's time in the future, Miss Monckton was a well-known bluestocking. Yet in the midst of this fashionable gathering at the very place where Sidney composed his *Arcadia*, Boswell "was sunk and nonchalant" and Paoli "tired exceedingly" (Journal, 21 April 1775). By the end of the three-day visit Paoli, who did not tire easily, had succumbed to the great enemy of an exile deprived of his profession, boredom. He did not thereafter reduce the frequency of appearances at social gatherings but very likely was more discriminating, and certainly less disposed to commit himself to long visits. There is no record of any host complaining of Paoli's behavior; on the contrary he was usually described as gracious and good-humored, with a vivacity in conversation which gave every sign of an engaged and happy mind.

Paoli's membership in the Royal Society, which had signaled his acceptance by the establishment of cultivated gentlemen of accomplishment or at least of exceptional curiosity, also brought particular pleasure to Boswell, who one day in 1776 was able to enjoy the company of such members as Captain Cook, Joseph Banks, Sir John Pringle, and Daniel Joseph Solander.[51] The year 1776 was a watershed for Paoli, a time for settling down for the long wait without succumbing to complacency. This year arrived his close companion for the rest of his stay in England, "the gallant [Antonio] Gentili who took Capraja, an amiable man whom I had seen at Sollacarò, though we did not remember one another."[52] Young Gentili could probably lay claim to the rank of colonel by the time the Corsican army disbanded in 1769. He was ultimately to become a general of France and fight against Paoli and the English. Now he was just what Paoli needed in a companion, a man of stable, reliable character and high intelligence who could discuss animatedly concrete plans for the future of Corsica. The age difference—more than twenty-five years—did not appear to matter. Gentili's ill health as frequently as Paoli's induced the two to escape

from London to Bath. When, years later, Paoli broke with
Republican France and was then abandoned by many of
the Paolist republicans, it was only the loss of Gentili which
gave the General deep personal pain. Contrary to reports,
they parted in sorrow, not anger.

In 1776, also, Boswell heard from the General, "in confidence, some important intelligence concerning Corsica
and himself. My mind was roused by it, though it was as yet
imperfect. It recalled his high dignity to my imagination."[53]
The intelligence may have had something to do with the
general amnesty the French government was now finding
it expedient to grant to the former Corsican rebels. At the
suggestion of Corsican leaders, private negotiations were
undertaken in the name of the King of France to offer
Paoli the royal pardon. The affair finally terminated in
1778 with Paoli's refusal—the conditions imposed unac-
ceptable restraints—and at this time Paoli's goods and
property were confiscated.[54] Another possibility, even
more speculative, is that the British government at long
last was considering the notion of acting against the
French, who already had busy agents in the colonies.

It is convenient now to gather what we know about Paoli
for the more than twenty years of his exile under headings
which derive logically from those used in the description of
the General in *Corsica*: his physical appearance and general
character, his knowledge, his views on religion and morality, on education and the arts, on politics; to which can now
be added an account of his principal friendships in England.

The last reference to Paoli's appearance was Johnson's,
on his lofty "port," a phrase which leads immediately to a
recollection of Boswell's quotation from the General on his
"unspeakable pride." It was a defensibly Christian pride.
Paoli was the chosen head of a free people now held in
bondage. All their hopes rested in him, and he was fated
to carry this sense of mission, this unspeakable burden,
even into his second exile in England in 1795. Corsica's
spirit of liberty incarnate; he could never forget, although
his easy social manner, his amiability, made others forget.

Within three years Boswell and Johnson believed they detected a change, the latter saying "he thought General Paoli had lost somewhat of that grandeur in his air and manner which he had when he came first to England. The observation is just," continued Boswell, "and the fact is easily accounted for. When he came first here he was just arrived from being at the head of a nation. Wherever he had passed, and even here, he was addressed in that high character. But after having been near three years just in the style of a private gentleman, much of the majesty of his deportment must insensibly be lost."[55] Yet James Beattie, who did not meet Paoli until the following year, found the great leader of Boswell's *Corsica* intact:

> Paoli is of a fair and florid complexion with dark and piercing eyes, and about five feet nine inches tall (as I guess); strongly made, but not in the least clumsy. He uses many gestures in his conversation as other Italians do, but they are not finical; and there is a freedom and dignity in his whole manner, equally free from assurance on the one hand and from affected reserve on the other. He looks and speaks like one who has been accustomed to command, yet there is nothing rough or assuming about him, but on the contrary the utmost politeness.

High character and grandeur in air and manner are not easily discerned where there is no high place, but Cosway's portrait of Paoli, painted in the late 1780s, shows a man of emotional intensity, dignity, and claim to power. John Wesley, who spent above an hour with Paoli on two different occasions in 1784, twelve years after the observations by Boswell and Johnson, wrote of him as "well-shaped," "graceful," with "something extremely striking in his countenance." Although "about sixty years of age . . . he does not look to be above forty."[56]

Of course it was not to be expected that the Paoli of Boswell's *Corsica* could survive intact a twenty-year exposure to the rigors of British society. People saw what they were able to see. The imagination of young Fanny Burney did not carry her beyond regarding Paoli as "a very pleasing man, tall and genteel in his person, remarkably well bred and very mild and soft in his manners," who spoke English

"pompously" and sounded "comical" when doing so. Time
held in store for Fanny some knowledge of what it meant
to be a General; now it was not surprising that she found
no more than her bluestocking friends. One might have
hoped for more from Mrs. Thrale. When the Thrale party
and Johnson reached Carnarvon on the tour in Wales,
1774, guns were firing in salute to the Corsican General,
who had just landed. The friendship with Paoli appears to
have become warmer after the marriage to Piozzi. Yet
when Paoli as the head of his nation once again was per-
ilously contending with enemies on all sides, Mrs. Piozzi
characterized him as "an old Goose" whose "meddling"
would probably lose him his head.[57] Only among the
Corsicans and some of the French did Paoli's stature survive unaltered during his twenty-year absence. Englishmen who thought they knew Paoli had to see him in
Corsica to detect the real man. Sir Gilbert Elliot and Lieutenant Colonel John Moore, of the British mission to Corsica in January 1794, found it necessary to revise their
opinions of Paoli which had been formed in England, the
first in a letter to his lady assuring her that she did not really know Paoli from recollecting him "only at the *Tabby* assemblies in London," the second in an entry in his *Diary*:

> Having never seen the General but as a well-dressed man
> going to court and routs, I had conceived, without better
> foundation, a poor idea of his abilities. I soon changed my
> opinion. . . . He struck us all as a very superior man.[58]

Thus, apparently, must it ever be for the leader in exile,
no matter how generally he is liked and esteemed. A singular exception in the large catalog of English men and
women who spoke in praise of Paoli was Horace Walpole.
During the Corsican struggle for independence Walpole
was a strong partisan and admirer of Paoli. But after the
defeat he saw the General in a different light, as a man who
had failed properly to dignify "the catastrophe of his
story." Writing to Mann of his first meeting with Paoli at
Court, he used much the same language he was later to
adopt in the *Memoirs of the Reign of George the Third*, saying
that he took Paoli for a Scotch officer, although he soon

concluded otherwise when he saw the King and Queen take great notice of him. Without identifying himself, Walpole told Paoli that he was Mann's particular friend. "He said he had written many letters to you, but believed they had all been intercepted." Mann chose to overlook the implications and turned Walpole's description into high compliment. "I am glad," he wrote, "that you have seen and conversed with Paoli, and can well conceive the impression that his first appearance made upon you. It is certain that in an English company he would never pass for a stranger. . . . In the meantime Paoli deserves every personal attention and support."[59]

Over the years Walpole's attitude towards Paoli developed from cool disapproval to downright nasty animosity. When Benedict Arnold arrived in London, Walpole observed that he "cannot do better now than consort with General Paoli." The record of "Tickets given for seeing Strawberry Hill" for 25 September 1784 shows that Maria Cosway brought Paoli to visit the showplace. According to Farington, Walpole returned the courtesy "by leaving a card at his door without asking for him"—an act only slightly removed from insult. After hearing that Admiral Hood had attempted to assist Paoli against the French in October 1793, Walpole wrote: "I wish he had not been complaisant to that dirty fellow Paoli. I would not send a man to the latter, unless it were his panegyrist Boswell, whose pigmies always are giants, as the geese of others are swans."[60]

For Walpole, Paoli's unforgivable offense was accepting the pension from George III; but the General compounded his faults by enjoying the best of too many worlds. A Plutarchian hero? "I always despised his conduct," Walpole told Farington. "A man is not obliged to be a hero; but if a man professes himself to be one he should die in the last ditch. Paoli to secure his pension fled from his country, and left many of his friends to be sacrificed." The General enjoyed the status and perquisites of a gentleman; yet the masses of people admired him. In the house at Vienna where Paoli stayed, Walpole heard, a mob surrounded the house "not to pull it down but to show attention to the person they supposed in it."[61] The General was treated as a friend by George III; yet he was on good terms with many distinguished members of the Opposition. Enough—Walpole's was on the whole a rare, dissonant note.

Moving now to Paoli as a specimen of a tolerably learned and eminently rational man, one finds much to remark upon. His literary interests were wide-ranging. "He has a strong understanding," Wesley concluded, "and seems to be acquainted with every branch of polite literature."[62] In Corsica, Boswell had been "diverted" with the General's English library. It was indeed fragmentary and diverse, but for a young and busy head of state in a country where English was not spoken and hardly regarded as important, the possession of volumes of the *Spectator* and *Tatler*, of Pope's *Essay on Man* and Swift's *Gulliver's Travels*, of Barclay's *Apology for the Quakers*, and of *A History of France* in what Boswell called "old English," suggests a man self-taught but on the whole leaning towards good exercises in the language if not consistency in the study of its accumulated culture. In the classics, aside from Homer and Virgil, his interests lay mainly in the historians and biographers. "Livy is a god, Tacitus a man of good sense, Sallust a philosopher," he told Boswell.[63] Of later writers his knowledge of Tasso was comprehensive enough for Johnson to call upon him to recite a passage appropriate to the discussion, and in his own century his familiarity with another Italian poet, Metastasio, which probably began when he was stationed in Italy, developed further during the stay in England. Paoli "has a general good taste in the Belles Lettres," Hannah More conceded in 1782, "and is fond of reciting passages from Dante and Ariosto. He is extremely lively when set a going; quotes from Shakespeare and raves in his praise. He is particularly fond of Romeo and Juliet, I suppose because the scene is laid in Italy."[64] Paoli's knowledge of other English authors is not fully documented. In the *Life*, Boswell shows Paoli rescuing Goldsmith with a gracious compliment: "Mr. Goldsmith is like the sea, which casts up pearls and many other things of beauty without being aware of it" (15 April 1773). The act was social and friendly—remarkably so in view of Goldsmith's previous attack on "Revolution"; but it was also discerning. Paoli, reading in a foreign tongue, apparently could still seize upon the particular talent of the author. Among "Memorabilia Paoli" in the Boswell collection is the following: "I said Lord Pembroke had wit. 'No,' said the General. 'He has been in the galleries of great men and he shows their *bijoux* [jewels]; but he is not a Goldsmith to make anything. He cannot polish a rough diamond'"(M 211).

Paoli's views of literature extended in both creative and scholarly directions. When he was informed by Boswell that his newly introduced guest, Thomas Sheridan, was a student of language, Paoli said "a great language, or a noble language, was a language in which great men have written; for it is by being moulded and animated by superior souls that a language becomes superior." When, on his first meeting with Johnson, his comments elicited an extravagant compliment from Johnson, they were again on the subject of language, its being formed on the particular ideas and manners of a country, its essential allusiveness. [65] Even when Johnson appeared to have "stunned" the General's faculties, the latter was able to voice an acute perception on Homer, which, as was all too often true, Johnson quickly dismissed: "He said he did not imagine Homer was so ancient as supposed, because there are circumstances in him of a refined society in a colony which we find were not in Greece itself when Thucydides wrote at a later period. . . . Dr. Johnson maintained the antiquity of Homer."[66] Paoli had perceived a problem which only later scholars were to find it easy to explain. The habit of intensive reading continued into Paoli's later years, once causing Maria Cosway to chide him for being "always immersed in philosophy or literature" (1798).[67]

In the sister arts Paoli had friends among painters—Brompton, Poggi, Cosway, and particularly Reynolds—but this fact could signify only that he enjoyed being among persons who could speak Italian. As for Reynolds, the friendship of itself demonstrated no more appreciation of art than it did for Johnson. For the General it may be said on Boswell's authority that he was a keen observer of the beauties of nature, that he at least thought about the "meanings" of emblematical or historical pictures, and spoke appreciatively of Sir Joshua's use of color. He was perhaps thinking merely of durability when he said that Sir Joshua as a sculptor would have won eternal fame, but the phrase denotes admiration; its critical acuity is of course debatable. We may leave the subject with one of Paoli's characteristic sallies on Reynolds, still indicating admiration: "He has a horn only at one ear; if he had one at both he would be a Jupiter."[68]

It is obligatory, before leaving the subject of Paoli and the arts and belles lettres, to take into account the surprising exchange between Paoli and Johnson on the art of printing:

> The General maintained that the art of printing had hurt real learning by disseminating idle writings. Dr. Johnson said if it had not been for the art of printing, we should have now no learning at all. . . . The General maintained that a diffusion of knowledge among a people was a disadvantage, for it made the vulgar rise above their humble sphere. The Doctor opposed this and said that while knowledge was a distinction, those who were possessed of it would naturally rise above those who were not. That to read and write was a distinction at first, but we see when reading and writing have become general, the common people keep their own stations. In the same proportion will it be with respect to other kinds of knowledge (JB Journal, 11 April 1776).

These views coming from a man who believed in education for all, who had the honor of bringing the first printing press to Corsica, are shocking.[69] Boswell, publishing them in the *Life* while Paoli was overburdened with problems in Corsica, transformed "The General" into "A gentleman." The Tory advocate of proper subordination has exchanged roles with the enlightened hero. Actually, Johnson is consistent. In *The Rambler, No. 4,* he had indeed attacked what could be called idle writings, but these were fictions which undermined instead of reinforcing the moral sense, and certainly had nothing to do with making the vulgar rise above their humble sphere. In his more pertinent review of Soame Jenyns' *Free Enquiry* Johnson, without denying the propriety of a society based on subordination, eloquently defended the need for education, which, to be sure, he did not tie to the maintenance of an unfettered press: "Those who communicate literature to the son of a poor man consider him as one not born to poverty but to the necessity of deriving a better fortune for himself." Such, one would think, were the views of Paoli; he had expressed them earlier, was to accept and reinforce them when he returned to Corsica under revolutionary France, and finally was to embody them in his testamentary wishes. The only possible explanation is a temporary lapse, induced perhaps by the violent and scurrilous outpourings which shocked him upon his arrival in England. Before he ended his exile he was to express himself quite differently on this subject.

The treatment of Paoli's views on literature and the arts should not be ended without a further glance at his knowledge and study of languages. Boswell had noted in the *Tour* that Paoli understood English and spoke it "tolerably well" (pp. 321-22). He read English more frequently as he tried to follow the course of British political opinion in the years 1765-69. During his first week in England he was interested enough to take a lesson in English from Boswell, and on the same occasion demonstrated his reading ability by translating Peggie Montgomerie's *"most valuable letter"* with "elegant spirit into Italian" (Journal, 25 September 1769). His progress in speaking and writing English was slow, and in company where Italian was not known by all who were listening he usually spoke French, in which, as he readily acknowledged upon first seeing Boswell in London, he lacked fluency. Even with practice he never became fully at ease in that language. With three known exceptions the General wrote his letters to Boswell in Italian, and Boswell wrote in English. The first exception is a paragraph, apparently written 6 May 1784 (C 2162), which

Paoli wrote at Dilly's after being too late to greet Boswell
upon his arrival in London. He asks why Boswell did not
immediately come to his house. Come soon, he continues.
"Any engagement would have been postponed for the
pleasure of embracing you and drinking a tombler to your
Political Endeavours." Boswell showed the note to Johnson
with pride; the latter observed that it was quite correct except for the spelling of *tumbler*, and at first doubted that it
was actually written by Paoli. The second, 10 March 1787
(C 2166.8), quite correct and idiomatic, is an inquiry about
Mrs. Boswell's health which accompanied tickets to the op-
era. In a long note to Boswell six days later (C 2167), concerning the date at which they are to dine at the Chaplain's
table at St. James's Palace, Paoli demonstrates that he can
now write in English with some ease when he chooses to do
so. Johnson's earlier doubts were probably occasioned by
the character of Paoli's spoken English, which in its 1782
form has been preserved by Fanny Burney. Boswell scholars have always been interested in one of the several paragraphs:

> "He came," he said, "to my country, and he fetched me
> some letter of recommending him; but I was of the belief he
> might be an impostor, and I supposed in my minte he was
> an espy; for I look away from him, and in a moment I look
> to him again, and I behold his tablets. Oh! he was to the
> work of writing down all I say! Indeed I was angry. But
> soon I discover he was no impostor and no espy; and I only
> find I was myself the monster he had come to discern. Oh!
> is a very good man; I love him indeed; so cheerful! so gay!
> so pleasant! but at the first, oh! I was indeed angry."

Burney was good, no doubt of it, but Boswell did not
have to yield to her as transcriber, and no doubt could
have recorded reams of Paoli's English. Yet among the
mountains of his papers no more than occasional words or
very short passages are to be found. Fanny Burney herself
explains why. Her introductory statement, "His [Paoli's]
English is blundering, but not unpretty," is bland enough;
but her final comment makes Boswell's reasons clear: "This
language, which is all spoke very pompously by him,
sounds comical from himself, though I know not how it

may read."[70] Superiority to one who speaks broken English is purchased very cheaply even by the most illiterate. It is a measure of Boswell's profound respect that even in the privacy of his diary he would not place the General in what in a weak moment he might consider an unflattering light.

One cannot turn from the subject of Paoli's knowledge of modern languages without taking note of Hannah More's complaint: "He will not talk in English, and his French is mixed with Italian. He speaks no language with purity."[71] It is worth observing that she started the paragraph by admitting that she had "not spoken seven sentences of Italian these seven years," and that in the midst of it she wrote that Paoli quoted from Shakespeare; but the critical statement is the last, that Paoli spoke "no language with purity." To defend Paoli's Italian from Hannah More is perhaps an uncalled-for exercise; aside from what she had forgotten there is the question of what she had never known, and there is always the consideration of which dialect of Italian deserved primacy. Paoli's reading in Italian was wide, and his experience in speaking involved Naples, Sardinia, Tuscany, and Genoa-Corsica. His letters should be sufficient to establish his competence. With reference to these, it is useful to remember that many were written in great haste. John Symonds, later Gray's successor in the chair of modern history at Cambridge, was one of those to whom Boswell, at Genoa, had so effectively communicated his enthusiasm for Corsica that Symonds himself then made a journey to the island. In a letter to Boswell he wrote, "I never found a person of a more liberal improved conversation than the General." Now Symonds was concerned that Boswell would not do justice to Paoli's literary powers in printing the General's letters in *Corsica.* "His letters are written generally in a common familiar style. He is above thinking much when he dictates, and indeed would not have time if he was inclined to it; else how would it be possible to dictate from twenty to sixty letters in a day, as he actually did when I was at Corte?" The style of Paoli's letters for this period, which in part covers the Paoli-Choiseul exchanges, nevertheless needs no defense.[72]

The range of Paoli's ideas on other subjects—metaphysical, philosophical, religious, and political—is suggested in the *Tour* and *Life*, but considerably enlarged by materials in the Boswell collection and elsewhere. The General sounds like the young Akenside when he speaks of the possibility of our some time being able to calculate moral events scientifically; but on the whole his religious views are consistent with statements in the *Tour*. John Wesley, after remarking that Paoli appeared "to have a real regard for the public good," added that he also had "much of the fear of God." Like any good Catholic Paoli attended Mass; to Boswell he "talked steadily of his faith in Revelation." His statement, "The miracles of freedom are more frequent, more grand, and more beneficial than those of Saint Anthony of Padua," has the ring of unorthodoxy, but it would not have upset the lower clergy and monks who worked so closely with Paoli in Corsica. God manifests himself in many ways; the passage quoted, written just before the onset of the French Revolution, was preceded by observations which placed Catholic France in a bad light compared to its Protestant neighbors, but their emphasis was simply on the effective practice of Christianity, itself miraculous and wonderful: "The lands of France are cultivated; but the masses of workers do not know and do not feel any pleasure from their toils. There are more kitchen spits and cooking pots on the fire in England, in Switzerland, and in Holland than in all the rest of Europe. In these places one does not see a barefoot man with a face marked by hunger."[73] When, under Republican France, Paoli curtailed the power of the bishops and confiscated their lands, he only concluded the process he had begun over twenty years earlier. He honored and respected the traditional acts of worship of the pious Catholic, and, like Johnson, he revered the truly Godly man.

On a subject which Boswell insistently brought up even though it agitated Johnson, the fear of death, Paoli at one point sought to calm Boswell with the image, "Nature withdraws her hand from us little by little until we have fallen asleep." Further discussions elicited a somewhat different response. "Dr. Johnson was much pleased with a remark which I told him of Paoli: That it was impossible not to be afraid of death; and that those who at the time of dying are not afraid, are not thinking of death, but of applause or something else which keeps death out of their sight, so that all men are equally afraid of death when they see it." Elsewhere Boswell elaborates the "something else" to include "imaginations of future felicity"—more appropriate for a devout man. Many years later Paoli was frequently requested by Maria Cosway to join her at Mass, which he did quite willingly. In one letter to her he wrote: "[Your letter] has edified me, and has altogether disposed me to follow your wise, good, and saintly counsel. . . . [The Church's] dogmas will endure so long as the world lasts, and I believe them by the authority by which she has manifested them, and in this put aside all the doubts which the weakness of the human mind would strive to pass off as arguments to the contrary."[74]

On the subjects of politics, government, and the organization of society, Paoli's views cannot now be as simply labelled as they might have been if based solely on *Corsica.* For one thing he clearly liked being a kind of ex officio member of the ruling class, to the disgust of some ardent and articulate republicans who themselves enjoyed the perquisites of affluence. Like the wealthy he preferred to leave London for the country in the summer; like them also he took the waters at Bath and there joined the company of high society. He entertained foreign dignitaries, took fashionable airings in his coach, made tours to places of interest. All this, nevertheless, was to a large degree on the surface. Although not a leveller, his basic physical needs, as he had demonstrated earlier in Corsica and was to do again, were essentially simple. He was in Corsica a man of authority, waited upon and guarded gladly by his people; but he there lived austerely. In England, if he wished to enjoy any intellectual stimulation, most of all if he wished to exert any influence, he perforce had to move

in circles which on the whole set him off from those who
wanted him to use all his powers to bring reform to England.

A few touchstones suggest Paoli's position. The quarrel
with the American colonists he wanted settled quickly one
way or another, so that Britain could be free to tend to its
proper concerns in Europe. It was wishful thinking, not
sound military judgement, which made him say to Boswell
and Johnson that America was like a man mortally
wounded, still holding the sword but in despair. Boswell
opined, more correctly and with a revealing change of sex,
"She's only scratched" (Journal, 5 April 1778). Some days
later Paoli, now considering principles, "argued for the
American resistance, not because Britain had not the right
to tax them, but because the exercising that right made
them *apprehensive* of slavery" (Journal, 17 April 1778). A
close observer of British affairs both internal and external,
Paoli saw them as foreign to his interests except as they
concerned Corsica. The formal treaty of friendship between France and America naturally placed the conflict in
a different light. Nevertheless, Paoli's attention was drawn
more to struggles of the same magnitude as those which
he and his people had experienced. Thus, speaking of the
past but thinking of the present, Paoli wanted books on
small-scale wars, not books like those by Folard, which
dealt with large masses of troops and consequent large cas-
ualties (Journal, 30 March 1778).

On constitutional and legislative matters Paoli kept to
the long view. With Oglethorpe he could join in admiration of the Jews. "Where," he asked, was there "such a legislator as Moses?" (Journal, 11 April 1778.) On the whole
he approved of the British constitution, at least for the
British, but when real reforms were in the air in the early
1780s he no doubt privately supported them. His admiration for Burke and friendship with William Johnstone-Pulteney are the most tangible clues supporting this
inference. He had no illusions about the masses or their
leaders; but he was probably thinking of Boswell's political
ambitions when he said: "Mankind as individuals are cun-

ning; as a multitude they are drunkards. Take care of them. If you are a pleasant bottle companion they will not employ you as a lawyer; they will not trust you with their property. But they will give their voice to make you a minister of state."[75] The inflammatory rhetoric and the vicious techniques of rabble-rousing which Paoli saw in England had no doubt appalled him. Nevertheless he could hope for the British the achievement of a sufficient approximation to the ideal society which appealed to him as a young man in Italy. When General Oglethorpe said of Johnson that "he thinks there is no misery in England because he does not see it," he demonstrated unbelievable ignorance of the life and views of Johnson. His further comments were in a vein to please Paoli. Now, he said, there were too many lawyers, physicians, and their underlings taken from labor: "Labour is the real riches of a country." Earlier in the day Boswell had remarked to the General "that the servants of London were a great body, lived well and happily, and, were they united, might be a body of great influence. . . . He said no. As individuals they had influence, but could not as a body. They were well called Knights of the Rainbow. There never could be a society of influence when there is no object of dignity to keep them together, when they are despised and are not admitted into company." To this should be added Paoli's comment when told by Boswell that Burke said "it was of great consequence to have a British peerage, for each generation is born in a great theatre where he may display his talents. 'It is true,' said the General, 'he is born in a great theatre, but he is applauded before he acts.'" It is fair to conclude that the passage of time found Paoli adjusting to the flow of events by occupying a middle position on government. He once told Boswell that he was going to propose, as a conversational gambit, the paradox that a republic should have a king and a monarch should have a republic, "to correct each."[76] It should be remembered that the Corsica to which Paoli returned in 1790 was under the government of a France which gave every indication of establishing a constitutional monarchy.

As we approach the end of the section on Paoli's first exile we cannot properly omit consideration of his close friends in England. For James Boswell, about whom much has already been said, Boswell's biographer may be expected to continue to place his friendship with the General in appropriate perspective. Now, it must be sufficient briefly to describe that friendship so far as possible from Paoli's point of view. Efforts like Boswell's would have made anyone a valued friend of Paoli. Their first days together in London were marked by exhilaration, admiration, and devotion on Boswell's part; on Paoli's, gratitude, of course—the pension, even the choice of England as the place of exile, would have been unthinkable without Boswell. Had this been all, Paoli, true to one of Machiavelli's maxims, would have tired of, even turned against Boswell. But quite the opposite took place, and the mutual affection so well described by Professor Pottle in a passage quoted early in this study deepened as the years wore on. Everything Paoli had—his house, his coach, his table, even his purse—was at Boswell's disposal. In his journal for 2 April 1776 Boswell writes of the General, after noting an additional borrowing of money: "His kindness to me, and his perpetual good sense and good temper, made me admire him more and more. I lived in his house with as much ease or more than if it had been my own. He was glad to see me at all times, for at all times I freely tried his civility. Yet he exacted no attention from me. My breakfast was brought into my bedchamber. I might have it carried into his. I might go out when I pleased. I might dine at home when I pleased. I might come home at any hour, and go quietly to bed. Giacomo Pietro, a Corsican, the General's own servant, shaved me and dressed my wig, and Jacob, a Swiss servant, went messages for me. Then I had the General's coach whenever I had occasion for it and he had it not out, which he seldom had."

Paoli was the indulgent father who encouraged Boswell's dear ambitions, even to enter politics and to settle in London—the last to be reversed as Boswell grew older. Yet he always sought to correct Boswell's errors, and though forgiving was unyielding in principle. Two passages not many years apart will illustrate. The first, concluding one of Paoli's many lectures on Boswell's drinking, finds Paoli comforting, then exhorting:

> Your friends did not think ill of you. I scolded your faults, but threw a shining veil over them; covered them with gold lamina. . . . I will offend you, [but] I will be your friend. For all my regard, if the King would send you as secretary with me to Corsica to restore our affairs, I would say "I will not have him. From his fault, I cannot trust him" Cure [yourself] of this, and you will be asked by men in power; it will be their interest. But you must appear to them. They will not draw you from the waves. The malignity of human nature likes to see you struggle. But get to shore; be firm, be able, and they will have you. (Journal, 7 May 1781.)

In the second Boswell was "much cast down" when Paoli said: "You are past the age of ambition. You should determine to be happy with your wife and children" (Journal, 6 July 1786). Boswell, an able advocate, did not reply: "And you, fifteen years my senior, are you not past the age of ambition?" Instead, now as always he accepted Paoli's correction, knowing that it was meant kindly and wisely for his and his family's good. With this father he never felt resentment, never quarreled.

Paoli was of course speaking of Boswell's political ambition, for Boswell had already published the *Tour to the Hebrides* and had not dismissed from his mind the immense project of the *Life*. It was great place or even not-so-great place rather than literary fame which for Boswell was the irresistible ignis fatuus. There is no need to deal here with Boswell's political career, which Professor Brady has so neatly chronicled and analyzed.[77] It is necessary only to mention that a dominant concern in the letters exchanged between Boswell and Paoli during the years 1780–86 is political. The exchanges have not yet been published; a running account with brief selections will serve here.

For the reader of the journals, Boswell's letters contain few surprises. The journal entry for 18 May 1778, for example, reveals Boswell's ruling passion and the depth of his affection for Paoli:

> He said at present I would be all things: keen in little things as well as great. I said, "Shall I ever be great? I'm unhappy not." "Yes, when you have taken a *caractère décidé* pour quelque état sérieux" ["A settled character for some serious office"]. Wished I were in Parliament. I was sorry to part with him. . . . Then to General's and packed all up in hurry. Should have packed in forenoon, but left all till night. Adieu to Gentili, General abroad. Better to be without adieu.

Add bouts of melancholy, unhappiness at being in many ways still a dependent of Lord Auchinleck, concern for Mrs. Boswell's health, desire for the life of London, and we have all the essential themes. However, Paoli's letters are more than extensions or elaborations of passages in Boswell's journal.

The surviving exchanges in England begin in the spring of 1780, when Boswell writes that he has "not been so long silent and all the while in good spirits." Unhappily, partly because of the illness of Lord Auchinleck he will not be able to go down to London this vacation, a fact which makes precious "the last rich though short harvest . . . which I enjoyed with your Excellency." He expresses pleasure in knowing that Paoli has made the acquaintance of Lord Bute. Has he seen Dr. Johnson lately? He forwards his wife's best compliments and sends regards to M. Gentili, as he is to do in all his letters. In his reply Paoli expresses satisfaction in hearing that Lord Auchinleck is better. He is not yet in a position to introduce Boswell to Lord Bute, but still believes coming to London would help advance Boswell's career. He had been counting on Boswell's companionship, for he too has been feeling dull and out of sorts. Apparently without hearing again from Boswell, Paoli two months later sends him a description of the Gordon Riots.[78]

Boswell is thankful that Paoli was unscathed by the "storm of Protestant barbarity"; indeed, "during this reign there has been such a ferment that we have really grown blotched from licentiousness." He hopes that Paoli will not

conclude that the British "constitution is a little too sanguine." He is sending the letter by his brother Thomas
David, whom he recommends as a banker to Paoli and his
friends. The two sons had spent four weeks with their
father at Auchinleck, "the romantick seat of our ancestors
which you honoured by liking it." He must decline Paoli's
kind invitation to resume his place under the General's
roof, but hopes to come in the spring. They then can make
plans for "a compleat tour through Ireland" for some
future year. In his reply Paoli expresses regret that he is
unable to help T. D. Boswell in a business way, "but you are
familiar with my circumstances and know that their measure falls short of that of my good will and my obligations.
I offered him your apartment, at least for the time it will
take him to become settled in the city; but he, seeing that
I was on the point of leaving once again for the country,
refused to make this his home at this time. He has promised
me for my return, which will be within three weeks, the
consolation of frequent appearances here." The elections
are almost finished. Fox will represent Westminster, and
"your friend Sheridan has found a borough to send him to
Parliament. The city of Bristol has refused to elect Burke,
who, it is said, wishes to retire and lead a private life.
Neither his virtues nor his vices are of the kind that should
allow him to be relegated to the quiet of obscurity. His
speech to the people of Bristol is in my opinion a master-
piece; it savors a little of the pulpit, but is not worth the
less for that; his mind and his political principles shine
forth nobly. . . . Autumn comes in, very wet, and we foresee
a severe winter; both seasons will be more tolerable, in
spite of the *ennuis* of November and the frosts of January,
since you have consoled me with the knowledge of having
you in this house at the beginning of spring." With Gentili
joining their councils, they will be able to agree on a plan
for the Irish excursion.[79]

Boswell now takes five months to reply. He begs forgive-
ness for his long silence, caused by a severe fit of melancholy aggravated by his brooding over "the perplexed
question of Liberty and Necessity," and asks how Paoli

overcame such worries. The reader recognizes with dismay that Boswell could have written exactly the same words over seventeen years earlier; indeed, in *Corsica* (pp. 349–50) he had already asked the question of Paoli, who explained that he never felt a moment of despondency. The reader of Boswell's journals and his correspondence with Paoli now knows that in exile the General admitted to moments of despondency; but he did not let Boswell or any of his English friends discover the true depths of his melancholy. To return to the letter, Boswell writes that his spirits are lifted by the expectation of leaving for London in two weeks (27 February 1781: L 1009).

In the *Life* for the London visit of 19 March to 2 June 1781 Boswell hews more resolutely than usual to the subject of Johnson and does not mention Paoli. Paoli and Johnson during this period are together at least twice; Boswell's journal as it relates to Paoli will be gleaned at the proper time, when among minor items his interview with George III on 30 May 1781 can be given appropriate attention.[80] When Boswell leaves for Scotland he enjoys the company of Johnson as far as Squire Dilly's in Bedfordshire, as related in the *Life*. Once in Scotland, Boswell writes to Paoli of the pleasures of the journey and the settling of his family in an agreeable little house; but even so the clouds of depression have returned. In this state he attempts to cheer Sir John Pringle, who has returned to die in his own country. His conversation with George III is "exactly written down." He cannot resist hoping that Paoli will tell the King that he wishes "to be near his person" (27 July 1781: L 1010).

Writing on 7 August 1781, Paoli tells of the apprehension caused by Boswell's "long silence." This characterization of a two-month period emphasizes the degree of Paoli's concern. He tries to cheer his friend up, ascribing the melancholy to Boswell's troublesome inflammation of his eyes. Further, "It is not strange that a new way of life and a sudden change to dull and tedious labour should affect the spirit and the machinery of the body." From here it is only a step to a caution against "a certain slight excess into which there is often danger of your falling again. . . . from a calmer and more constant spring draw your good humour and the better side of your nature." Paoli goes so far as to praise T. D. Boswell for lending "no ear to the followers of Bacchus. . . . Take thought of returning to London soon; otherwise this brother of yours, with the easy affability of his character, will take absolute possession of the spirits of all your friends." It is clear that the General knows how far he can go; and with respect to Boswell's drinking he repeatedly goes far indeed. To return to the letter: Paoli praises Boswell's letter to Lord Mountstuart, with whom he has had a pleasing conversation dealing in part with Boswell's talents. (Mountstuart was one of those through whom Boswell unsuccessfully sought preferment.) A moving portion of the letter is occasioned by thoughts on Sir John Pringle, "that most worthy and honourable man," to whom he sends "a hundred thousand expressions of esteem and affection." Paoli, twice torn from his native land, is entering the thirteenth year of his second exile. His sentiments suggest the influence of Rousseau, but Paoli has no more need for Rousseau's ideas on love of country and the simple life than he had had for Rousseau's laws:

> It is from Nature that we receive that instinct which you call prejudice in our old friend. Such an instinct is the same thing as love of country. For it, even in the arms of the beautiful Goddess, Ulysses could not forget the rock of Ithaca; and for it a friend of mine would not sell for any price the remains of a ruined tower situated upon a rock and amid the ancient tufted oaks of his park. Man is unwilling to persuade himself that he is mortal, and after he has acquired fame and riches he is by nature impelled to return to his native land, where a pleasing illusion (from which society derives so much good) makes him believe that he converses with the shades of his forefathers and gives them pleasure. This passion has been common to all times and to all men; indeed it must have a rational source. . . . for my part I believe that the sum total of happiness enjoyed in one small Swiss canton is but little less than that enjoyed by all the inhabitants of the Monarchy of France, where all men are at the disposition of others and are virtually forced, without respite, to do something they are either unable or at least unwilling to do (7 August 1781: C 2155).

Boswell waits close to five months, until 8 January 1782, to reply. His depression has deepened, this time in part for the very good reason that Mrs. Boswell has been displaying more alarming symptoms of illness. Margaret Boswell's condition was a subject for concern as early as 1774, and by 1776 she feared she had consumption. On Boswell's visit to London in 1777 he apparently forced Peggie's sickness below the threshold of his consciousness, for he led Johnson into telling him he should bring his wife to London as soon as he could (Journal, 20 September 1777). In the brief journal notes for 5 January 1778 Boswell records that Margaret Boswell "spoke of what might happen, and that I must be both father and mother to my children. This terrible." In the above-mentioned letter to Paoli, dated a few days later, he writes of Mrs. Boswell's recovery. In addition he expresses a wish for an end to the war with America, and sends a memorial asking Paoli to use his influence with General Sir George Howard to have a humble acquaintance excused from military duty. Finally, he asks if Paoli sometimes calls on Sir John Pringle, that gentleman apparently having decided not to wait for death in Scotland (L 1011).

Paoli as usual replies within a short time. He is led to "hope for the advantages of having you here for some time during the spring. Come to admire or to pity Lord Cornwallis and to make the acquaintance of Arnold," both of whom are momentarily expected in London. Writing about public affairs now only violently upsets me, he continues. "I will only say that my poor compatriots are converging from every quarter upon Leghorn, there to find passage to Minorca, where there are at this moment hundreds of them. They go willingly and in good order, showing at once their resentment and their gratitude. Now they understand what they could have done." In a postscript he tells of going to visit their friend Sir John Pringle, only to find that he had died during the night (22 January 1782: C 2156).

The ministry which succeeded Lord North's in March 1782 agreed on little other than ending the disastrous war with America, and even on this issue proceeded to quarrel among themselves. A coalition of the Rockingham and Shelburne groups, it consisted of Rockingham himself as First Lord of the Treasury, Fox and Shelburne as Secretaries of State, Lord John Cavendish as Chancellor of the Exchequer, and Burke as Paymaster of the Forces. Pitt, although supported by Shelburne, was denied a position on grounds of youth and inexperience. Writing to Paoli on 19 April 1782, Boswell expresses regret that the lack of funds and any pretext for bringing legal business before Parliament will prevent him from going to London this season. Now that his friends are in power, he has made application for the office of Judge Advocate of Scotland to Burke, Fox, and Lord Pembroke. Perhaps, he adds, the new administration will do something for Corsica also. Paoli, replying on 26 April, says he will do all he can by speaking to Boswell's friends. But, since the courtesy visits following the change of ministry, "I have not yet been able to talk with anyone but Mr. Fox. They have too many irons in the fire." Come and ask for the office yourself, he adds. "The trip will cost ten guineas; it will pay with interest in time. If you consult your father he will be of my opinion. . . . The day before yesterday Dr. Johnson, on his way to dinner with Paradise at the Bishop of St. Asaph's, came to pass an hour with me. . . . May Mrs. Boswell and your father accept my respects and not take amiss the counsel I give you, to come here for a while and fish in these troubled waters." The General, too much a realist, says nothing of Corsica.[81]

Boswell was to make no trip to London in 1782. Writing on 4 July, he speaks of his own illness and of the more portentous consumptive symptoms of Mrs. Boswell. He is grateful for Paoli's generous offer and expresses a sense of delicacy about hurrying up to London just when his friends have come into office. It is "too much like a hungry Scot." He may come in the autumn with Mrs. Boswell, and then also pay a visit to Burke. At least one exchange of letters during the next few months is missing. Boswell certainly wrote to Paoli following the death of Lord

Auchinleck on 30 August; and Paoli on his side wrote a letter of condolence, for which Boswell expresses deep gratitude in his letter to Paoli of 18 January 1783. He has been "a better man" since his father's death, and "as moderate a wine drinker as yourself." He had actually set out for London in the autumn, but was recalled by a message that Mrs. Boswell had been taken very ill. His hopes of office have been revived since Lord Mounstuart's return from abroad.[82]

Paoli is moved by Boswell's deep seriousness. "I have always cherished your letters, but that of the 18th of this month has become so dear to me that I have determined to keep it in a place apart so as to have with me always a token of the friendly confidence which you place in me. Yesterday I encountered your brother. . . . I told him of the consolation you have given me, and you may imagine how great was our pleasure when you consider that I sincerely participate in whatever interests you, with the affection and the friendship of a true brother." Paoli goes on to speak of a long conference with Lord Mountstuart, who he is sure will do what he can to further Boswell's aspirations. He writes of Burke's situation, and of the signing of the preliminary articles of peace with France and America. "I do not hope for any talk of Corsica at this juncture." Lord Pembroke is a great man at court, and should be able to help Boswell. Besides the usual expressions of respect for Mrs. Boswell, the letter closes with news of Johnson's health and of Mrs. Thrale's plan for going to Italy in the spring. "She too has her Blue Stocking meetings and from time to time bids me come. But oh God! can I see myself there!" (P to JB, 24 January 1783: C 2158.)

The next exchange of letters takes place within a month, Boswell expressing pleasure that his "last letter gave so much satisfaction" to Paoli, and venturing the hope that when next in London he will be able to persuade the General to revisit Auchinleck. In response Paoli repeats what by now should have been unnecessary, the assurance that so long as there is a room in his house there will be a bed and a welcome ready for Boswell. Nothing would have pleased him more than to revisit Scotland, but much has happened to prevent him—most important, concern for his brother Clemente, who has been at death's door but has almost miraculously recovered.[83]

The record of Boswell's stay in London, 20 March to 30 May 1783, his first as a *Laird*, shows him first of all anxiously visiting Johnson. His other concerns, political and social, remain essentially unchanged. In the *Life* Boswell refers to the new Ministry, in which "those who had been long in opposition had attained to power, as it was supposed, against the inclination of the Sovereign," and quotes the remark of "a respectable friend": "You need not be uneasy about the King. He laughs at them all; he plays them one against the other." Boswell's unidentified "friend" is Paoli (Journal, 22 March 1783), whose genuine liking for George III is enhanced by a respect, not generally shared, for his political skills. Johnson, normally well enough disposed to think highly of his monarch's abilities, diagnoses the political situation more correctly than does the General: "Don't think so, Sir. The King is as much oppressed as a man can be. If he plays them one against another, he *wins* nothing" (22 March).

At Paoli's, Boswell finds his room ready; and among the company every day two new Corsican faces, those of Pietro Colle and Filippo Masseria. Colle had been one of Paoli's most trusted and daring captains in the struggle against the French. Masseria, also an officer, was to remain with Paoli in London—how long as an inhabitant of the general's house is not clear—until 1789, acting as secretary, lieutenant, or agent according to circumstance.[84] (Gentili was more an associate than a lieutenant.) Paoli and Boswell on separate occasions visit George Dempster and Bennet Langton. Boswell's cousin, Captain Robert Preston, at one time joins him at dinner with Paoli. The General, Boswell records, when speaking of these friends was in "fine spirits. . . . He called Preston 'floating Bob, who thinks the Landed Interest not worth a pinch of snuff,' and spoke of 'Langton's geese fluttering, and he a reed shaken with the wind'" (11 May 1783).

As often happens, Paoli makes the first effort to write to
Boswell after the latter's departure from London. He also
has news, particularly regarding Johnson's health, tells of
a distinguished party of foreigners about to visit Edinburgh, and recommends one of them, the Marquis de
Biencourt, to Boswell's notice (28 June 1783: C 2160). Boswell does not write until 8 August, when he apologizes for
his long silence. He has not yet emerged from "a state of
dreary dejection . . . so dull and discontented in this narrow country . . . that life seems a burthen." When so many
have seats in Parliament and important offices he must
waste his time in "provincial obscurity." He emerges from
self concern to express disappointment that Paoli is not to
visit him this year—an annual but nonetheless sincerely felt
ritual not only on the part of Boswell and his wife but also
on that of the General—and to speak of Johnson's stroke
of palsy as an "awfull prognostick." The foreigners have
been taken care of. Boswell and Sir Alexander Dick joined
in the pleasure of entertaining the Marquis de Biencourt
(L 1016).

The next letter from Boswell to Paoli in the Boswell collection is dated six months later than the above, on 9 February 1784; quite possibly one exchange is lost. Boswell
writes of an indisposition which, though it has confined
him to the house, has not affected the health of his mind.
He anxiously awaits the next month, when he can go to
London and perhaps allay the anxiety he has felt concerning Johnson's health. Mrs. Boswell is now fully recovered,
his children promise well, he ought to be happy. "But ambition troubles me; and my soul is impatient of this narrow
sphere of action." Dilly has been asked to present Paoli
with a copy of *A Letter to the People of Scotland on the Present
State of the Nation.* Paoli in his reply rejoices in Boswell's recovery and permits himself parentally to support Boswell's
resolution: "Now more than ever you need to be firm in
your desire to lead a different life." He gives news of Johnson, as related earlier, and then advises at length: "You
have entered the field of politics, and amongst the people
you will encounter there your convivial nature, which used

to earn you such warm welcome everywhere, will avail you little. These men are composed wholly of amour-propre and see nothing in their rivals and opponents but faults, which they magnify; and those virtues which they cannot deny they strive to make look dangerous. . . . [The *Letter*] has caused a stir. You have entered the lists; you must now fight, for your new friends feel obliged to you for what you have done in their behalf, in equal measure perhaps as your old friends have cause to be disgusted and offended. . . . I should like to warn you . . . that although you have differences of opinion with your old friends you must not evince a want of esteem for them, for they will always be able, if not to be of use to you, at least to impose barriers to your desires. Have regard for them as persons, and let them know so when you wage open war upon their principles. Excuse me for this confidential warning." He has moved from South Audley Street to a place in Portman Square more capable of sheltering the number of people living with him.[85]

Boswell arrived in London on 5 May 1784. Paoli sought him at Dilly's the next day and, missing him, left the first of his extant notes in English. "For what reason did you not alight in Portman Square"? he asks. (This stay in London, Boswell's last before Johnson's death, was dealt with earlier in the discussion of the Johnson-Paoli friendship.) Boswell bade adieu to Johnson on 30 June, spent another day in London with the hope of talking to Lord Thurlow about support for Johnson's proposed sojourn in Italy, and then left for Scotland. Within two weeks he had resumed his " station at the bar," he writes Paoli, and now is in a very melancholy state, not at all helped by the efforts of his friends and relations to dissuade him from trying his fortune at the English bar (17 July 1784: L 1018). Paoli then sends Boswell his most significant letter of advice. He is being treated by Sir William Fordyce for the " family disease" which afflicted his father severely to his last days, and tormented his brother. What it was precisely we do not know, but it affected at various times his leg, knee, arm, and hand. Its consequences were arthritic-like symptoms

which later permitted Napoleon and other enemies to
gloat over the fact that the General had difficulty in moun-
ting his horse. What interests us now is the lecture, which
in essence is no more than the Rambler and Lord
Auchinleck had said many times; in style it is London-vin-
tage Paoli:

> Within ourselves we carry everywhere the feelings of ennui
> and discontent; and remedy, if there be any, can be found
> only in one's own reflections. If in the bosom of your lovable
> family you are melancholy in Edinburgh, a city now full of
> affairs for you and peopled by an urbane society with which
> it is to your interest to mingle, how much more would you
> be wearied in London, where you would not encounter in
> the streets a single person of your acquaintance? All the
> beau-monde is in the country, or at least, in order to appear
> to be there, keeps its windows tightly closed and allows itself
> to be seen only in hasty flight. . . . Come here to recover
> from melancholy? There is still much time for you to con-
> sider your plan to settle here. First I believe you will wish to
> grasp all the conditions of qualification for these Courts,
> and will wish lengthier and more exact proof of the power
> of the good will of your friends. The hopes of success in
> these Courts must be founded upon the regard in which
> you are held by the Ministry, whose influence can procure
> clients for you and give you that reputation which is often
> worth more than a hundred volumes of studies. There [in
> Scotland] your prospects are neither slight nor poor nor
> distant; there is no need to abandon them save after mature
> consideration. If you obtain your father's Office, with your
> popularity naturally increasing, I believe that by coming to
> London once a year to amuse yourself and to converse with
> your friends you would be of greater importance and have
> greater advantage at Court than if you were a member of
> Parliament obliged to vote as your friend wishes or else
> forced to offend him by following your own lights and the
> dictates of your conscience. From there your advantages
> can become great, for they are supported by your talent and
> sustained by your family connection and especially by the
> consideration of your substantial independent possessions.
> From there you can negotiate and manage more firmly be-
> hind your entrenchment; here you become subject to the
> disposal of others. . . . It is not lucre that moves my friend
> Boswell. His generously ambitious mind, which is familiar
> with the turbulent political state of this country, will not find

my opinion ill-founded, and will perceive that I respond with sincerity to the confidence with which he consults me. Of these things we shall speak at greater length when you are here with your wife. Meanwhile, make your interests respected among your countrymen. Popularity in Scotland you see can give importance even to Lord George Gordon!

Paoli's letter is followed the next month by one from Gentili in which he tells of the turn for the worse in the General's health and the necessity of putting off once more the trip to Scotland. Readers of the *Life* will recall that Boswell frequently had sought Johnson's approval for his removing to London, and that at about the same time as he wrote the letter which elicited the above reply from Paoli he also wrote to Johnson asking that he write down the arguments supporting the move. Johnson complied in a letter marked by neither enthusiasm nor characteristic force.[86]

The death of Johnson on 13 December 1784, though not unexpected, badly shook Boswell. He received the news about five months after he had last written to Paoli; he waited two more months before writing, sure that his long silence would be understood. There is reason for him to be busy, first with publishing his journal of the tour to the Hebrides, and then with the life of Johnson, for which he has been collecting materials for upwards of twenty years. Now he is coming to London to explore his prospects at the English bar. Paoli replies, admitting he felt a little hurt by Boswell's long silence, but quickly forgives, especially with the joyous prospect of having Boswell under his roof the next month. They will be able to discuss Boswell's problems and projects together.[87]

In 1786, against the advice of his friends, Boswell goes through with his plans to settle in London and practice at the English bar. For the first time in many years he does not stay with Paoli but instead takes a house, even though he does not expect his wife and children for several months. The account of the relationship so far mainly illuminated by letters will now draw upon other materials. "The solitude of my house in London I thought sunk my

spirits," Boswell records in his journal. Gentili does his best
to help Paoli cheer his friend up, and at the former's suggestion Paoli gives a dinner for Boswell and his English
relations. Boswell also has a standing invitation to Paoli's
Sunday dinner, always attended by "a select company of
foreigners." It is like "dining on the Continent"; but ultimately Boswell, after once counting a company of seventeen, resolves that it is wrong to make a practice of being
there. (Thomas David, both foreigner and native, has no
need to resist.) However, in the lonely summer of 1786,
when "good Gentili proposed that I should resume my bed
at the General's," Boswell strongly feels the urge to move.
"Luckily my room was not properly prepared."[88]

Boswell's journal for September and October 1786 , after the settling of his family in London, records frequent
exchanges of visits between the Boswells and the General
and Gentili. November finds Paoli and Gentili at Bath. In
response to Boswell's note asking when they will return,
Paoli explains that the "waters agree with Mr. Gentili's
stomach, and as he believes he is recovering I want him to
drink them for at least the ordinarily prescribed term of
four weeks." What follows could be drawn from the letter
of an English gentleman taking the waters:

> Even here we have some very cold days, but not cold
> enough to prevent us from going out on horseback. This
> climate is indeed quite mild, and the situation of this city is
> truly delightful. The River Avon, which washes it, disperses
> the mists which rise from the mineral baths, and the sur-
> rounding hills shelter it from the wind. There are numer-
> ous ways out into the country: one cannot take a step
> without being in the presence of a landscape of hills and
> valleys of the most charming and picturesque sort. Never in
> any other place have I seen country so full of pleasing varie-
> ty. If you did not have your family with you now I should
> have liked to urge you to come here and stay with us. We
> have a room to spare, suitable for a friend, and our quarters
> are in the South Parade, in my opinion the most delightful
> situation in this city. At the moment society is not at its most
> numerous; one finds nevertheless many persons of rank
> and elegance, and our time passes very agreeably.

Paoli then refers to Maria Cosway in a way which will require our attention later.[89]

Boswell's family is of special interest to Paoli, the General at one time entreating Veronica to play the harpsichord at a concert, at another hosting Betsy and her father at tea. But their mother is his real concern, and when late in 1788 Boswell takes his wife with Euphemia and Betsy back to Scotland it is safe to assume that the General is glad Boswell has seen fit to accede to Peggie's wishes, much as he admires her and enjoys her company.

What remains to be said of Boswell's friendship with Paoli can be assimilated later into the general narrative of Paoli's last years. By late 1789 Paoli's attention is riveted on France, and Boswell, when he can, is struggling to write with the more immediate support and assistance of Edmond Malone. Paoli continues as the bed for Boswell's "rock," but once he leaves England he steps into the irrecoverable past.

Margaret Montgomerie Boswell deserves a special place in the history of Paoli's affections. It is difficult to read Boswell's journals and letters even across this great gap of time without feeling the ache of sympathy, the recurrent wish to comfort, to reduce in some way the misery which so often tormented Margaret Boswell. Yet she was beloved, and enjoyed moments of great happiness. James Boswell could not have loved anyone more. A quite unmixed pleasure in exploring Margaret Boswell's relations with General Paoli is the discovery that, once her apprehensions of having to stand in his presence at the wedding ceremony were disposed of and their meeting was finally effected, they never thought of each other without warm and deep affection. If she later remembered what she had once written to James, she must have smiled at her fears. "I seriously wish he [Paoli] may not come, but if he does, and you signify to me your desire to have him, you may believe I shall agree, whatever it should cost me. . . . Remember, with advantages vastly superior to mine, you yourself was uneasy in the presence of the illustrious chief" (31 October 1769).

Boswell's journal for the period of Paoli's visit to Scotland nearly two years later does not survive; later references show that the charm the General had for Peggie was unlike that which as a matter of course was duly noted with pleasure by other women.

On Paoli's departure from Edinburgh, 12 September 1771, Mrs. Boswell herself gave him "a convoy as far as Haddington." The following spring in London, Boswell records, "The General spoke much of Scotland; and what gave me much pleasure, he commended highly my dearest wife, said she had something of the Italian manner, a frankness, an attention, a politeness" (24 March 1772). We may pause to allow the Scotsman and Corsican to remember their Italian women: Boswell certainly not forgetting Moma Piccolomini, and Paoli recalling faces and bodies from the time of his young manhood when, as he put it to Boswell, he "very seldom deviated from the paths of virtue." Returning to the above journal entry: Paoli particularly remembered Mrs. Boswell's giving him the convoy as far as Haddington.

Margaret Boswell and Pasquale de Paoli were not to meet again for fifteen years, but the General continued to send his respects to her. The many references by Boswell and Paoli to the prospect of another visit to Scotland were not simply polite formalities. The General missed his young friend surely enough, particularly in those years when Boswell failed to come to London at all. Nevertheless he had the satisfaction of seeing James reasonably often. The seriousness of his intention to revisit Scotland stemmed primarily from his wish to see Margaret Boswell. We are indebted to Gentili for the specific statement. Writing to Boswell on 26 August 1784 (C 1362), he tells of the General's ill health and expresses regret that "this year we must once more put off the trip to Scotland we have been planning to take. I pray you, again in the name of the General, to present our most respectful compliments to Mrs. Boswell, and to assure her that this journey had been planned more for the sake of bearing to her direct witness of our esteem than from any other motive." On a later occasion Gentili forwards Paoli's wishes for uninterrupted health for Boswell's family, "your lovable wife first of all" (10 January 1786: C 1363).

When the Boswells moved to London in 1786 Paoli at once took in the situation and acted more than the dear concerned friend. It was doubtless with Margaret in mind that Paoli had told Boswell he was past the age of ambition and should determine to be happy with his wife and children. Earlier, it had probably been more than a professional appraisal that prompted Paoli to be "clear for my not becoming an English barrister" (Journal, 25 November 1785). A journal entry for 30 May 1787, when the Boswells were entertaining at dinner a small group which included Malone, Wilkes, and Courtenay, speaks volumes about the feelings of the sick Margaret Boswell. "Wilkes and Courtenay very improperly attacked General Paoli. My wife, with a just warmth, drank his health, declaring her high respect, and desired there might be no more of it."

In Corsica, Boswell was persuaded that had Paoli been a private gentleman he would have married and proved "as good a husband and father as he does a supreme magistrate and a general." In England, Paoli has become a father both to Margaret Boswell, who had lost her parents years before she married, and to James Boswell, who had lost his mother and too often found in his natural father an inescapable adversary. Paoli's letter of condolence to Boswell upon Margaret's death, hitherto available in print only in a limited edition published over forty years ago, demands a place here.

London, 19 June 1789

I have learned from your brother of the loss which you have suffered. Our long friendship and the esteem which I had for the character and virtues of your wife will not allow you to doubt that I sincerely share your affliction. I would do anything I could to lighten your burden now, knowing that you are especially oppressed by many new cares and obligations connected with the education of your family and the management of your domestic affairs. But exhortations and moral reflections are more tiresome than useful, and from personal experience I have learned that they are utterly powerless to lessen the sense of that grief which comes from real affliction, and which acquires its greatest force from the deprivation of those objects and habits which form the dearest support of social existence. Time alone will be the first to alleviate your anguish; Time, which dulls the poignancy of our pleasures, also takes away the harshness of our griefs, and causes them at last to pass away. Yet while you await this relief which cannot fail, I beg you not to hesitate to turn to me if there is anything, however small, in which I can contribute to your relief. You must know from experience that the more difficulty I have in expressing myself on the most urgent occasions, the more I feel the duties of true friendship. I shall say no more, save to subscribe myself, as always,

> Your sincere friend,
> De Paoli

Writing over two years later, Boswell remembered how often the General, not the nagging sort, chided Boswell when speaking as Paoli put it of "her of whom I was not worthy."[90]

James and Margaret Boswell shared their Corsican father with one other, the vivacious Maria Cosway, wife of the distinquished miniaturist Richard Cosway. There is no evidence that the two women ever met; Margaret would have been shocked to learn that Paoli felt an attachment for this young lady reputed to have beaux, perhaps even lovers, by the dozen. The blue eyes surrounded by golden curls that look at us from Maria's portrait could well belong to Pope's Belinda, who had only to smile to make all the world gay. Maria Cosway, occasionally with the aid of her husband, presided over elaborate concerts and entertainments. Horace Walpole considered her "pleasing," and found reasons to gravitate toward "a great concert" at Mrs. Cosway's. Maria herself would occasionally join the distinguished performers, playing on the harp or harpsichord when not moving among the admiring company. One time Walpole heard there the famous male contralto, Giovanni Battista Rubinelli; another, he found among the company a notorious transvestite, three foreign ministers, and John Wilkes and his daughter Mary.[91] Paoli undoubtedly preferred visits to the Cosways when guests were few; on several of these occasions he was accompanied by Boswell.

Maria Louisa Catherine Cecilia Hadfield Cosway (1759-1838) had not long been accustomed to attention in fashionable society when she first met General Paoli, probably some time in 1783.[92] Her father, Charles Hadfield, was already a wealthy merchant in Manchester when he decided to move to Florence and there establish the hotel which became the resort of English nobility and gentry who visited Italy. Maria, the first daughter to reach maturity, was very much her father's girl. She remembered him as a man who "had a great taste and knowledge of the arts and sciences," and who had "in every way contrived to furnish my mind. . . . Everybody knows what my father was and the education he gave me. My gratitude has never ceased." Certainly her achievements went far beyond what was expected of a convent-educated girl. As a very young lady she played the organ at the Monastery of the Visitation in Florence. She could also play the harp, harpsichord, and pianoforte; she could sing; she could compose tuneful songs and duets; above all she could paint, and at the age of nineteen was honored by election to the Academy of Fine Arts at Florence. Her beauty and talent brought predictable results. James Northcote, after meeting her in Rome when she was eighteen, said "she had been the object of adoration of an indulgent father who unfortunately for her had never checked the growth of her imperfections." To be sure, she was indeed talented and "not unhandsome," but also "active, ambitious, proud, and restless." When Maria's father died she felt a sense of calamity from which she took years to recover. With some difficulty her mother prevented her from taking vows. Maria's was not a sudden impulse; in a letter to a biographer written when she was seventy-one she wrote: "My inclination from a child had been to be a Nun."[93]

Mrs. Hadfield was relieved when, at the suggestion of Angelica Kauffmann, who became her sponsor, Maria in

1779 went to England. By the next year she began to exhibit at the Royal Academy, and her circle of admirers could not but please her mother. The successful suitor, Richard Cosway (1740–1821), promised to provide for Mrs. Hadfield and settled £2,800 upon Maria. Perhaps early in the marriage, which took place 18 January 1781, there was happiness and mutual affection. James Northcote believed that at the time of the marriage Cosway "adored" Maria, "but she always despised him." Northcote's observation, often quoted, does not accord with Maria's statement when writing to her husband in 1815 concerning "how many years we were happy." The pair's affections certainly cooled, but nothing in Maria's later behavior supports Northcote's emphasis.[94] Maria Cosway as painter, composer, and musician displayed real though minor talents. Her husband as miniaturist had few peers; even without the advantages of moving in the fast crowd of the Prince of Wales he undoubtedly would have achieved the material and artistic success he conspicuously enjoyed. His short stature and flamboyant dress made him the object of some satire; but his fellows in the Royal Academy recognized the merits of his work.

Maria Cosway's salon was fashionable. The guests, whether talented artists, tainted or pure high society, or merely wealthy patrons, usually found her attractive; as one contemporary put it, she was "a golden-haired, languishing Anglo-Italian, graceful to affectation and highly accomplished, especially in music."[95] The absence of reference to drawing or painting, her most notable accomplishments, characterizes the impressions of visitors. Cosway himself was considered by some to be good company. Walpole, though he soon discovered he could believe very little of what Cosway said, nevertheless characterized his "glibity" as very entertaining.[96] Boswell enjoyed Maria's company, but found the husband's boring (Journal, 28 July, 19 September 1785).

When Paoli was first invited to the Cosways he would have been justified in looking upon the marriage as essentially typical for a couple in their class and profession.

Maria couldn't help hearing that she had rivals, but such
gossip, like that concerning her extramarital affairs, was in
its early stages, normal and properly to be discounted. The
General and Maria undoubtedly valued the pleasure of
conversing in Italian. Probably very early in their friendship she ceased to disguise her true emotional state, and
Paoli, it is not too much to assume, found his heart going
out to this lovely fellow exile, doomed to a cold climate and
an indifferent husband, far away from the sunny skies and
church bells of what she never ceased to look upon as her
native country. Of Maria's unsatisfied needs, Paoli in particular understood the deep pietistic force which, if ever
revealed to others, was no doubt dismissed as a convent
girl's foolish nostalgic talk. Her gaiety and liveliness, her
coquetting, singing, performing, even her painting, were
attempts to divert her inward gaze from the melancholy
truth that she had taken the wrong turn; now she saw
clearly that for her all was vanity. Boswell gives us only
samplings of Paoli's social life; even so, the frequency of recorded visits to and from Maria Cosway in 1785 suggests
the close bond. Evidently the General and Maria took
many excursions together, probably with one or two other
companions for the sake of propriety. Such was the trip to
Strawberry Hill on 25 September 1784, when tickets were
issued to "Mrs. Cosway, Prince Ranusi, and Paoli and one
more."

Pretty Maria's reputation for breaking hearts naturally
obliged Boswell to put himself to the test, not with all the
charm he could command, possibly because he really was
not physically attracted and also because his interests at the
time lay elsewhere. Nevertheless he made something of
two occasions when he was asked by the General personally
to extend invitations to Mrs. Cosway. On the first, not finding the lady at home, he left a note—or, since he played the
role of ambassador—"dispatches" with appropriate literary
references which he hoped "will make you laugh away the
war between two Powers which should ever maintain the
strictest alliance. I pray you let my first *diplomatick* attempt
be successful, and come and dine with us tomorrow"

(30 June 1785: *L 382). The "war" was not between the General and Maria. A month later Boswell wrote another note, this time in Italian, still assuming the "carattere" of ambassador, inviting Mrs. Cosway to join the General's party in attending Astley's circus, which offered a well-known act using trained dogs. Astley, Boswell writes, gives dogs a human semblance while you, he continues (now breaking into English) "*treat men like dogs*" (28 July 1785: *L 384). Perhaps playing the game was in itself a sufficient end.

If the husband was mocked and derided by some for the pretentiousness of his dress, the wife was praised, and the virtues of her person by contagion spread to her art. Walpole paid extraordinary homage in "Verses on seeing Mrs. Cosway's Pallet," for the *Morning Chronicle*, January 1784.

> Behold this strange chaotic mass,
> Where colours in confusion lie,
> Where rival tints commix'd appear,
> *Here* tints for water, *there* for sky.
>
> Kept in imagination's glow,
> See now the lovely artist stand!
> Grand visions beaming on her mind,
> The magic pencil in her hand.

After two more Collins-like stanzas praising her art, Walpole asks her to preserve Ossian, pursue the endless subjects in Shakespeare, and even turn to Rowe, Otway, and "Sweet Prior." He concludes:

> To these, sweet artist, give thy youth,
> Their thoughts embody with thy hues:
> Grateful the offering to their shades—
> Canst thou the glorious task refuse?

"Peter Pindar" (John Wolcot), for whom writing was by nature a personally satisfying expression of malice, took in both Cosways in his eighth ode:

> What vanity was in your skulls
> To make you act so like two fools,
> To expose your daubs tho' made with wondrous pains out?
> Could Raphael's angry ghost arise,

And on the figures cast his eyes,
He'd catch a pistol up and blow your brains out.

The reader must not omit the close, however:

Muse, in this criticism I fear,
Thou really hast been too severe;
Cosway paints miniatures with truth and spirit,
And Mrs. Cosway boasts a fund of merit.[97]

In the late summer of 1786 the Cosways went to France on a journey which, as was usual for the husband, would combine business with pleasure—securing commissions for paintings while at the same time bringing the enjoyment of hospitality and conversation with the nobility and members of high society, and possibly even affording him an opportunity to add to his very fine collection of paintings, furniture, and objets d'art. Maria preferred the company of artists. One of them, the American John Trumbull, introduced Thomas Jefferson to the Cosways.

At this point Jefferson scholars, who are far from being of one mind concerning their subject's amours, take over. According to Helen Duprey Bullock, Jefferson's "capitulation [to Maria] was immediate and complete;" Fawn Brodie more recently writes, "if ever a man fell in love in a single afternoon it was he."[98] Many of the male Jeffersonians insist that the "love" never went beyond the verbal stage. For the ordinary reader Fawn Brodie's presentation of evidence, circumstantial though it is, supports the conclusion that Maria and Tom—his fall from grace sanctions familiarity—enjoyed an ardent, happily consummated love affair. For Maria, Jefferson was possibly not her first earthly lover; he was very likely her last.

In 1945 Helen Duprey Bullock printed for the first time twenty-five Maria Cosway-Jefferson letters which had been found in the estate of Thomas Jefferson Randolph, Jefferson's grandson and executor, who at the time he discharged his duties apparently did not deem the letters yet appropriate for public scrutiny. (It tells us something of Jefferson's feelings that he preserved Maria's letters and the copies of his own.) Brodie finds the letters unequivocal.

For more than a month following their meeting Maria and Tom were able to see each other almost every day, many times without distracting company. When, unhappily, the Cosways left for Antwerp, Jefferson sat down and wrote one of the most extraordinary letters ever penned, a long —over four thousand words—dialogue between "My Head and My Heart" (12 October 1786).

When Maria returned to London she could think only of her lover. I spend my time, she writes to him, "in painting, playing on the harp, the harpsichord, and singing." But "there is something so very heavy in this air that whatever I do seems to make me sad."[99] Writing to Boswell from Bath on 8 November 1786 (C 2166), Paoli, calling Maria "our Tenth Muse," asks Boswell if he has seen her since her return from France. "She hasn't written to me since her return to London, and as I don't know whether she has come back from France as a friend or as an enemy I have no wish to precede her [in writing first], all the more for her telling me the last time she wrote to me from Paris not to think of her any more. I almost feared lest that knave of a friar she had about her as a French teacher had succeeded in persuading her to enter a convent to paint Saints as formerly she had enjoyed painting Giants and Monsters. If you go to see her do not convey my compliments but rather my disappointment." The General pouting because he has been neglected is an image one regrets to accept, but the long silence of a close friend, particularly of a girl thirty-four years one's junior, intensifies sensitivity. The phrase "friend or enemy" reinforces the interpretation, but of course Paoli is not serious, the overtone going beyond personal pique to indicate the ever present sense of France as the possibly seductive enemy. The mention of the convent reveals how fully the General understands Maria, anticipating her actions by only a few years. The belittling of her talent, or the application of it, besides soothing his wound establishes the proper tone for the reader, Boswell. To the modern scholar Maria's injunction to Paoli, "not to think of her any more," suggests at least as much as Brodie supposes for this period. That Paoli entertained only the highest esteem for Maria's moral character is indicated in a statement in the letter to Boswell suggesting that "Miss Boswell [Veronica] would benefit from her company; the two could practice music together."

For the next several months, while Maria languished and despaired of going to France again, there is no information on Paoli. One must suppose that he saw her, guessed at the cause of her deeper melancholy and comforted her as best he could. Suddenly, in the summer of 1787 when it became clear that Cosway had no intention of going back to Paris, Maria found the courage to go alone. This stay of over three months, under the cloud of her Church's disapproval and of her husband's rage and possible abandonment of financial support, is examined by Brodie.[100] There were moments of happiness; but something went decidedly wrong, and at the very last Maria departed without keeping a breakfast engagement with Jefferson.

Jefferson was so angry at Maria's abrupt departure that he did not write to her for seven weeks, during which time she wrote him two letters expressing deep anguish and pain. "I'm perfectly sure it was my fault," she wrote in the second. If you will only come to London, she told him, "I promise to make myself and my society according to your wishes." When he finally did write Jefferson as compared to his former self was, as Brodie puts it, "frostiness itself." It is, however, impossible to agree with Brodie when she concludes that "what Maria Cosway seems to have wanted was a rescuing father, not a lover, a role Jefferson refused to play." Maria had a kind and compassionate father in London. She wanted again the raptures of love she had experienced the year before; that Jefferson was many years her senior enhanced that love, no doubt. Maria did not quickly cease to hope that she and Jefferson might be rejoined. Jefferson, with his eyes on the comely young mulatto half-sister of Martha Jefferson, Sally Hemings, found it possible to bank the fires more easily than did poor Maria. Still, as he embarked for America he wrote to her: "The ensuing spring might give us a meeting at Paris

with the first swallow. . . . remember me and love me."[101]
The disconsolate Maria did penance in resuming her conjugal role. When her daughter Louisa Paolina Angelica
Cosway was born, in July 1790, the given names signified
attachments—godmother, Louisa, Countess of Albany;
godfather, Pasquale de Paoli; friend and guide, Angelica
Kauffmann. The confinement had been difficult. Some
weeks later Maria set off to recover her health in the south
of Europe; perhaps also to seek the peace and eternal love
which had beckoned to her from childhood. The rest of
Maria's story will wait until we arrive back in England for
Paoli's last exile.

To the very short list of Paoli's female friends in England
are we justified in adding lovers? For a biographer of Paoli
the evidence is maddeningly slight. Writing to Boswell on
1 February 1775, William Johnson Temple, who had read
and admired *Corsica* in manuscript, states: "It is splendid
and illustrious actions and events that exalt history above
simple narration. I wish you would dignify another Paoli,
but where are Paolis to be found, and how long will they
continue so? How I grieved the other day to hear from
Lord L. [Lisburne, Temple's patron] how rapidly your hero was descending to the level of common men. It seems
he can amuse himself with a French mistress as well as any
other man of fashion. Such is the effect of situation and the
manners of those we live with, and so difficult is it to per-
severe in a uniform tenour of singular and illustrious
disdain of sensual gratifications. I can excuse the man, but
not Boswell's hero" (C 2758). The Rev. Mr. Temple, as
Boswell's friend certainly privy to the ways of untamed
sensuality in this world, never sounded more like a
preacher. Said of Johnson, the accusation would have
rushed Boswell into an exhaustive investigation. But in the
Boswell manuscripts, in printed pieces devoted to scandal,
there is nothing to substantiate Lord Lisburne's bit of
gossip, which nevertheless could have been based on fact.
It is reasonable to believe that Boswell did not consider
sexual continence obligatory for one in Paoli's situation; on
the contrary, Paoli would have seemed something less than

a complete man—certainly less than a complete product of Mediterranean civilization—had he never permitted himself "sensual gratifications." At any rate the matter still stands exactly where Temple left it.

One woman, however, appears certain to have enjoyed Paoli's love. Returning to England in 1796 the General wrote: "Here I have few of my old friends left. . . . She is dead who would have been helpful to me in times less uncertain than these." On the basis of information supplied to him by "one who heard from this woman a hint of modest confession," Tommaseo expressed a belief that the loved one was a Corsican.[102] For a distinction of this kind, suggested only by hints expressed after Paoli's death, hundreds of candidates might reasonably have been expected to step forth.

We must accept the fact that Boswell, although he found pleasure in periodically gathering sayings of Paoli, never intended to explore Paoli's life; the hero in Corsica too far surpassed, particularly in public interest, the gentleman in exile. It nevertheless comes as a surprise that one of Paoli's closest personal friends, the Rev. Andrew Burnaby, is not mentioned by Boswell after the first meetings in September 1769. Perhaps Paoli recognized Boswell's envy of Burnaby's initial privileges as the King's agent, and never made particular efforts to bring them together again. In any event, the letters from Paoli which Burnaby published in 1804 established that the friendship was close and of long standing.[103] It was of course a quite different kind of friendship from that with Boswell, who was younger and in need of emotional propping and personal favors. Paoli many times, appparently, stayed with Burnaby at Baggrave Hall, Leicestershire, talking of old times and future prospects. Burnaby probably also visited Paoli in London on several occasions. The likelihood of Boswell's meeting every one of Paoli's friends who did not himself have an established place of residence in London was not great, particularly if Paoli made any effort to manage his calendar.

It is through a lucky accident that we learn of another friend of Paoli, not a close one, perhaps, but close enough for Paoli to spend some time with him in the country. The source is the Rev. Dr. William Adams' letter to Boswell, 1 May 1778, in which he mentions that Paoli was staying with William Johnstone-Pulteney (1729-1805), whose service in Parliament extended from 1768 to 1805. John-stone-Pulteney, friend of Adam Smith, George Dempster, and David Hume (the last censured him as a Wilkite in June 1770), was of course known to Boswell, who must have envied him his political career. In this same year, 1778, Johnstone-Pulteney published a pamphlet sympa-thetic to the Americans. The previous year he had offered to go to Paris to negotiate with Franklin; this year he did go, unofficially, and did speak with Franklin. Like many friends of the colonists, Johnstone-Pulteney balked at granting independence. Late in 1783 he and Boswell both wrote pamphlets attacking Fox's East India Bill. The re-viewers on the whole praised Johnstone-Pulteney's work more highly, though Boswell thought it inferior to his own.[104] By 1784 Johnstone-Pulteney's speeches were almost invariably favorable to Pitt, but he nevertheless continued to enjoy a reputation for independence. How many friends Paoli had of this kind—principled, inde-pendent, favorable to liberty, but not remarked con-spicuously in histories—it is impossible to know, but it is reasonable to assume that there were a modest number.

It is time now to look at Paoli in the political arena, the gladiator unarmed except for the immense moral reserve which he had accumulated in Corsica and which he now protected by receiving courteously any advances which added to the circle of partisans and by keeping his defenses active. Among these latter were his imperturbable civility and his wit. Samples of his wit have cropped up several times in the present work. Of this quality Boswell com-plained: "General Paoli said more good things than almost anybody, yet he talks of them with contempt. I told him he had always *bon mots* about him, which he used like foot-balls—he threw them down and gave them a kick."[105] Paoli's wit was social and critical, suggesting a man always quite wary even when at ease. When John Wesley said to

Paoli, "he had met with much the same treatment with that of an ancient lover of his country, Hannibal, he immediately answered, 'But I have never yet met with a King of Bithynia.'"[106] Hannibal had found refuge from the Romans in Bithynia. When Rome demanded his surrender, and the King of Bithynia showed signs of complying, Hannibal took poison. I am not a mere refugee but still the leader of my country, Paoli implies, and I have not met a sovereign who will betray me. Wesley went away most pleased, probably, with Paoli's classical learning.

What Paoli understood to be strongly on his side, of course, was the historic rivalry between England and France. Most lovers of liberty approved the pension given to Paoli; but the government of George III did not award the pension to advance liberty—not in Corsica, not in America, not in Ireland, and most of all not in England. Boswell, notwithstanding his romantic notions, was under no illusions. When a clergyman complained that Paoli was doing nothing but eating English beef, Boswell replied: "He is a game-cock, ready to fight whenever there is a main [match between cocks]. In the mean time he must be fed—George the Third, feeder" (Journal, 25 March 1775). The king's views are finely summed up in Boswell's conversation with him on 30 May 1781:

> KING. When must you be in Scotland for your law? BOSWELL. The 12 of June, Sir. Our term begins that day. KING. Have you practiced the law long? Ever since you returned from abroad? BOSWELL. Yes, Sir. KING. Ever since you came from Corsica? BOSWELL. Your Majesty is pleased to recollect my having been there. KING. When did you see General Paoli? BOSWELL. I saw him today, Sir. I live in his house. KING. Do you? That's but fair. I think him a man of an excellent heart. BOSWELL. He is indeed, Sir; and is always very sensible of your Majesty's goodness to him. But though your Majesty is pleased to make him very comfortable as a private gentleman, I, who have seen him in Corsica, am sensible that it is a sad change. KING. Was it not like to kill him at first? But I believe he is a philosopher. BOSWELL. He is, Sir. But I remember when he was amongst our mountains (for he came down to us to Scotland), I heard him have this soliloquy: 'Ah, que cela me

fait souvenir que je ne suis plus rien.' KING. When he saw
your hills? BOSWELL. Yes, Sir. Old Ambassador Keith said
of him at my house, 'This is the most sensible man I ever
saw.' KING. I believe he was a greater politician than a
soldier. BOSWELL. The French have been at great pains to
depreciate him as a soldier. But from what I have been informed, I trust he had courage enough (or acted very
well). KING. I don't mean he was deficient. But that his
forte was being a legislator—in short, putting law into a
people who were *lawless*. 'Yes, Sir,' said I, 'and he did it
with great ability." After saying that General Paoli had an
excellent heart his Majesty added, 'He is a great deal better
than the people among whom he was. They were wild' (or
some such word). 'They were a brave people, Sir,' said I. I
was exceedingly happy at being allowed thus to talk with the
Sovereign. . . . I was in very fine spirits, and related to the
General all that had passed at Court.

On Paoli's public character and particular achievements
George III was expressing the views of informed members
of the Administration. There is evidence here and, as we
shall see, elsewhere, of a genuine liking for Paoli on the
King's part, a liking that was reciprocated. The "intolerable
coldness" Paoli once sensed at Court had thawed out early.
On 10 November 1788 the King's illness affected Paoli so
deeply that he wrote the following to Boswell:

> In these days of such anxiety and public affliction I have not
> the heart to attend any banquet; therefore I beg you to re-
> lease me for next Thursday and to defer to another time the
> appointment with our good friend the Bishop of Killaloe
> and with Sir Joshua Reynolds. Yesterday I could not speak
> two words with the people who habitually, and as you know
> without special invitation, honour me with their presence on
> Sunday. The condition of the King, and of the Queen, who
> is also ill, make every pleasure insipid and inappropriate,
> especially to those persons who owe them so much respect
> and personal devotion—like your good friend, who, with so
> many enemies, can live in this world only through their
> generous protection and benevolence (C 2168).

In the years of exile, then, Paoli did not find need to
worry about the attitude of George III, whom, however, he
recognized as unaggressive and excessively ˙ concerned

about military expenditures. Rather, Paoli watched the political actors closely. He had friends in the Administration;
changes beneficial to Corsica, however, he knew could
come if at all only with a change of Ministry combined with
so far unlikely developments on the continent. As the war
with the colonies grew into a European war posing increasingly unsettling dangers to the home island, the fall of
North became inevitable. Some of North's eminent opponents, like Burke, Fox, and Sheridan, Paoli knew personally. Shelburne he had reason to approve of, particularly for what he had done in the shadow of Chatham; but
it is not clear whether he enjoyed Shelburne's acquaintance. Wilkes, who apparently never ceased making
unfavorable noises concerning the General, was by now a
cipher.[107]

Paoli's acuity in appraising those whom he knew personally or saw directly in political action had not deserted him.
Where can one find a more penetrating short observation
on Charles James Fox than what Paoli wrote in a letter to
Boswell on 2 October 1780? "[Fox] has the boldness and
the arrogance necessary for making his way in a populous
city like this. When, with time, he acquires a little more
moderation, he will be a great figure in this country; he has
many talents and a lofty mind" (C 2154). Paoli's praise of
Burke in the same letter has already been noted. Burke of
course drew much attention from all who approached the
Johnson circle. When Paoli said of an occasion, "Burke did
not dawn, but walked round the Sun of our table," he was
paying tribute to Burke's restraint and to their common
admiration of the "Sun," Johnson. Speaking more fully to
Boswell, he said: "Burke is truly a great man: a good husband, a good father; and he sometimes goes round the at-
mosphere and takes such a flight that our eyes cannot
follow him. But when we think him lost in the clouds, he
is conversing with the gods and throwing light on human
knowledge."[108]

The time came for the momentous changes in administration, or as it turned out, for the creation of a succession
of administrations. The discredited North was succeeded

by a coalition of the Rockingham and Shelburne groups in
March 1782. Within four months it in turn was succeeded
by the Admnistration of Shelburne, who at last was able to
bring young Pitt into the Cabinet. It was Shelburne who
had to make the general peace which all deemed necessary, and then to be damned for it. Shelburne, like his
mentor Chatham, believed in what today, at least in America, would be called nonpartisan government. But he had
no control over the Fox faction—Fox nominally headed
the followers of Rockingham upon the death of that leader
—and the North faction. A Fox-North coalition brought
Shelburne down and established its Administration in
April 1783, with Burke as paymaster again. Within eight
months the resentment against Fox, North, and Burke
enabled Pitt, backed by a general election which demonstrated confidence also in the king, to secure power. It was
with Pitt's first administration, 1783–1801, that Paoli found
himself dealing for the remainder of his active life.

To go back some eight months. On 22 March 1783 Boswell recorded: "Burke was in high glee from a belief that
an Administration to his mind was by that time settled."
The depressed Boswell brought the news to Paoli, who assured his friend that the King "played them one against
another." More may be found here than Paoli's desire to
comfort his friend and his excessive belief in the abilities
and powers of the King. What lurks below the recorded
statement is Paoli's disenchantment with the political process in England. England's form of government was
basically as good as any to be found—Paoli was later to
stake his place in history on that belief—but it was flawed
by too much jockeying for position, too much compromis-
ing with principle, too much eagerness to embrace the corruption of power. Even Burke was not exempt. Two
months before the time of Burke's "high glee" Paoli had
written to Boswell: "Your friend Burke will have difficulty
in emerging from the shadow in which he has allowed
himself to be obscured. He has offended many. His talent
excites admiration amongst the common, but envy
amongst those who are in power to help or harm. . . . This

is not a comfortable state for one like him who does not take his pleasure in the rightness of his intentions and is not willing to be content with the high rank in which he appears in the society of Sublime Talents" (22 January 1783: C 2158). It is probably fair to say that Paoli approved of George III's idea of a patriot king, and of Chatham's idea of a government above faction or party.

And so Paoli watched and waited. He undoubtedly was acquainted with Pitt and many others in power; at the same time he was too wise to hope from any of them more than sympathy, which he despised. He still believed himself destined to escape from the social rounds of his northern hosts, and meanwhile continued to make his life in exile one of study, movement, and independence. When the Piozzis returned to England in 1787 Paoli proved himself constant in friendship. Another household where he could converse in Italian certainly had its special appeal, but the General's frequent visits were not made on such trivial grounds. Mrs. Thrale is not a source for many insights on Paoli, but one entry in *Thraliana* can move us forward. If he could change places with any person in history, Mrs. Thrale records, "General Paoli desired to be Julius Caesar." The General once told Boswell, when reasoning on the possession of greatness, "I have known it fifteen years. . . . I was educated to it—It was like going from one room to another." It was with a fitting sense of drama, then, that Paoli observed to Boswell after nine years in England, "his life [had fallen] in four acts: Corsica, Naples, Corsica, England. Said I, 'In [the] fifth [we] hope for [a] glorious catastrophe.'"[109] But when? While this our Caesar fed upon hope and George III's lean meat, across the channel there suddenly materialized legions to fight his battles, though not under his banner.

When Louis XVI in August 1788 issued the official summons for the Estates-General, Corsica was granted four deputies in the proportion which held elsewhere: one for the clergy, one for the nobility, and two for the third estate (commons). The election for the representative of the nobility was bitterly contested. Matteo Buttafoco's faction finally won, but not before his opponents had accused him of having betrayed his country and grown wealthy and powerful as a direct consequence. The entire deputation consisted of the following: for the clergy, Charles-Antoine Peretti della Rocca; for the nobility, Matteo Buttafoco; for the third estate, Christophe Saliceti and Pierre-Paul Colonna de Cesare Rocca. Each of the estates prepared its notebook. Prominent among the requests of the third estate was that for "letters of pardon for all fugitives from Corsica who have not committed capital crimes." An indication that the desire for Corsican identity was not easily to be lost was the request that Corsican ships be permitted to carry the Corsican symbol, the Moor's head, on the white French flag.[110] The Corsicans at this time were certainly no better off than inhabitants of other districts of France, notwithstanding the claim in the present century of Louis Villat, that the islanders during the years 1769–89 enjoyed stability and economic recovery under the rule of a benevolent despot, whose agent for most of the period was the Comte de Marbeuf. A majority of the Corsicans would have agreed with the words of the young Napoleon, who described them as being weighed down by chains even as they kissed, trembling, the hand which oppressed them.[111]

In truth, the most talented Corsican youth had been skimmed off into the army and professions of France; and the plums of office in Corsica were given to Frenchmen. A memoir in the French National Archives, dated 1788, notes that these officeholders appropriated sums of money for their own use, and concludes that "Corsica is in the same state of poverty and misery as at the beginning of the conquest." It would be very easy, the author continues, for General Paoli with only modest assistance from the English to create a successful revolution. The discontented people of the interior would quickly join him. In England, the General wrote that the courage of the Corsicans had been broken. "They have been deprived of the pleasure of watching over and contributing to the common good; they no longer perceive any link between them and the general interest; they have seen these laborious, patriotic, and honorable duties accorded to Frenchmen, whose entire talent consists of joining numbers and tracing letters." Napoleon, meditating on his country's plight, wrote to Paoli from the barracks at Auxonne (12 June 1789), denouncing "the present administration" and attacking "the numerous band of French employees who govern our Island."[112]

The delegation did not arrive at Versailles until the end of June 1789. Buttafoco on the right and Saliceti on the left soon established themselves as the voices of their respective constituencies. In Corsica the events in France were viewed with an impatience which stirred up factional outbursts and riots, based in part on the fear that France might for reasons of state dispose of Corsica—barter away its freedom before it was ever realized. At the urging of Saliceti, therefore, the following was voted:

> The National Assembly declares that Corsica constitutes a part of the French Empire, that its inhabitants must be ruled by the same constitution as other Frenchmen, that from this moment the King is requested to send and execute there all the decrees of the National Assembly.

Hardly had the decree been adopted when Mirabeau offered another, proposing that all Corsicans "who, after having fought for liberty have been exiled following the conquest of their Island, and who, however, are not guilty of any violations of the law," be give the right to return to their country "in order to exercise there all the rights of French citizens." The left applauded and the right protested. Paoli and the possibility of a revolt for independence quickly came to mind. "It is necessary," declared an eminent jurist, "that Paoli himself learn to become a Frenchman," and he left no doubt of his conviction that this would come to pass. In a burst of enthusiasm Mirabeau declared that for him it was a question of remedying an injustice: his early youth had been "dirtied" by participation in the conquest of Corsica. Buttafoco's colleagues objected; and the Abbé Peretti proposed that at the least the exiles upon returning be required to take an oath of allegiance.

Saliceti retorted, "Their return will prove to us their fidelity to our institutions; the title of Frenchman which you give them is the surest of guarantees." When brought to a vote on 30 November 1789 Mirabeau's plan won by a great majority. In Corsica the news of the decree brought joy everywhere. Te Deums were sung, bells sounded, dances organized in the public squares. At night huge bonfires, a form of expression particularly enjoyed by Corsicans, were lit in the hamlets and cities. [113]

Paoli, following the deliberations of the National Assembly very closely, certainly was aware of the magnitude of the task which faced that body. His impatience, though understandable, was quite unreasonable. On 27 October 1789 he wrote:

> I wish there were fewer orators and philosophers in the Assembly. The Magna Carta of the English is comprised in a few lines; the Bill of Rights is also very brief: and these monuments and bases of British freedom were not the results of a mere few hours of meditation. In looking for the best they risk losing the good. They disdain the constitution of this country and move toward that of the Americans: they are building Chalcedon in the cast of Byzantium.

The Assembly's recognition of the Corsicans' gallant struggle for liberty moved Paoli to write, on 10 November 1789, "The freedom of my country is my only aim, and I would not wish for more than to assure it under such a great nation."[114] Filippo Masseria and then Antonio Gentili served as Paoli's eyes and ears at Paris. In a letter dated 8 December 1789 Paoli authorized Gentili to communicate his views and intentions. Paoli was sure that the Corsican people would demonstrate their wholehearted attachment "to the free constitution of the monarchy." As for himself, he would never do anything to oppose any measures of the National Assembly. If his stay in England gave offense or occasioned factional differences, he would retire into silence and renounce the hope of ever again seeing *la patria*. His gratitude for the kind welcome which he had received in England was "eternal." "I will not serve against the English, no more than I will lend myself to any undertaking, either on their behalf or on behalf of any other power, which might compromise the liberty and the peace of our Island. Whatever the hand which breaks our country's chains, I kiss it eagerly. . . . We have had enough wars and misfortunes . . . Do your utmost therefore to dissipate all suspicions: my conduct will never give the lie to your assurances."[115]

The Corsicans sent a commission to London to invite Paoli to return to his native land. "It was somewhat melancholy," Boswell recorded in his journal for 8 January 1790, "to think of the General as having acceded to the dominion of France over Corsica (however made palatable by its natives being admitted to a participation of French privileges), and that he was preparing to quit this country. I regretted his having interfered at all, as I hoped the French Monarchy would be reestablished." A few weeks later Boswell breakfasted with Paoli and "had from him a full state of his motives in his conduct as to France, and was satisfied that unless he had been active his great object, the delivering Corsica from oppression, could not have been accomplished" (Journal, 7 February 1790). Boswell interrupted the General's preparations by giving a farewell dinner party for him on 22 March, and a few days later wrote, for Paoli to sign and seal, two letters of recommendation, one for the General's coachman and groom and another for his footman, both English. The General's old friend, the Corsican *valet de chambre* Giacomo Pietro, was to continue to accompany him.[116]

There is no reason to question the degree of Paoli's hope and confidence when he first made the decision to return to Corsica. One could wish for details of his conversation with Boswell; but certainly Paoli spoke in good faith when he later embraced the new regime in Paris and in Corsica. The French constitution at the time for the most part embodied—or showed signs that it would embody—principles which he himself had been instrumental in putting into effect in Corsica a quarter of a century earlier. Paoli had not gone so far as wholly to confiscate Church property and secularize the clergy, but, though a devout Catholic, he had severely restricted the political power of the Church; and the general notion of religious toleration was congenial to him. Further, like the French revolutionaries, he had reduced the power of the nobles. However, in Corsica both the abuses and their correction had been less extreme: Rome had continued to view the Corsicans as being within the fold; and only a few of the important nobles had gone over to France when the issue of independence was first clearly joined in the 1760s. Now, as Paoli saw it, the Corsicans "in perfect union" with France would "consolidate reborn liberty and peace."[117]

As he prepared to leave, Paoli revealed his joy and hope in sending to Burnaby an extract from the letter of the Corsican deputation. "The brave heroes yet live," they wrote to him, "who shared your hardships, distress, and exile; from them their sons learned to love in Paoli the creator and protector of equality and liberty. . . . It will be our most sacred duty to demonstrate to France and to Europe that the Corsicans know how to reward true virtue."[118] At the end of March 1790 Paoli, who had lived on the bounty of England for nearly twenty-one years, departed for France.

son enough, perhaps, not to neglect the last seventeen
years of Paoli's life. I find further reason in the fact that
Boswell's *Corsica*, his journals, and his exchanges of letters
fittingly prepare us for the final chapters of his hero's life.
I will therefore glean from them what might interest those
who have been brought to Paoli through Boswell.

In Paris wherever Paoli appeared he was surrounded by
cheering crowds. That the experience paralleled his triumphal tour into exile of 1769 did not dismay him. The
National Assembly greeted him with wild applause. "This
is the finest day of my life," he told the deputies. "I left my
country a slave; I now find her free. What more is there left
for me to desire?" Of all the tributes paid him, that of Robespierre might have been expected to please him most:
"You defended freedom when we did not even dare to
hope for it."[1] Significantly, portentously, Paoli singles out
Lafayette in summarizing his impressions when writing to
Burnaby on 4 May. "He has a soul made of different *pasta*
than that of other men. His disinterested patriotism has no
parallel among men either modern or ancient. He is
knowing; he is not presumptuous; and he has an imperturbable spirit. There are some who envy him; but
none dares to deny his worth or to express doubt of his zeal
for a free constitution under the monarchy." Paoli goes on
to praise the patriotism and intelligence of the members of
the Assembly, excepting the few discredited aristocrats
who prefer the old despotism. "There may be conflicts, but
the great work as a whole goes well; and later they will correct actions taken a little hastily." This long letter to
Burnaby has no counterpart in the Boswell collection; to
balance it there is only Paoli's letter of the previous week,
one sentence in length, telling the silent Boswell that he is
well and that "this nation . . . seems to strive to emulate the
kindness and the warm welcome with which yours received
me in my misfortunes" (28 April 1790: C 2173). Paoli refused the honors of rank and remuneration which the
King was still empowered to bestow, making use of his
position only to give advice on procedures for extending
the decrees of the Assembly to Corsica, and to request that

the Duc de Biron be named commander of the troops in Corsica.[2]

On 14 June, as he prepares to leave Paris, Paoli writes a full paragraph to Boswell, concluding: "I long always to hear from you. In Corsica you will have a friend and a servant obliged to you in a thousand ways. I embrace you with feeling" (C 2174). The letter to Burnaby of the same day recounts his leave-taking of the King and Queen. "Both of them received me very graciously and spoke to me of Corsica, and of the pleasure they would have in seeing me there at another time. . . . Things here are going rather well; the 14th of July will be the most glorious day that the world has ever seen."[3] Soon Paoli was on his way toward Marseilles, where another deputation elected by the Corsicans was awaiting him, ready to join that which had been accompanying him from London. Everywhere he was received in triumph: in Lyons, Valence, Avignon, Aix, Marseilles, Toulon. At the end of his progress Paoli takes time to write a note to Boswell which ends:

> I beg you to continue in friendship with me, and to write to me as often as you can through Leghorn. Ships leave London every month for that place. Write to me at length and in great detail, so that I may always be informed of the affairs of that country which it is my lot to love and esteem all my life. Remember me to all our friends, and believe me always full of affection and true friendship for you and all your family.[4]

Upon reaching Corsica, Paoli kneeled and kissed the earth.

The wild celebrations which greeted Paoli as he moved through the island did not long prevent him from seeing that Corsica was as deeply torn by divisions as mainland France, but with appropriate differences. During the French occupation all except a few diehards had made their peace with France. The Revolution unleashed old hatreds and fostered some new. The three estates in Corsica corresponded roughly to those in France, with the added permutations occasioned by the facts that (1) Corsica was a poor country and did not have as relatively large and powerful a class of nobles, and (2) it had been torn by

a war of independence and was still strongly nationalistic.
It was earlier noted that among the nobles the Buttafoco
faction only with great difficulty succeeded in electing its
deputy to the Assembly. This wing was to be identified in
Paoli's mind with those who had betrayed Corsica in 1768;
in new terms they belonged to the *ancien régime*. In the
Church the lower clergy had always furnished Paoli many
friends and followers; they were also in his eyes among the
most important of secular functionaries, teachers. Paoli
had had his troubles with the bishops, and was to continue
to differentiate between the good and the bad. Here too
there was a kind of continuing thread—those who favored
Corsican independence in the past now accepted the new
constitution. The third estate drew men from all classes, as
in France. The leaders, for the most part born during
Paoli's generalship, were strongly nationalistic and
dreamed at one time or another of Corsican independence. By the time Paoli arrived, when the Revolution was
already a year old, their views were becoming more settled.
Saliceti had become as French as any Frenchman, and took
positions as radical as circumstances at a given moment
permitted. Pozzo di Borgo was finding his home in what
Palmer has characterized as the middle of his five spectral
groups; here could be placed such diverse adherents of the
idea of constitutional monarchy as Mirabeau and Lafayette.[5] Pozzo's friend, Napoleon, in these early years indulged himself with strongly nationalistic sentiments.

At the first session of the General Assembly of Corsica,
on 9 September 1790, Paoli was unanimously elected President. He reaffirmed his faith in France and its constitutional King, expressed his gratitude towards England,
described the welcome he had received in Paris, and urged
the Corsicans toward union and a loyal respect for the law.
The rivalry between France and England, he believed, was
now at an end; putting aside all jealousy they surely would,
"through a system of enlightened politics, cultivate mutual
friendship and thus assure the peace of the entire world."
Paoli refused a proposed appanage and argued against a
further proposal that a monument be erected to him. "The

most flattering monument for me is the one which you have built in your hearts. Do not lavish praise . . . on a citizen whose career is not yet finished. Who can assure you that the last days of my life may not stir much different sentiments from those which you manifest toward me at this moment? My end is not far off: please defer your judgment on the services I have rendered our country; later you will disclose your opinion freely and without offense to my modesty." Nevertheless the Assembly decreed that a statue be erected immediately at Bastia, and made a generous allowance (upon which Paoli drew only for postal expenses). At the same meeting the Assembly elected Paoli commander of the National Guard.[6]

Paoli soon appeared to justify the hopes of his supporters in the French Assembly, who looked upon him as the only leader who could unify his country and at the same time keep it loyal to France. He did not hesitate to take firm action and express clear principles. He expelled Royalist-tainted army officers, among them Gaffori, Buttafoco's father-in-law, and disbanded their unreliable battalions; at the same time he asserted that old feuds between families and past political alignments must be forgotten; the only test was to be loyalty to the new constitution. Corsica as a Department was now organized under the French administrative system. Each Department had an Administrative Council composed of thirty-six members, and a Directory composed of five. The head of the Department's Directory was the Procurator General Syndic. In recognition of his services Saliceti was made honorary Procurator General Syndic, while Bartolomeo Arena was given the active office. When the new Council met in October, Paoli was formally elected President. Gentili and Pozzo di Borgo were named to go to Paris to extend Corsica's thanks for the freedom and institutions which France had granted, and to present to the King and Assembly the official record of the organization of the Department of Corsica. As for the actual government, Paoli said "I must not and can not any longer have a hand in it. . . . The machine is set up; good will and disinterest is all that is required in the ad-

ministrators to make it run well. If they keep me informed
and ask my advice, I will give it with sincerity and frankness. In this state of affairs we have nothing to fear."[7]

On 15 November 1790 Paoli again writes to Boswell and
Burnaby, mentioning further packets containing news and
pamphlets concerning the organization of the Department
of Corsica. Gentili, in Paris, has by now probably found an
Englishman to carry the packets across the channel. "I long
to have news of you," he tells Boswell. "My health is much
better under my native skies. . . . I live as an ordinary
citizen, and never shall use the 60,000 francs a year granted to me by the Department, but I have not refused the
guards it has given me. The Genoese still do not love me"
(C 2176). The letter to Burnaby, considerably longer than
that to Boswell, starts with the statement, "My country is
once more free and calm, under the good constitution
which all France enjoys." To Burnaby also he writes of his
improved health, but adds: "I have need of it, because they
do not leave me one moment of peace. I am the advocate
of everyone."

From advocacy to action was but a short step. Paoli certainly had persuaded himself that he could refrain from
active participation in the affairs of government; and for
some time he succeeded in maintaining a state of near se-
clusion. The "machine," however, perhaps was not sufficiently perfected; more important, its operators were
either incompetent or dishonest, sometimes both. Further,
the citizenry, beneficiaries of all the plans created in France
and now so bravely implemented, had little idea of the
democratic process and could easily be stirred into acts of
lawlessness and violence. "I would never have believed that
twenty-one years of despotism could have destroyed the
public virtue which a brief period of liberty had caused to
shine in our country," he exclaimed. "Would that I had
been dead when the French gave us liberty! Of few could
it have been said that they had closed their eyes in the great
sleep more fortunately than I. . . . How heavily upon me
weighs the blood of so many martyrs spilled under my orders to give freedom to a people which is so unworthy of

it." Criminals often went unpunished, and corrupt officials when replaced were emulated by their successors. "If I go away disorders break out in the cantons. . . . When I am here all is calm, and I can at least keep them [the National Guard] ready to act in support of liberty and the constitution."[8] The constitution itself was not to be blamed. Burke's *Reflections* provoked Paoli to comment to Burnaby: "He speaks well of your constitution, but he has permitted himself too much license against ours." Perhaps he wishes to discredit the Revolution in the eyes of the British, but he should have "more regard for the Assembly of such a great and considerable nation. Be our constitution good or defective, a Frenchman must defend it: he cannot turn back without danger of falling into former despotism."[9]

During the first year in Corsica, Paoli when he was forced to act moved with the current of French history. Most conspicuous was his action against Bastia. As the most fully developed northeastern port city Bastia was the gateway to Corsica from the continent. Here the invaders usually had set up their headquarters. Bastia served as the capital of Corsica during the French occupation; it continued so to serve during the revolutionary regime. (Shortly after the troubles here related the capital was transferred back to Corte.) Hardy virtue and the spirit of fierce independence had historically found their home in the mountainous interior, whose inhabitants tended to look down upon the Bastians as corrupted by foreign ways. Now the years of French rule had left Bastia conservative, conventionally religious. In its midst the new government placed the headquarters of the Directory, whose radical, anticlerical chief, Bartolomeo Arena, took pleasure in enforcing decrees aimed at the *ancien régime*. Further, Filippo Buonarotti was now using Bastia as the base from which to write and publish his fulminations against God and Pope and King.

At Bastia tensions grew between the new revolutionaries and the Royalists, who courted the pious ordinary folk not caught up in the causes of the Revolution. The new civil constitution of the clergy required the reduction of the five

Corsican bishoprics to one; the one bishop refused to take the oath to uphold the constitution as decreed by the National Assembly. The Pope had indeed condemned the oath, and later in the year was to threaten any of the clergy who took it with the sentence of excommunication. The Corsicans simply elected another bishop, Paoli's old friend the Abbé Guasco. Paoli, although he made a practice as he put it of not interfering in "daily affairs," had participated in these events, doing all in his power to persuade the first bishop to take the oath, and, when unsuccessful, sending him to Rome to reconcile matters. The bishop in due course returned, but with the belief that he could persuade the people to oppose the decree of the civil constitution of the clergy. "The Court of Rome," Paoli observed dryly, "is not always well informed." Believing finally that he had brought calm to the city, Paoli permitted himself to depart on a leisurely journey through the mountains to Ajaccio. "My absence," he related to Burnaby, "gave courage to the fanatics," who at the time of the Rogation Days "held a most imposing barefooted procession, and wailed and wept for their endangered faith. . . . The women ran to abuse the house of the new bishop; at night the rabble insulted the Directory beyond measure. . . . Religion was no longer anything but a pretext. The movement was incited by the aristocrats, discontented with the constitution." The mobs stormed the headquarters of the Directory, dragged out Arena and his Secretary-General, Panattieri, and placed them, together with the hated foreign agitator Buonarotti, in a boat whose captain was given orders to take them to Italy. The three escaped, and Arena soon joined up with Paoli, who had hurried to Corte upon hearing the news. The grand council of the Department asked the General to place himself at the head of a body of five thousand men gathered from the National Guard to move on Bastia. When he reached the coast Paoli warned the commander of the fortress that he "would unhesitatingly turn the artillery against the city if it resisted." He entered the city without hindrance. As Paoli saw it, the mob had been seduced by the priests and the aristocrats, who assured them "that France was agitated by civil war and invaded on all sides by armies of princes united against the constitution. . . . I hope that they will no longer think so lightly of the affection of our people for its free constitution. Many good priests spoke against the briefs supposedly issued from Rome. The zeal of the people in this crisis seems to have acquired new vigor." The seditious bishop "did not see that obedience to the Pope must not be opposed to the first duty towards the homeland. . . . I pay no heed to the threats which our priests make to me from Rome."

Paoli's actions, and even more the tone of his letter, suggest a Jacobin in the making. The sarcasm and contempt, however, are tempered by what follows:

> I am sailing a sea full of hidden rocks: I must not be dismayed: my Pole Star is the liberty of my homeland and a loyal obedience to the free constitution of our monarchy. The Corsican aristocrats in Paris often denounce me for contrary sentiments. But these men are ignorant of the delicacy of the point of honor of an *onest' uomo*, and the good Frenchmen and the Assembly do not listen to them. Nor can I complain of the government, from which every day I receive fresh proofs of its approval of my conduct; there is no deference which they do not observe in my regard. . . . I could not require more respectful affection from my fellow countrymen, nor greater regard from the troops of the line. My way of living is the same which you saw me practice in Corte so many years ago. I always wear my boots, ready to mount a horse at any moment.[10]

The Royalist deputies from Corsica, Buttafoco and Peretti, cited the new troubles in Bastia as further confirmation of their recurrent charges against Paoli. Buttafoco published two tirades against Paoli. The following passage from one of them is sufficiently representative:

> No one denies that Paoli is intelligent and capable. He has the talent of a Venetian State Inquisitor, of a Parisian police-lieutenant—above all of a very active Visir's agent in Constantinople; but he has never been, nor has he ever shown himself to be, fit by inclination or principle for action within political institutions.[11]

Paoli did not lack supporters—Saliceti, for one, kept Buttafoco on the defensive; further, the two commissioners
sent to the Assembly, Gentili and Pozzo di Borgo, lost no
time in denouncing Buttafoco and Peretti. Napoleon, ever
watchful for an opportunity to engage attention, drew up
a protest in the form of a letter to Buttafoco in which he accused that nobleman of having sold his country to
Choiseul. The Patriotic Club of Ajaccio, which was af-
filiated with the Jacobin Club at Paris and numbered the
Bonapartes, even the sixteen-year-old Lucien, among its
vigorous members, had the pamphlet printed.[12] In Ajaccio, Buttafoco was burned in effigy for what he said and
wrote against Paoli.

Before he was able to mail his account of the troubles to
Burnaby, Paoli was given the shocking news of the arrest
of the French King and all his family at Varennes. He suddenly felt older, a victim of history rather than a shaper.
"Few years remain for me in this world," he added in a
postscript. "I find that I must create illusions for myself,
that I must make preparations to live in the memory of my
fellow countrymen, and in the good opinion of my friends."
Again his thoughts go to the King, and to the misfortunes
of those in high place. "He who might return fifty years
from now—how many new things would there be for him
to marvel at! And how then could he merely praise or
blame the conduct of the authors of this great scene! Your
sons, dear friend, will have this pleasure; . . . tell them to be
my advocates, only for errors of mind, nothing else." Although he became more wary, Paoli saw no alternative to
adhering to his firmly enunciated principles. The affair at
Bastia had brought forcefully to his attention the Directory's eagerness to settle old scores of the vendetta and new
scores of the revolution. He had of course already heard
many complaints; but his age, his poor health, and above
all his desire to let the new generation run things despite
its mistakes, made him reluctant to take action. Now he
concluded that he must intervene directly in political affairs. An opportunity came with the elections to the new
French Legislative Assembly in September 1791. The Di-

rectory expected to control the six-man delegation to the new Assembly, but Paoli determined openly to administer the Directory a rebuke and to see to it that loyal and honest Corsican adherents to the constitution (Paolists) represented the islanders in Paris during the critical times ahead. In this maneuver Paoli succeeded, although the entire delegation was by no means Paolist. The untrustworthy Bartolomeo Arena found favor by openly admitting past errors, and Pozzo di Borgo, whose talents for some time had attracted Paoli's respectful attention, took an independent line which permitted him to be reckoned among the faithful.

Paoli's efforts left him exhausted. On 7 October 1791 he sent messages to both Boswell and Burnaby by his servant Giacomo Pietro, who was going to London to see his family, telling them that he had not time to write but that Giacomo Pietro would give them news of Corsica and their friend. "Remember me to all our friends," he asks Boswell. "When you have the opportunity, write to me of events in that country which I shall always love, all the more now since our rivalries are at an end" (C 2177). The note to Burnaby, only a few words longer than that to Boswell, is much more revealing. "I have no cause to regret having come here" is his first and rather surprising statement after the preliminaries. "I have not been useless up to now, but it is a miracle that my health continues. I have little time to write, and little time to sleep. If once the affairs of our monarchy were firmly consolidated I could think about going away secretly with my brother to some place in Tuscany. We both need rest and quiet; and here it is not to be hoped for. . . . Remember me to all my friends; their good opinion is now the greatest comfort which I may have." This private man the Corsicans were not permitted to see; but, as if in response not only to the weariness of his body and spirit but to a premonition of disaster, during the next year especially he was to express in his letters again and again a desire to retire to remote peace. He was not to leave until requested to do so by George III in 1795. His enemies, first Corsican and French and then English, attributed his continuance to an insatiable desire for power. His letters show that he stayed because he believed he could not in honor abandon his people when they needed him.

The year 1792 saw the estrangement between Paoli and Saliceti, and between Paoli and the Arena and Bonaparte families. Increasingly, those Corsicans with antennae tuned to the strongest signals emanating from Paris looked upon Paoli as an obstruction. Yet he was vulnerable only to the degree that he used reason and compassion in moderating the effects of official decrees. For example, the National Assembly in 1790 decreed that monasteries and other religious houses be suppressed; yet in February 1792 the Corsican Directory found it necessary to issue an unqualified order for the suppression of the monasteries. If Paoli himself at this time detected danger from the left he gave no signs of it. Rather, he was concerned with developments on the continent. "In what a difficult role have I been placed in this little theatre!" he exclaims to Burnaby on 26 February 1792. Aware of the declarations of Austria and Prussia, he still does not believe there will be war. If it were to come it would be civil, "in the manner of those which shook England in former times."

> And who can reckon the results? This country at worst is the best situated: if the troops of the line are for the constitution—and there appears no reason to fear otherwise—no one will dare to attack us in our rocks and mountains. Let come what may, my principles of liberty will ever be my guide. Honor, liberty, *patria* would be the inscription on my banner if I had one. . . . Oh! how much would I give for ten years of robust health to enable me to respond to my obligations to the Assembly. Gentili is no longer in good health; he too would sacrifice future years for natural, active ones now. . . . When I write to my friends whom I have left in England, I open my heart and lose my sense of reserve; but friendship will excuse me to them. . . . the freedom of *la patria* so concerns me that I no longer see or feel anything else.

What Paoli is here considering is the possibility of a general war in which the despotic powers of Europe seek to overthrow the forces of the French Revolution; and he quite naturally allies himself with the Revolution.

Soon France declared war on Austria and Prussia. Uncertainties about France's fate and a concern for the direction of the political deliberations in Paris find expression in Paoli's letter to Burnaby from Corte, 30 June 1792:

If I were a statesman I would abhor those plans of government formed in philosophical cabinets. The good laws are those which the needs of the times and the will of the people have created; and these for the most part have the sanction of centuries. Everyone must rule himself according to his own experience. You have a government which has brought you prosperity and peace: a sign not contrary to liberty. You do well to be more than content with it. The French do not have such a government. Do not then join with the despots to prevent us from forming one for ourselves. If you give us time, we shall yet learn how to secure a balance so that man will have to fear neither the insolence of democracy nor the power and excessive wealth of an individual. When our affairs become calm, two peoples so close will be able to provide an example for all the world; or at least prescribe for it a perpetual peace.

"The insolence of democracy!" If the letter were intercepted—many letters, even those carried by friends or trusted couriers, somehow were—how the French radicals could seize on that phrase! The hope for a supervised or "prescribed" peace which Paoli has cherished since leaving England he realizes may be quite futile; the alternative forces attention:

If the military powers take the upper hand, we must look forward once more to centuries of barbarity. But where can I go? My health is rather good for my age, and I have need of it. This people and the government have graciously invited me to be close to the administration in these circumstances. . . . If I can once see the ship out of this storm into port, be assured that then you will hear that I seek repose in some corner withdrawn from the world: I cannot tell you where, because the states of Italy fear that the presence of free men will disturb their lethargic slumber. . . . Gentili no longer has his health. . . . I have found few of those men who were my companions when you were here. I am among new people.

Testimony that Paoli was believed to be in control of Corsica's destiny comes from Napoleon, who, after his activities in the island had alienated Paoli, Pozzo di Borgo, and even the people of his home city of Ajaccio, went to Paris and immediately waited upon the Corsican deputies to the Assembly. "Keep on close terms with Paoli," he writes to Joseph on 29 May 1792. "He is everything and can do everything. In the future he is going to be more than anyone foresees." Writing again on 18 June he tells Joseph, "You must try to see if Lucien can stay with the General. It is more than ever probable that all this will end in our independence."[13]

Disturbing news now comes from Paris. As the allies advance into France, the members of the Assembly brave enough to remain in session vote to suspend the King from his office and to authorize the immediate election by universal manhood suffrage of a National Convention that is to prepare a republican constitution for France. The Legislative Assembly, before relinquishing its powers, takes the precaution of appointing Paoli General of the army division in Corsica. The appointment, which now puts Paoli under direct military orders, the General accepts under protest, pleading his advanced age. The period from the suspension of the King on 10 August 1792 to the assembling of the National Convention on 21 September is one of anarchy in Paris. Saliceti, the devoted follower of Robespierre, is the Corsican who rides most high. Pozzo di Borgo and his fellow Corsican deputy, Pietri, disappear from public view and soon show themselves in Corsica.

The election for deputies to the National Convention provided Saliceti his last chance to contest the power of Paoli in Corsica. Paoli was stricken ill, many feared mortally, and Saliceti intrigued actively with the Directory, some of whom had not recovered from Paoli's criticism of their conduct. Saliceti managed to secure the election of the majority of his candidates on this occasion. But in the election which shortly followed, for the administrators and justices of the island, the Paolists completely dominated. Such was the situation by the end of 1792: in Corsica a people united by Paoli, with the political and judicial apparatus for the first time completely under his control; in France opposition from Saliceti and his followers, already finding expression in criticism of Paoli's sympathy for the old monarchy.

Toward the end of his three-month period of convalescence, on 24 December 1792, Paoli writes to Burnaby that the people had been "wearying the heavens with their prayers. If I had need of other incitements to be completely dedicated to their destiny, this last token of their devotion [furnishes them]. May I think of nothing but to see their liberty firmly established." Later on he states that he longs "for the time of peace" in order to resign his commission of lieutenant general and the command of the army division in Corsica. "If I once succeeded in fulfilling my duty toward *la patria*, I would give all the favors of the world for an hour's peace of mind, and for conversation with my friends." In a postscript he adds that the "health of Mr. Gentili is not better. . . . Father Guelfucci also has been practically given up. . . . We are old; we must all think of giving way to youth."

In France the political campaign against Paoli began in the summer of 1792, with the circulation of rumors that he was secretly in league with the British. After France declared war against England, 1 February 1793, the charge was made openly in the Convention. Asked to furnish four Corsican battalions for an expedition to liberate Sardinia, Paoli made no secret of his doubts concerning the wisdom of the undertaking. He furnished about 1,800 troops out of a total of 10,000. "I will do as much as I can," he wrote, "but I will stay on guard so that if the undertaking does not succeed they will not think they can charge me with its failure. I have reason to fear that they wish to make trouble for me."[14]

Paoli's fears proved well-grounded. Saliceti persuaded the Convention to remove Paoli from Corsica by issuing a military order asking him to join his comrades in the army of Italy. Paoli expressed his regrets, pleading old age and infirmity. Saliceti in Paris and Arena in the south of France intensified their campaign against Paoli, accusing him of having aborted the expedition to Sardinia, of seeking independent and dictatorial power, and, in order to achieve his ends, of conspiring with England. The Corsican Directory responded with charges of personal corruption against the former syndics, Saliceti and Arena, and offered proof. Saliceti was not above lining his pockets with multiple salaries at public expense, or expropriating property for personal gain; nevertheless his position as the dedicated revolutionary and chief of the anti-Paolist forces was not in the least shaken. The Convention dispatched three commissioners, Saliceti and two native Frenchmen, ostensibly with orders "to examine the coast" with a view toward improving defenses. In reality they were to assess the political and military situation and if possible to counteract Paoli's influence. Saliceti went so far as to make a brief visit to Paoli at Corte in the role of mediator—with some success, he thought. The Bonapartes began to shift towards the Saliceti faction. Joseph attached himself to the commissioners from the Convention shortly after they arrived in Bastia. Lucien, who had been repulsed in his application for a post on Paoli's immediate staff, crossed to France in March 1793 and in the Jacobin Club of Toulon denounced Paoli as a traitor, guilty of treason, fit for the guillotine.[15] Napoleon did not commit himself.

The radical factions in Corsica and France dismissed Paoli's defenses with impatience. It availed him little to write: "Freedom, country, constitution—these are my guide. He who defends them will find me . . . at his side. The enemy will never make me change opinion or language."[16] What was now the "constitution"? Not only his refusal to veer with the wind but his outspokenness made Paoli dangerous. Could a man be permitted to continue in power who believed that his enemies "would like to make Corsica a nest of assassins, now that they have destroyed the freedom of Europe"?[17] The Corsican Directory, among them the new syndic Pozzo di Borgo, still sought to influence the Convention, writing to the Corsican deputies Bozio and Abbé Andrei: "They must be convinced at Paris that we are free, that we are aware of our rights, and that we will reject calumny, intrigue, and arrogance, now evidently the established means of determining policy against the Corsicans."[18]

While the commissioners were still at work in Corsica the Committee of Public Safety issued, on 2 April 1793, a warrant for the arrest of Paoli and Pozzo di Borgo. Saliceti was caught by surprise. He believed, perhaps without very much justification, that he was making some progress in his open negotiations with Paoli and in his secret intrigues with lesser patriots. Now his work was undercut; he stayed on to salvage what he could. The decision to arrest Paoli had been triggered by the aforementioned speech of Lucien Bonaparte, which had been adopted by the Jacobin Club at Toulon and in expanded form presented as an accusation before the Convention. Upon hearing of the warrant Napoleon, who as an officer in the expedition to Sardinia knew how groundless were Lucien's assertions concerning that action, immediately came to Paoli's defense by drawing up an address to the Convention in the name of the Jacobin Club of Ajaccio.[19] Napoleon was not driven by a passion for truth; he still saw Paoli as the chief power in the island, and believed that his family's and his own future lay in coming to an accommodation with the General. In the eyes of the Paolists, however, this action by one of the Bonapartes came too late. Paoli already had in his possession an intercepted letter from Lucien to Napoleon in which he exulted, "I have dealt a decisive blow to my enemies. . . . I am impatient to know what will become of Paoli and Pozzo di Borgo."[20] Napoleon barely escaped to San Fiorenzo, where he joined the commissioners from the Convention in attacking Paoli. "Make up your mind to it," he wrote to his mother, "this country is not for us."[21] On 11 June 1793 Napoleon with his mother and other members of the family set sail for Toulon. For nearly four years Napoleon had spent more time in Corsica than in France. Within three years, as commander of the French Army of Italy, he was to look upon his homeland as significant enough strategically to warrant the taking, but as otherwise deserving little attention.

Only two weeks before he was informed of the warrant

for his arrest, Paoli for the first time since leaving London received direct news from Boswell. Boswell's letters upon arrival had somehow been placed in a box or case for books at Bastia, and only when the case was moved to Rostino were the letters found and forwarded to Paoli at Corte. The bundle was small—two letters totalling four folio leaves—and thus easily lost among the absent General's belongings. The first letter, dated 10 December 1791, must have seemed to the beleaguered Paoli a message from another world. Boswell apologizes for his long silence: "The alternate agitation and depression of spirits to which I am unhappily subject has innumerable times prevented my sitting down to write what my heart never failed to feel." The recent history of Paoli and his countrymen "is almost equal to any of the delightful stories of Romance. Thousands of hours has it animated my thoughts and excited an earnest desire to be again in Corsica, that I might gratify my eyes and ears with the actual impressions of so amiable and so glorious a restoration." All Paoli's friends in England rejoice; among them Boswell mentions the Generals, Sir George Howard, Robert Melville, and Cyrus Trapaud, as well as the Bishop of Killaloe (Thomas Barnard). Another close friend, Sir Joshua Reynolds, is, alas, extremely ill. Boswell is now sending a copy of "my *Magnum Opus*, the Life of Dr. Johnson, requesting your indulgent perusal of it." The extent of the sale and the praises of critics bring satisfaction.

> But as to obtaining a proper settlement in life, I am as yet at a loss. I found my connection would do me no good, and I resigned the Recordership of Carlisle. I attend Westminster Hall, and have chambers in the Temple, but I have very little practice, and I feel myself miserably unoccupied. I went to Auchinleck last Autumn, hoping to exert myself in the arrangement of my affairs, which my accurate, judicious and friendly Brother had the year before gone down and put into a pretty clear train. But the *Place* brought back upon me with much additional sadness the loss of *Her of whom I was not worthy*, as your Excellency used justly to say. Melancholy seized upon me, and I have not yet recovered from the gloom in which all objects seem to be involved. In

such a situation, I peculiarly feel the want of your Excellency's most hospitable house in Portman Square, in which I at all times found consolation.

He tells Paoli of his children, who, he believes, "are all improving." The old Boswell will not down. "I still flatter myself that I shall get some preferment." Thinking of Paoli's new life: "Pride, a noble Pride must be best gratified in Corsica, but you surely enjoyed more pleasure in London. I hope we shall yet see you here again. But if that cannot be, I believe I shall pay a second visit to Corsica, and carry my eldest son with me" (L 1023). This letter Boswell does not send until he joins it with the next, dated 16 August 1792, at the same time sending a copy of the *Life*. Reynolds has died; he, Boswell, has achieved a more tolerable state of mind (L 1024).

Boswell's appalling obtuseness in not even faintly imagining the desperate concerns of one in Paoli's situation, his failure to recall that Paoli in his life had one "great object"—or worse yet, his implied conclusion that that object had already been achieved—these must have disappointed the General, but disappointment doubtless immediately gave way to sadness. Paoli's reply, on 20 March 1793 (C 2178), displays the old warmth but quite naturally places matters in a new perspective, and not only because France had declared war on England some weeks earlier. "When I have a little time to myself I shall send for your *Magnum Opus*, to peruse it and to be in imagination with you and with so many good friends mentioned in it." He writes of the dangerous disease from which he is still convalescing, and of the renewed demonstrations of the people's loyalty and affection. "Through fatal misfortune our nations are now at war. Could they have agreed on their plans all Europe would have become free in a short time. Providence, which rules over the Fate of Nations, will untangle this knot. Our vision is too limited for us to discover the means by which it will bring peace to the poor peoples oppressed by the ambition and pushed to the brink of ruin by the ignorance of their leaders. . . . I embrace you and your sons, and I should like to say a thousand things to your lovable daughters, to make them accept my attentions." Imagine Paoli's not dropping everything to read the *Life of Johnson*! Boswell's silence for nearly two years may properly be attributed, however, to many causes other than hurt pride.

Paoli's initial response to the decree for his and Pozzo di Borgo's arrest had been one more of sorrow than indignation. To the deputy Abbé Andrei in Paris he wrote on 19 April 1793:

> My feelings for liberty are hereditary and habitual, but they are nonetheless founded upon the most serious political considerations. . . . the freedom of France will never be an object of indifference to me. If that country returns to servitude, goodbye forever to every hope of liberty, especially for the small states. This is and will always be my way of thinking: and if they wish to meet me in this life, they will know me ever firm and unfailing in the intention of seeking for my country a freedom combined with that of the French. May Heaven grant that the other determinations of the Convention be more just and better reflected upon than that which they have taken against me![22]

To the Convention Paoli sent a long formal reply on 26 April 1793. After expressing surprise at being ordered "to your bar with the same precautions which are used with a convict of the State, who must account to you for his lies and his misdeeds," he goes on to express his regret that his feeble state of health has made it impossible for him to cross "more than two hundred leagues" to present himself before them. If he were to appear, he continues, "of what crime would I need to justify myself?"

> My indebtedness to England has been spoken of, and the motive which this must give you to fear that I may serve its interests to the detriment of those of the Republic. Certainly I am not ungrateful; but I am even less a perjurer. I cannot forget my duties toward my homeland, nor the obligations which bind me to the cause of liberty and of equality. Neither can I renounce the esteem of the nation in which I lived for twenty years, and give it cause to be ashamed of the generous interest it had shown me.

To the charge that he has made excessive and improper use of his influence with the Corsican people he replies:

> My conscience, however, provides me the satisfying testimony of not having ever made particular use of it, except for the defense and for the relief of the widow and of the orphan; to strengthen liberty; to humble fanaticism; to maintain peace and tranquillity in this Department, in the midst of the agitations which ordinarily accompany every revolution; to preserve, finally, this Island from the horrors and from the atrocities with which the enemies of liberty have dishonored the revolution in so many other places in the Republic. . . . If you believe, citizen representatives, that for the peace and security of this country, and to reaffirm liberty and equality in Corsica, it is necessary that my presence no longer give pretext here for hatred, distrust, or jealousy, speak: I will go away without a murmur from my native land which has honored my life and my name.[23]

The Convention, beset with a seemingly endless number of critical problems, decided to suspend the decree of 2 April pending the report of a new commission which was to go to Corsica. The commission already in the island, however, was taking actions which could not be reversed. To one of his administrators Paoli wrote, "I sincerely pray for the liberty of the French, since if the despots succeed in overthrowing it and in introducing an arbitrary government into that vast country, no other nation can dare hope to preserve its liberty." The Department, he continues, which before the arrival of the commissioners was "so tranquil and loyal," is now "on the point of being placed in insurrection and exposed to the horrors of a civil war." The small bodies of French troops being deployed in various areas bring alarm and unrest. A good Frenchman could not rejoice:

> Corsica in ruins is no longer valuable for France. But I believe that the whole thing reduces to the miserable scheme to see out of the Island three individuals of one family, all decrepit and oppressed by infirmities. Tell them to reestablish peace and mutual confidence, and I, my brother, and our poor sister will go elsewhere to finish our days in peace.[24]

By this time all correspondence from interior Corsica
was being intercepted, and Paoli's people kept in isolation
from France. The commissioners dissolved the De-
partmental administration and authorized the formation
of new, loyal Republican battalions of Corsican troops.
Saliceti threatened into silence the Corsican delegates in
Paris (except for Abbé Andrei, who in expressing himself
seriously jeopardized his life). To the Convention Saliceti
wrote on 14 May 1793: "The commission has dismissed the
administration of the Department. . . . We are sure not to
be obeyed. The rebellion has started, and under the name
of Paoli the Corsican people runs to plunge itself into an
abyss from which it will never emerge."[25]

In response to the commission's actions Paoli called for a
General Council (*Consulta*), which met at Corte on 26 May.
Over a thousand delegates representing nine-tenths
of the population overwhelmingly declared for the General. Paoli still hoped that a break with France could be
avoided. For the time being the Council satisfied itself with
proclaiming its own authority within Corsica, supplanting
the commissioners from France; and with declaring that
Saliceti, Multedo, and Casabianca were no longer authorized to represent Corsica at the Convention in Paris. It
then called upon the citizens enlisted in French battalions
and in the National Guard to return to their homes.
Saliceti circulated his charges in an apologia "much more
virulent than that of Buttafoco," noted Paoli; "the two
principal enemies are myself and Pozzo di Borgo."[26]

On 17 July 1793 the Convention in Paris declared Paoli
a traitor, and ordered the executive council to dispose its
forces on land and sea for the execution of the law and the
defense of Corsica.[27] The Corsicans responded by naming
Paoli Generalissimo, calling back many of the exiled clergy,
and organizing the resistance. For the last time Corsica
proclaimed itself an independent nation. At this juncture
some of the Paolist republicans abandoned the General.
For Paoli the great single personal as well as national loss
was the withdrawal of Antonio Gentili, his companion in
exile in England. It was clear enough to Gentili that, unless

France collapsed, Paoli would be forced to seek help from England, and at a price. As Paoli's gentleman-satellite Gentili had been treated kindly enough in England, but he had developed no very deep attachment for that country. He chose France without a fanatic's enthusiasm, fully aware that his decision like Paoli's would be judged in the light of developments neither could possibly foresee.

History appeared to be repeating itself. As in 1768, Corsica could claim to be a sovereign nation in full control of its territory except for some seaports occupied by the French and their sympathizers. But much had happened since the time when Paoli sternly rejected the English spy's suggestion that England, if it chose to help Corsica, would expect certain permanent reimbursements such as harbors and the like. Now Paoli knew that Corsica could not long maintain its independence in the midst of powerful warring nations. France, far from moderating its views, was moving towards a new despotism; for Paoli, England appeared to offer the only hope for the kind of support which would not enslave his people. By the end of August the General initiated official overtures.[28]

In October, Paoli began to seek sympathetic understanding of his position from the British public. To Burnaby on 11 October 1793 and to Boswell on the next day (C 2179) Paoli sent letters along with all printed matter issued by the Corsicans since the time of their dispute with the National Convention.[29] Forgetting that Boswell could no longer call up the energies of his youth, Paoli tells him to "take up the defense of your old friend," and ends his letter: "Remember me to your Brother and to our friends. I embrace you warmly." Paoli also asks Burnaby to remember him to "our friends. I hope my conduct will not be censured by them." To Boswell, Paoli does not confide remarks like these to Burnaby: "My health holds up tolerably well. But the sciatica no longer permits me to walk even a mile on foot; and you know how unsuitable this country is for traversing on horseback. May God grant that for the second time I may exit with honor from the political scene, which I have entered not prompted by ambition but only

by necessity and my duty toward *la patria.*" A few days
before Paoli wrote to Boswell a small British naval attack
supported by the Corsicans drove the defenders from
much of Capo Corso. It was at this time, apparently, that
Paoli's agent, Masseria, quietly left with the British to
pursue his mission in London.[30]

The England toward which Paoli turned in 1793 he considered little changed from the country which he had left
three years earlier. It had the same King, the same Prime
Minister, and the same form of government. Toward
George III Paoli held feelings of trust and affection. After
a decade of waiting upon and observing Lord North, Paoli
was not inclined to trust any English Minister; but William
Pitt bore an illustrious name and appeared to understand
where his country's interests lay. As for the English political system, Paoli admired it more than did most of its
citizens. True, in the early 1780s it failed to move forward
to adopt the reforms which seemed obviously desirable to
lovers of democracy. Yet imperfect as it was, it responded
to public will to a degree which Paoli found remarkable.
Meetings, petitions, pamphlets, general noise: if necessary
one or all could be used to implement electioneering. And
somehow the mechanism politic incorporated an im-
perceptible system of checks and balances; no individual or
faction could succeed in assuming despotic powers. England, as Paoli was to observe to Burnaby, had a Parliament
that could restrain executive power; and the people, when
the abuse became intolerable, were somehow able to
restrain Parliament.[31] Ironically, even as Paoli was seeking
freedom under England's protection, that country was
moving to restrict political meetings, to suppress "riots,"
and to enlarge its internal spy network.

The proximity to Corsica of British naval and land forces
was owing to the unexpected opposition to the French
government which in July 1793 had arisen in the cities of
southern France—Lyons, Avignon, Marseilles, and Toulon. The rebels were soon crushed except for those at
Toulon, who had called in England and its allies and turned
over to them thirty ships of the line plus twenty-odd

frigates and smaller vessels. The British army commander at Toulon, General Charles O'Hara, led a force inland into the arms of the Republican forces.[32] His successor, General David Dundas, refused to venture far outside the perimeter without additional help. Admiral Hood paced the deck of H.M.S. *Victory* from August to December, sure that all that deprived him of victory was the lack of a bold and intelligent army general.

Hood had been joined in November by an agent of Pitt's ministry, Sir Gilbert Elliot. Elliot was one of the first of the Portland Whigs—successors to the Rockinghams—to move toward the position of Pitt, without however renouncing allegiance to his leader. His appointment "in a ministerial character, for transacting all affairs of a civil and political nature" which might arise in the south of France pleased his friend Burke, who, however, found in "the dead stupidity" with which news of the success at Toulon was generally received "the worst possible augury of the sense and public spirit of England."[33] Sir Gilbert set foot on land on 19 November; by 17 December he was shipping back his papers to the *Victory*; and the next morning he joined Hood aboard. Of twenty-seven French ships of the line still at Toulon, three accompanied the retreat. The British succeeded in burning nine ships; the remaining fifteen, a quite significant force, were later to appear in the fleet which went with Napoleon to Egypt, there to be destroyed by Nelson in 1798.[34]

On 19 December 1793 the fleet got safely out of Toulon roads. Elliot expected to return to England after he had assisted the refugees immediately under his care, mostly widows and orphans. The future Viceroy of Corsica was consciously decent, compassionate. To Henry Dundas, Home Secretary, he wrote: "My opinion is—and I trust it is yours—that we have been too closely connected with them in the events which have preceded this calamity, as well as in the last scene itself, to shake them off at this moment, and leave them to their miserable and certain fate, while we pursue our own better fortunes with indifference."[35]

In the more than four months since Paoli had approached England, Lord Hood had obliged with the minor naval actions mentioned earlier and then, beginning early in December, with a squadron under the command of Nelson which so closely blockaded Corsica that neither troops nor supplies had been able to enter, nor had vessels been able to escape.[36] For all this Paoli was duly grateful. But there was no sign of commitment; Hood in the Mediterranean was silent or evasive, and the Ministry in London kept Masseria, the bearer of Paoli's offering, dangling. Finally, toward the end of the year, after the unexpected power of the French Army of the South had brought about the hasty allied withdrawal from Toulon, Corsica was given more concentrated attention. On 10 January 1794 Elliot boarded a frigate "to settle," as he put it, "the cession of Corsica to England." Lord Hood and the fleet were to follow in a few days.[37] By the time the British mission landed, on 14 January, Paoli was both angry and suspicious.

The mission consisted of two Lowland Scotsmen and one Hessian: Lieutenant Colonel John Moore, Sir Gilbert Elliot, and Major George Frederic Koehler of the Royal Artillery. They found "every Corsican, not excepting the priests, in arms. . . . I do not believe," observed Elliot, "there was a man, woman, or even a young child amongst many thousands whom we saw, that came within hail of us without calling, 'Viva Paoli, e la nazione Inglese!'"[38] After the first exchange of compliments, during which Elliot delivered to Paoli a letter from Lord Hood explaining the nature of the mission, the General, instead of speaking to Elliot addressed himself to Koehler and Moore. Moore, quite puzzled, found it necessary to make it clear to Paoli that, although Koehler and he were to coordinate military operations with the Corsicans, both were under Sir Gilbert Elliot, who was one of the King's Commissioners in the Mediterranean, and until the General had had some previous conversation with the Commissioner, Koehler and he could not enter upon the subject of the mission. Paoli "made some odd answer to the effect that he was tired of Ministers and negotiations." He however then turned to Sir Gilbert. The reasons for Paoli's uncharacteristically insulting behavior toward Elliot soon became clear. After requesting several people in the room to withdraw, he said to Elliot that he was sorry to find by Lord Hood's letter that he "continued unexplicit and diffident of him."

> In affairs of this kind it is necessary to be open and candid. "I wrote long ago to the King and to his Ministers; I have also repeatedly written to Lord Hood that I and my people wished to be free, either as subjects of Great Britain, which I know does not want slaves, or free under the protection of Great Britain, as the King and the country may hereafter think most convenient to adopt; having said this, I can say no more. Why, therefore, does his Lordship tease me with more negotiations? *That man* has already injured me with promises of succour which he has always withheld. If it is meant to include my compatriots in any arrangement which may hereafter be made with the Bourbons, I can have no hand in it. I shall retire. All I wish is to see, before I die, my country settled and happy after the struggles of these past three hundred years. I think my countrymen will enjoy a proper degree of liberty under the protection or government of the British nation. I have told them so, and they have that confidence in me that they believe me and wish to make the experiment!" The General seemed much affected; the tears came into his eyes whilst he spoke.

Moore notes in his diary that "the General is much broken since I saw him in England," and mentions his recent illness and the death of his brother.[39] Paoli's visitors had little conception of what it had cost the General to arrive where they saw him. How much he thought might still lie ahead the reference to the Bourbons painfully disclosed. During the previous thirty years he had seen Great Powers deal with small nations. Corsica, he had written in 1771, was a "poor rag . . . placed at auction by the powers of Europe." Poland had been partitioned in 1772 and now was being partitioned again. His own people were not to be disposed of casually, let alone returned to a Royalist France as part of a peace settlement. Unhappily, factions like that of Buttafoco would be only too willing to take over for this kind of arrangement.

Moore admired Elliot's composure: "Sir Gilbert never attempted to interrupt him, though some of the General's expressions with regard to Lord Hood were not the most polite. When he had finished he calmly told him he had misconceived Lord Hood's letter, that no advantage was meant to be taken of the General or his countrymen. The object of his mission was to know if any method could be taken, by assembling the states or otherwise, of getting the public assent of the Island to what the General said was their wish. The General said, 'How can this be done at present? The enemy must first be expelled. It is then my intention to call the states together. In the meantime I know what is their wish and can answer for them.'" The next day Moore learned that Elliot and the General had arrived at an agreement. The Corsicans were to be given every assistance in expelling the French from the island; and the particular mode of government was to be left to future discussion. Moore and Koehler then discussed military plans with the General. On 20 January the party set out on their return, except for Koehler, who remained behind at Paoli's request. "Paoli was afraid that, if we all left him, it might have a bad effect on his people."[40] The week on the island thoroughly convinced Elliot of the Corsicans' passionate attachment to Paoli. That the multitudes were acting upon orders was inconceivable. Further, "whenever we talked of making them independent they rejected that idea, and said they would be English." Neither did Elliot doubt Paoli's intentions. "He is old, extremely infirm, harassed and fatigued beyond his strength, and impatient to return from this scene of labor, perplexity, and danger as soon as he has brought his country safe into a British haven."[41] The similarity of these views to those expressed by Paoli in letters to Burnaby indicates accurate reporting.

Lord Hood officially concluded the convention with Paoli, by which it was agreed that the British forces should assist the Corsicans in the expulsion of the French from the island, and that its annexation to Great Britain should be the immediate consequence. Pending the success of the military operations no further diplomatic action would be taken. Elliot, who was now entrusted with the commission of generally superintending political affairs in the Mediterranean, returned to Italy and the problems of the

French refugees, for whom the leaders of the various Italian states offered much sympathy but little help. Finding places of settlement, and then persuading the refugees to accept their miserable new life, occupied many weeks of Elliot's time.

The French were forced to abandon San Fiorenzo on 17 February 1794, leaving some forces to destroy arms, ammunition, and roads while the main body retreated to Bastia. Paoli was pleased with the progress so far, although he naturally had hoped for speedier success. His hand being too numb to permit him to write himself, he dictated accounts of the battles to send to Burnaby and [Tiberius] Cavallo. The Corsicans had fought bravely; too much praise could not be given to Major Koehler, Colonel Moore, and Captain [Edward] Cooke (R.N.). "I cannot write to everyone," he tells Burnaby, and begs him to give news to Boswell and his other friends. The next day, 23 February 1794, he finds time to add a postscript to his letter to Burnaby and to dictate a short letter to Boswell after all, the intent of which is apparently to let Boswell know that he has not been forgotten and that he can expect from Burnaby and especially from Cavallo a summary in English of the events in Corsica. "I have charged them with the task of informing you of my letters" (C 2180). In the letter to Burnaby, Paoli expresses his gratitude to England, which "kept alive the ardor for liberty in Corsica during twenty years of tyrannical oppression." He longs to see his friends in England again, and to return to "that country in which I have lived longer than any other, and where I would wish to end my days after the happiness of seeing *la patria* free under the protection of, or in union with Great Britain."

On the same day Paoli wrote the above letters to his English friends Hood sent a note to Paoli "on the success of your brave people"; but in reality the English were furious at the Corsicans, who had failed to accomplish the one coordinated task assigned to them, that of cutting off the French escaping from San Fiorenzo to Bastia. By the time Bastia fell, on 22 May, essentially because the blockade by sea and land had brought the city close to

starvation, Moore's disillusionment with Paoli was complete. Paoli, Moore now concluded, was merely a "politician," essentially ignorant of military matters. "The great
cause of the failure of the expedition has been the failure
on the part of General Paoli and the Corsicans. Instead of
the active, warlike people I took them to be, zealous in the
cause of liberty, they have proved to be a poor, idle, mean
set, incapable of any action which requires steadiness or
resolution, and have been absolutely of no use to us since
we landed."[42] Moore had only himself to blame for equat-
ing lucidity and intelligence in conversation with a capacity
for acting in the field. We should also remember that
Moore was to achieve eminence not only as one of Britain's
greatest generals but also as an authority on the training of
soldiers. It would have been surprising if the ragtag bands
of Corsicans had come up to his standards.

The siege of Bastia also brought an intensification of in-
terservice rivalries. Admiral Hood went over General
Dundas' head; Moore, from tip to toe a professional, was
adamant in refusing to act upon or to acknowledge Hood's
orders. Koehler had succeeded in obtaining a transfer;
Dundas was now glad to leave. Dundas' successor, D'Aubant, found no more reason to take initiatives, especially
when suggested by Hood; but he sprang forward with
alacrity once the flag of truce emerged from Bastia. In this
state of affairs the arrival of D'Aubant's successor, General
Charles Stuart, just after the fall of Bastia, was looked upon
rather desperately as a harbinger of harmony.[43]

Elliot, who had come from Leghorn with General Stuart,
found he was in time to celebrate victory and, with Hood,
to sign the convention for the surrender of Bastia. From
this ceremony Paoli was conspicuously omitted. Moore discussed the siege with the commander of the defending
forces, General Gentili. "I expressed some surprise . . . that
with so strong a garrison he never made a sortie. He said
a sortie would not have given them bread; that besides, he
wished to do his duty, but no more; his property was in
England. He found fault with us for trusting the village of
Villa upon our right flank to Corsicans. It could have been

attacked with success; in which case we must have retreated to our ships with the loss of our guns." Gentili's state of mind should have made him susceptible to persuasion by Paoli. "He would not speak of capitulation as long as he had a mouthful of bread and beans," Paoli wrote proudly of his old friend. But Gentili had cast his lot. "I am sorry," wrote Paoli of him, "that he desired to go [back] to France, even though he is not without fear of being ill-received there. Like all those generals who have acquired a reputation in the service of their so-called republic, he believed that his honor demanded that he expose himself to this risk."[44]

The British continued to press Paoli to hold a Consulta. On 21 April 1794, while the siege of Bastia was still in progress and the attack on Calvi only in the early planning stage,[45] Hood and Elliot addressed a letter to Paoli requesting action that would "bring to a final conclusion . . . the particular form and manner of relationship which must . . . be established between the two Nations. . . . His Majesty . . . is therefore determined to conclude nothing without the general and free consent of the people of Corsica. We therefore request Your Excellency to take the appropriate steps in order to submit these important matters to the judgment of your fellow countrymen." Paoli complied with a long public letter to his "Most Beloved Compatriots," dated 1 May 1794, in which he reviewed the recent history of oppression, and gave reasons for seeking "the protection of the King of Great Britain, political union with the English Nation, which demonstrates to the universe the prosperity and the power of entire centuries as proof of the excellence of its government." To this address he attached a translation of the letter from Hood and Elliot.[46] Paoli requested a General Consulta in Corte on 8 June. In electing deputies he urged each of his countrymen "to propose to himself the one whom he judges most useful to *la patria.*"

What Paoli saw as the imposition of a condition which showed a lack of trust in him as spokesman, made him all the more anxious to extract maximum expenditure and involvement from the British before yielding to them. From their point of view the British had reason to require extraordinary assurances before committing themselves to defend a remote land and its people. Perhaps Paoli could at the moment "answer for them;" but with Paoli retired from the scene—an imminent condition as understood on all sides—would the Corsicans still attach themselves fervently to George III?

Elliot was in high spirits as he approached Corte for the meeting of the Consulta, which had been delayed until 10 June. Corsica, he wrote to Lady Elliot, "is really a fairy land." In a revealing passage he spoke of himself as Bolingbroke. "I met and embraced *Old Richard* at his door. However, the likeness does not hold, for although I am a sort of successor he would have more God bless him's than I, and could send Bolingbroke into the kennel without the help of Roan Barbary,."[47] Elliot was to prove unable to shake off this sense of competition with the "king" he was displacing.

On 19 June General Paoli in the name of the Corsican people tendered the crown of Corsica to his Majesty the King of Great Britain, represented by Sir Gilbert Elliot as his Minister plenipotentiary. The Assembly named Paoli President, and he in turn chose Pozzo di Borgo as Secretary. "I call God and man to witness," Paoli then said, "that I have used all the means which moderation and love of peace suggested to me, in order to dissuade the French from their cruel resolution to kindle an internal war of extermination in Corsica."[48] Before disbanding, the Assembly heaped such titles on Paoli as Father of the Homeland, restorer of liberty, tutelary genius of Corsica; further, it decreed that a bust of Paoli should be erected in the hall of Parliament as a perpetual reminder of the services of the General and the gratitude of his people. Paoli was given the honor of naming a deputation of four members who were charged with presenting an address to George III (written by Pozzo di Borgo) from the Assembly, expressing the feelings of love and fidelity of the Corsican people for his British Majesty.[49] The resilience, the stubborn endurance of Paoli's battered capacity for hope broke forth in his final exclamation: "Blessed, blessed, O my compatriots, the blood which your fathers spilled, that which you yourselves have shed for freedom; blessed the wounds, the hardships, the persecution, all the misfortune that you have suffered for it: here is the fulfillment of the prayers of our forefathers, here is the end of our sighs, our wrongs: *la patria* is free, *la patria* is independent: now there is a Corsica." Elliot found the proceedings eminently satisfying, confiding to his wife that "I was crowned last Thursday . . . and I send you My Majesty's speech, which was spoken in French; it produced on my new subjects a kingly effect."[50]

The constitution which emerged from the deliberations guaranteed individual liberties, free speech and press, freedom of conscience and religion. While Catholicism was acknowledged as the only established religion, other religions were to be fully tolerated. Legislative power was granted to an Assembly—now to be called Parliament—composed of representatives of the people; all laws or decrees or rulings were subject to the King's (i.e. the Viceroy's) approval. With respect to domestic affairs the constitution resembled the Corsican document of 1768, modified somewhat to conform to English practice. Suffrage was limited to males above twenty-five years of age who possessed property—a matter of little moment because all Corsicans considered themselves landholders. Two modifications probably were the work of Sir Gilbert. The first stipulated that a candidate for Parliament should be a qualified voter possessed of land worth at least six thousand lire; the second provided that the members of Parliament defray their own expenses. The King's representative, who would have the title of Viceroy, in addition to his powers of veto would control the military affairs and foreign policy of the island with the administrative assistance of three Secretaries of State or Ministers, two of whom were to be drawn from the Supreme Council, appointed initially by the Consulta and later by the Parliament; the third Secretary of State was to be an Englishman

appointed from home. The King had the right to dissolve
Parliament, with the proviso that he convene another in
forty days; in its turn Parliament had the right to request
the recall of the Viceroy.[51]

Paoli was aware of shortcomings. "Under the present
circumstances, surrounded as we are by enemies who are
jealous of our independence, I could not have proposed a
better constitution than the one we have adopted. I hope
my compatriots will not have occasion to be discontented
with me for this deed. It is a great thing for the people to
have the authority to choose their Parliament. It can at
times be corrupted, but the people have the knowledge
and the power to remedy the abuses of authority. [I hope
those who govern will be persuaded] that the best way to
assure dominion is to use the laws, and to be gentle in following them." There was no reason for Paoli not to believe
that his hope when he called in the English was realized—the Corsicans would "now be at least as free" as the
English, and more fully insured against "internal
vicissitudes." As for the alternative, Paoli was fully revealing in his strong comment to Burnaby: "I am petrified
when I perceive a considerable number of Englishmen so
dazzled by the French revolution as to wish to introduce
innovation into their own government. The cure would
certainly be more dangerous than the disease. That in other countries there should be discontent and insurrections,
considering the despotic tyranny . . . with which they are
governed, may not appear unnatural. But England, which
has a Parliament that can restrain the executive power,
what could she possibly gain by permitting the multitude
to new-model her constitution?"[52]

Elliot and Paoli, as members of the commitee to draft the
legislation required by the constitution, worked together
during the summer mainly in the district of Orezza, a
beautiful mountainous area with abundance of shade and
water. To Burnaby Paoli wrote of Elliot: "He seems as happy with these places as my compatriots are with him. He is
gentle and affable; he speaks the language well; and every
day he advances in our people's affection and esteem"

(9 August 1794). Not many days later Paoli again wrote to Burnaby, still sanguine about developments in Corsica. "I no longer desire anything but to retreat to private life. . . . if *la patria* had need I would not spare myself as a simple citizen; but I can no longer subject myself to any burdens of responsibility. If peace were assured I should like to see Rome, and then spend some time in the temperate climate of Bath" (19 August 1794).

What of Elliot? Before the ceremonies of union he had confided to Lady Elliot that he had "a real ambition to be the founder of what I consider as likely to prove [Corsica's] future happiness. My wish, therefore, would be to settle, as representing Great Britain, our connection with Corsica; to be the first representative of British Government there; to prepare its new Constitution; to see the machine fairly launched and floating with a favourable breeze, and then resign the helm."[53] Now, at Orezza, where in his own words he receives from Paoli "every mark of personal kindness and confidence," Elliot submits a bill of complaints to the Duke of Portland, his old political leader who in the previous month (July 1794) had joined Pitt's Cabinet as Home Secretary, Henry Dundas shifting to the new post of Secretary of War. From the beginning the Corsicans had wanted an open declaration that Corsica was part of the British Empire, as safe from attack or dismemberment as, say, Canada or even Ireland. In the absence of such a commitment, signified in appropriate formal documents and by the appointment of a Viceroy, the Consulta as its last act on 19 June 1794 invested the Executive Government provisionally in the persons who before composed the Administration. According to Elliot this government, headed by Paoli, has taken "vindictive" actions against those whom it considers disloyal. Elliot, on the contrary, had he been given power, would have endeavored "to unite and attach to the new system all description of men in the country." All these evils, continues Elliot, were trifling "compared with uneasiness which the conduct, and I fear the character, of General Paoli have given rise to during this interval." He distrusts us. The delay in the arrival of

dispatches from England has led him to believe that we are
" treating with every power in Europe for the surrender of
Corsica. . . . What I have said will lead your Grace to conceive that Paoli's total retreat from this country would be
a desirable if not almost a necessary thing. It has struck me
that something might be done at home to relieve us from
this perplexity. I took the liberty of suggesting in my
despatch from Corte [June 1794] that a letter from His
Majesty would be received by Paoli as a flattering and a
most gracious mark of his royal favour and condescension.
If a desire to see him in England could be introduced into
His Majesty's letter, it might have a very happy effect. I
took the liberty also of recommending a renewal of his former pension."[54]

Elliot now yearns mightily for power, all the more so because his home government has frustrated him: no formal
commission as Viceroy, not even a document authorizing
transfer of power. "The delay," grumbles Elliot, "is, beyond
anything I ever heard of, strange and culpable. It is impossible to describe the mischief it has occasioned and is
occasioning. . . . We have neither justice nor revenue nor
any other business transacting here."[55] Even as Elliot
looked upon Paoli as a bitter old man exulting in a last
chance to destroy his political enemies, so Paoli developed
the misconception that Elliot was working hand in glove
with the Ministry to keep Corsica dangling as a minor prize
to be bargained away if something more to Britain's advantage could be obtained. Actually, the Ministry was exercising its right to be impenetrable to Corsican and British
agent alike. Two months after they had left the island the
members of the Corsican deputation were finally received
by the Duke of Portland, who informed them that they
would have to postpone laying the Corsican address at his
Majesty's feet until George III had made a trip to
Weymouth and returned—some six or eight weeks later.
This news from the deputies joined the other unfavorable
omens. As Paoli wrote to Burnaby two years later, he
began to suspect that "this Ministry had little desire to preserve our country."[56] It is probable that no one in London,

not even Pitt, could have given a very sound reason for delaying the sending of the commission as Viceroy to Elliot, other than that more pressing matters required attention.

Finally, more than a year after Paoli had first approached the British, a dispatch dated 9 September 1794 recognized and praised Paoli's services, and informed him of his Majesty's pleasure in bestowing a pension of one thousand pounds per year; further, it announced that the King was sending Paoli a gold chain with his Majesty's picture set in diamonds. "So peculiar a mark of distinction," Portland had suggested to the King, "only so lately imagined by your Majesty and conferred only for the most eminent public services, would be the most desirable gratification which he could receive, and by being constantly worn by him whenever he appeared in public would be the proudest testimony which could be given him of your Majesty's opinion and sanction of his conduct." The Duke took upon himself the pleasure of writing to Paoli from London, 17 October 1794, to offer his "most cordial congratulations on the very unexampled mark of distinction which the King has conferred upon you by directing his Viceroy to decorate you with His Majesty's picture, appendant to a gold chain; and to desire you, in his royal name, to wear it as a badge and testimony of his high sense of your great and meritorious services."[57] Paoli was vastly pleased. Although nothing was written from London suggesting that the General should take advantage of his pension to return to England, it was perhaps natural enough for the English to believe that Paoli would retire from the island shortly after the formal appointment of a Viceroy.

To Paoli's dismay the portrait never reached him. In London the Corsican deputies were unable to arrive at any better explanation of the affair than that Viceroy Elliot himself had pocketed the picture, diamonds, gold, and all. In relaying this story to Elliot the Duke of Portland said that, upon hearing their charges, "I fairly lost my temper and told them plainly that if Corsican gentlemen were capable of so misunderstanding the character of English gentlemen, the sooner they and this country ceased to have any relations the better." The Duke had never developed a high regard for the members of the Corsican deputation, who had been praised by Elliot at the time they were sent on their errand. "They soon manifested a disposition to intrigue," wrote Portland. "This I thought natural from the observation I have made on the characters of all foreigners in general, and in particular those who are members of second-rate states."[58] Paoli never accused Elliot, but the conclusion appeared inescapable that only the King's Ministers could have prevented the publicized mark of the King's favor from reaching him. Disappointed more than he dared tell, Paoli officially disposed of the affair in a gracious letter to Elliot: "The material picture of his Majesty, and the ornaments with which it may be adorned, could not enhance or make more vivid that which his royal virtues have long since imprinted on my mind."[59]

Elliot's commission as Viceroy at last arrived at the time of the above affair; however, as Paoli noted, "his commission was not signed by the King, nor secured with the great seal of the nation. It was a simple letter from the Secretary of State, and on this the Provisional Government of Corsica did not want to place any value." Paoli persuaded the Provisional Government to "frustrate the artifices of the ministry, if it was employing any, by making it perform some public act by which Europe would see that the King had accepted our constitution and consequently was pledged to uphold it." Thus, if at some treaty of peace France should raise an objection to the annexation by England, Corsica would not be placed under the dominion of another country; at the least it would be "guaranteed independence." The official commission, with the King's signature, did arrive the next month.[60]

We come now to the period in which Paoli's behavior provides the occasion for the most widely known characterization in print: "crotchety, suspicious, impossible to cooperate with, and unable to accept anyone as his superior or even as his equal in the conduct of Corsican affairs."[61] This was one view, Elliot's, the official view—echoed, elaborated, intensified as it moved within the Ministry and finally to the King. Other evidence, bountifully provided, paints a quite different picture. First, Paoli, equally biased to be sure, had occasion to speak for himself in many letters, in particular one which he later wrote to Burnaby which could be titled "What Went Wrong with British Rule in Corsica." Further, there is the running journal account of Colonel Moore, no admirer of either Paoli or Elliot, and not involved in the differences or quarrels between the two men until his last days on the island. Finally there are facts. Surely it is significant that Paoli's departure was followed by uprisings which Elliot took military measures to quell; significant, too, that Elliot thought it necessary to place a British officer over each Corsican officer, and all this before Napoleon's successes in Italy could be considered a chief incitement to insurrection. And what is one to make of the successive changes in army command over which Elliot presided? Generals Dundas, D'Aubant, Stuart, and Trigge, not to mention high officers like Koehler and Moore? It tells us something that Elliot did not receive what he considered adequate cooperation from the army until he had finally removed the subordinate Moore so as to be left with Trigge, spineless, unimaginative, incompetent.

Certainly it would have been difficult for any Viceroy to measure up to Paoli's hopes. What must be recognized also, however, is that above all Paoli wanted the new government to succeed. All his efforts, however wayward and disruptive they may have seemed to Elliot, were actually directed toward making that offical and his government approximate principles and modes of action to which the Corsicans could accommodate. Had Paoli been able to read the mails of Elliot or the Ministers during this period he would have found more than enough grounds for being "suspicious." In a remarkable dispatch to the Duke of Portland dated 30 December 1794—some time before the Corsican Parliament was to assemble for its first meeting—Elliot wrote that, should it become necessary for Eng-

land to declare a "disunion," Great Britain should
"stipulate either for the independence of Corsica or for a
complete amnesty" from the French.

> I consider the condition of amnesty as a *sine qua non*, and as
> not less essential to the King's honour than due by every
> principle of justice and by every tie, human and divine, to
> the people of Corsica. . . . The same necessity which should
> oblige us to renounce and surrender our Corsican friends,
> or a single emigrant, to the vengeance of their enemies,
> must make us, I think, surrender the Tower of London if
> summoned to do so.

The dispatch does credit to Elliot's humanity and his hon-
or as an Englishman. Aware from firsthand observations of
the decay and weakness of the Italian states, aware also,
perhaps from discussions with his friend Horatio Nelson,
of the dissipation of large English forces in efforts across
the seas, Elliot went on to warn that "unless Great Britain
were prepared to make a very great and vigorous exertion
in the war, Corsica, as well as Italy, must inevitably suc-
cumb to the arms of France."[62] The warning, fifteen
months before Napoleon was given command of the Army
of Italy, demonstrated a degree of prescience not fully
shared by the Ministry or its military planners.

In this same month of December Lady Elliot arrived at
the home in Bastia which her husband had prepared for
her. "It is impossible to see anything more beautiful," she
said of Corsica. If the country were "in a state of civilisation,
it would be Elysium; but I am not reconciled to see every
peasant carrying a knife, gun and pistol. . . . It is too hot
[in Bastia] for summer, but on a winter's day one might sit
and bask and feed one's eyes with beauty, and be beyond
the nuisance of the dirty town. All that Nature has done for
the island is lovely, and all that man has added filthy."[63]
Few natives besides Pozzo di Borgo and his close associates
were to find favor in the eyes of Lady Elliot. Sir Gilbert
thought nothing more natural than that the government
should move to Bastia also. In this decision the elements
cooperated. Parliament was scheduled to met at Corte on
15 January 1795, but heavy snows rendered the mountains

impassable for a great many of the members. Parliament was then adjourned to Bastia, where it was to gather on 9 February. For Corsicans the memories of Bastia as the seat of the foreign conqueror were still fresh. Further, as Paoli noted, "they dance there; they have also formed a sort of theatre." Against these "miserable allurements," Paoli complained, the virtues of the mountain citadel of Corte counted for little in the minds of the British and their minions.[64] Yes, compared to the gracious guest in London of just a few years earlier, the old man was "crotchety." He had aged rapidly, and now with power slipping and time running out he was desperate lest this last gamble not succeed.

During the few months following 14 August 1794, at which time Paoli had expressed to Burnaby his desire to retreat to private life and enjoy the "temperate climate of Bath," he tried to allay the fears and suspicions which had been nagging at him. Elliot's commission arrived in October and arrangements for transfer of authority and establishment of the new government with its Parliament were made, but nothing had yet been done to reinforce the defenses of the island in the face of growing evidence that France was planning an invasion. Nevertheless, writing to Burnaby on 24 January 1795, Paoli gives no voice to his misgivings and expresses his intention to leave Corsica after making "a tour through the Island to take leave of my friends. I will probably want to wait in order to see and hear the opening of this Parliament. Everyone is confident that things will take the desired turn."

Prior to the opening of Parliament, Paoli's fears concerning the failure to strengthen land defenses were heightened further. Since May 1794 General Charles Stuart had commanded all the troops in Corsica and indeed the whole of the Mediterranean except Gibraltar. With his opposite number in the other service, Admiral Hood, he had conducted the siege of Calvi. When difficulties arose between the services, Hood and Nelson blamed Stuart's conduct on the influence of his subordinate, Colonel Moore; thus Stuart remained beyond

challenge and criticism. Although as the son of the third
Earl of Bute he could claim privileges of influence, all who
knew him, including Moore, judged him an able and deserving officer. Problems, however, arose as soon as Elliot
received his commission, upon which occasion he asserted
his right to the command of the army. Stuart claimed to be
"at present responsible for the conduct of the army and for
the military operations in the Mediterranean. Till such
time as your commission gives you the powers of a Com-
mander-in-chief," he advised Elliot, "you will do well not to
attempt to interfere in military matters." In January 1795
Elliot obtained letters from home which established his
claim to powers similar to those of the Lord Lieutenant of
Ireland. "The General, of course, departs immediately,"
noted Moore. "It will be long probably before I serve under an officer for whom I have so much esteem and attachment."[65] Moore expected to leave soon, but whether
because of romantic attachments—the handsome young
officer had an eye for the ladies and they for him—or because of the challenge the defense of the island offered
him, he stayed on.

On 9 February 1795, with appropriate ceremonies, including the singing of the British national anthem in ac-
cents strange, the Parliament at last officially began its
session. The unfurled flag bore, beside the Moor's head of
Corsica, the coat of arms of Great Britain. The members
then witnessed the unveiling of the bust of Paoli which the
Assembly at Corte had authorized. Paoli, who was not
present, characterized the rites of unveiling as "incense for
the dead."[66] To his worries concerning the inadequacy of
the island's defenses were now added another set concerning the political conduct of the new overlords. When the
Corsicans declared their independence in 1793 the inhabitants were all "Paolists"; those not in sympathy with Paoli's
principles nor satisfied with his leadership had, on the left,
gone to France, or, on the right, settled outside the island
among fellow Corsicans who had prospered under the *ancien régime*. With independence, to be sure, there had been
a modest influx of clergy and of some families who had lost

favor with the increasingly radicalized representatives of the French Republic.

Elliot wasted little time in making fundamental changes. Prior to the opening of Parliament he invited back to Corsica "those rash exiles," as Paoli called them, "who until now had been opposed to the liberty of *la patria*." Paoli had no complaint against the principle of general amnesty for all who pledged allegiance to the King, or against Elliot's grandly proclaimed refusal to allow British authority, money, or soldiers to be used for or against any of the Corsican factions. "On this point I have been inflexible," he wrote, "and during the whole time of the Provisional Government the Corsican and British powers were on this matter pulling in different ways. I think it my duty to prefer the Paolists to others, but not to the exclusion of others."[67] This duty, defensible as a principle, Elliot honored mainly in the breach. Some months later he put his name to a decree which provided for the confiscation of the properties and goods of the Corsicans of Bastia and Calvi who had gone to France after the fall of those fortresses. At the time of the surrender the English-Corsican government had guaranteed that property rights would be respected. The decree further declared that all Corsicans who had fled to Republican France were traitors, and that their property also was to be confiscated.[68] The contrast between Elliot's treatment of the Republicans and that he extended to the aristocrats was not lost on the inhabitants.

Elliot's task in finding Corsican subordinates for his administration had not been easy. Moore early appraised Paoli's "cabinet" as a generally imcompetent lot. The chief member, Carlo Andrea Pozzo di Borgo, young, ambitious, and in promoting his interests certainly quite competent, did stand out from the others. It was Pozzo, acting for Paoli, who had received the money from the British and disbursed it. According to Moore, Pozzo so managed affairs that the Corsicans were "allowed to be in want of everything." Moore was willing to believe those who asserted that Pozzo "pocketed the money intended for the public use." When Elliot upon becoming Viceroy needed an able

Corsican assistant Paoli recommended Pozzo, who before long became Elliot's chief adviser even though, as Moore understood it, he was "universally disliked and generally thought to be a scoundrel." By February 1795 Moore felt able to render a complete judgment: Pozzo di Borgo "is a low, mean-minded man, with some cunning and intrigue, but totally devoid, in my opinion, of talents. The Viceroy, whose friendships are passions, is completely blinded by this man, who has already led him into several scrapes. Pozzo has entirely broken with Paoli, and the airs he gives himself to the Corsicans are perfectly disgusting."[69]

With respect to the external threat of invasion from France, Elliot had early stressed to the home government the need for strengthening the naval arm, for which he admitted a strong partiality. Here Elliot met with moderate success; but land forces remained pitifully weak. "I fear," wrote Paoli, "that Pitt wishes to sustain the fleet, but no longer wishes to make outlays for us. And the Viceroy is irresolute. . . . They [Pozzo di Borgo and his colleagues] have the art of keeping far from the Viceroy all who can enlighten him on the state of affairs."[70] Moore had made it his business, frequently in the company of Paoli, to become acquainted with the island's terrain, particularly places likely for the enemy's landing as well as those suitable for initial and subsequent defense. He was disgusted with the incompetence of his superiors and the absence of support from home. "I fear if ever we are [attacked] we shall cut a disgraceful figure, though, were proper measures taken, the Island is capable of a considerable defence, and of adding much to the reputation of the officer who conducts it."[71] Napoleon believed that Corsica was France's for the taking. "With 8,000 or 10,000 men and twelve warships an expedition to Corsica at this time of year would be just a military parade," he had written the preceding September.[72]

Nelson, after investigating the state of the French fleet at Toulon, noted in October 1794 that an expedition was in readiness, although he could not tell whether it was intended for Corsica.[73] By February 1795 the French had detached to Toulon a force of eighteen thousand men for the invasion of Corsica, but held the transports in the harbor until the fleet should achieve a favorable decision. The French and British fleets finally came in sight of one another on 11 March. What followed in the next few days could not be called a naval engagement. Two French vessels, one crippled and in tow of the other, were rather easily captured. Nelson wished to pursue the enemy, but Admiral Hotham was satisfied to have them take flight. "We should have had such a day as I believe the annals of England never produced," exclaimed Nelson. For the time being France abandoned the expedition against Corsica, and attached the troops which were intended for that action to the Army of Italy.[74]

For Paoli and for Moore the repulse of the French fleet failed to remove the threat of invasion. The danger, though less imminent, nevertheless compounded fears and discontents in the island. Elliot's government was revealing its character. The comments by both Moore and Paoli, who neither worked nor thought in concert, are remarkably similar. Paoli:

> No posts were given except to those who obliged themselves to support the proposals of the administration; and if they faltered only slightly they were threatened with dismissal. This was true not only for those holding civil posts but also for those who held commissions in the army, particularly if they were also members of Parliament. Besides this practice, the profusion of money to buy votes was scandalous. . . . They [Elliot's administration] did not value the affection of the people; they longed to form a party for themselves.

In these actions, continued Paoli, Elliot further displayed "a very clear aversion toward those who had the most merit in the service of *la patria*, and a manifest partiality toward those who had betrayed it."[75] Pozzo di Borgo recruited from his generation Corsicans driven by ambitions similar to his own; and from the older generations those who had, prior to the Revolution, lived happily under the French Monarchy. To Paoli, Elliot appeared to be yielding foolishly to the desire for personal power and the pleasure of being surrounded by sycophants, with the consequent loss of loyalty on the part of the main body of Corsicans who had devoted their lives to Corsican democracy. From our perspective Elliot's actions, whether consciously so or not, also appear basically counterrevolutionary. [76]

On his part Moore recorded that "the avowed plan of Sir Gilbert's government is that of bribery," administered by his political manager for domestic affairs, Pozzo di Borgo. "No man who does not court this fellow . . . has the least chance of employment. Any person who opposes his views in Parliament, however scandalous, is damned forever. Several have told me that Sir Gilbert's government is the completest despotism ever exercised in Corsica. I expect daily a revolt in some part of the country."[77] These words, confided by Moore to his journal when Parliament was starting its second week, were to prove prophetic.

Compared to the above evils, those which now supplement the list in random order may seem secondary:

1. Ostentatious display and waste in an impoverished country. Elliot took the second syllable of his title seriously, being "infinitely dazzled," as Moore put it, "by the splendour of aides-de-camp, general ushers, etc." Shortly after Elliot's "crowning" the accoutrements of power multiplied—the Englishmen who served as aides, the Anglican chaplain and his staff, and the various Corsican military and household officers who had reached a settlement with Pozzo. Elliot's salary and expenses totalled the annual equivalent of over a million dollars today—fortunately for the Corsicans, not exacted from their incomes. [78]

2. Contempt for the feelings of the people, such as was shown in establishing court at Bastia.

3. Failure to establish the university which had been authorized in the legislation implementing the constitution—a project close to Paoli's heart.

4. The reintroduction of the salt tax, a hated device associated with government under the French monarchy.

Perhaps Corsica could have survived all of Elliot's mistakes if the economic base, particularly in agriculture, had been developed, and if the people had not feared for their lives and property in the struggle between France and England. Moore stated simply, on 20 April 1795, that the Corsicans had "lost all confidence in us." This feeling among a people who had to put up with the injustices of local government fostered by Pozzo di Borgo's mode of operation, occasioned a steady stream of visitors to Paoli's retreat at Rostino. Paoli listened sympathetically, but in most instances was unable to judge the legitimacy of the complaints. His few attempts to secure rectification by means of letters to the Administration or to members of Parliament only served to make the Elliot-Pozzo faction sure that Paoli himself was the original source of disaffection. "In Council," the General noted bitterly, "I and the good patriots who gave the crown to the King are called seditious. . . . Already Pozzo di Borgo is without restraint. He says that I am discontented because the King did not make me Viceroy. What a character!"[79]

So quickly did the general mood of dissatisfaction spread that early in May Paoli deemed it necessary to visit Bastia. There he spent several days, and had two long sessions with the Viceroy. To Elliot he owned the suspicion, which sounded rather like an accusation, that the English Ministry was deliberately withholding reinforcements in order to permit France to recover Corsica by an appearance of conquest, and thus avoid the disgrace of surrendering it by treaty. After the conclusion of the meetings Paoli began to speak openly against Elliot, and told Moore that he had written home. "The other has, I am convinced, written often enough misrepresenting Paoli," observed Moore.[80] At this time a motion made in Parliament by Pozzo di Borgo, that Lord Hood's portrait be hung in the hall, was defeated. This was a signal to the Elliot-Pozzo faction that it needed to purge or transform Paolists in that body.

At the beginning of June Moore made a fortnight's tour to acquaint General Trigge with the island. Some places he had visited "so often before"—Corte, Ajaccio, Bonifacio—but others in the deep interior he himself now saw for the first time. When he returned to Bastia he found that the Viceroy had decided to make a progress across the island to Ajaccio, to see the country and to allow its people a view of his Majesty's representative. "He takes an escort of troops, etc., and means to show himself in state to such places as Pozzo di Borgo may think it safe to introduce him." Moore evidently found no reason to forego the pleasure of irony in his private journal. Elliot, as the bodily extension of George III, was safe everywhere; it was Pozzo who needed protective guards. From Elliot's point of view everything went extremely well. On the third day the party arrived at Rostino, and Elliot passed the day pleasantly with Paoli. Paoli understood that good manners could not dispel unrest, but Elliot allowed himself to lapse into his earlier state. This sort of expedition, he noted, "appears to make the proper impression."[81]

Elliot believed that such reservations as Paoli might still have entertained about departing were now happily dispersed. The military danger had been reduced: early in July Admiral Hotham's fleet at San Fiorenzo was reinforced by six sail of the line, and the land forces by the 100th Regiment (Gordon Highlanders).[82] Unfortunately, Corsican discontents were multiplying. The true state of affairs was made clear to all by the response to the "assassination" of a bust of Paoli. The story survives in various versions; that believed by Corsicans outside Pozzo's circle went as follows: When Elliot was at Ajaccio some Corsican officers decided to give him a ball, using the town hall in which a plaster bust of General Paoli happened to be placed. When some of the officers were assembled to consult about preparing the hall Captain Colonna, aide-de-camp to the Viceroy, pointed to the bust and said, "What business has that old charlatan here?" He thereupon thrust it into a closet, and his companions joined in the fun by thrusting their stilettoes into it, shattering it into fragments. When Elliot became aware of the event and its growing repercussions, he questioned Pozzo and Colonna, who denied all charges, and took what he considered excessive pains to return to Ajaccio to visit the scene of the alleged crime. There was the bust "with no visible damage, but the thickness of a wafer rubbed off the tip of the nose, which appeared like an old sore." The Corsican version was that by this time Paoli's bust had been replaced by another, but Elliot did not believe it necessary to question witnesses or look into the official investigations by the Corsicans. It remained only for Pozzo to write to Paoli assuring him that the story was untrue. Paoli's answer was that Pozzo and his fellows would do well to clear their conduct with the people of Corsica; as for himself, he laughed at the story. Paoli indeed insisted on keeping the issue impersonal, joking about the "ridiculous piece of chalk which could be the subject of a poem on the model of that of *Secchia Rapita* [the stolen bucket poem of Tassoni]." No, the important issue was Pozzo di Borgo's responsibility for "the scandalous promotions, the corruption in Parliament, the fostering of laws harmful to the nation, the impudent boasting with which he says that he will no longer convene Parliament."[83]

In Elliot's view Paoli was using the invented incident as a pretext for inflaming the people. To Lady Elliot, cooling herself on the mainland at Lucca, the Viceroy wrote: "General Paoli is playing the D—— with a vengeance; the pretence is an absurd lie which was invented while I was first at Ajaccio. . . . He has had Pozzo di Borgo burnt in effigy in several villages, and a petition is being signed asking me to remove him. . . . Nothing in the world shall induce me to move one inch; if this Island is incapable of bearing a good government we had better give it up; it is not worth a bad one, even if we were capable of attempting such."[84] No, the removing would be of another kind. On 31 July 1795 Elliot wrote to the Duke of Portland asking the Ministry to enforce, by the most tactful and conciliatory means possible, the retirement of Paoli from Corsica. The basis for Elliot's request was evidence he claimed to possess for two rather inconsistent charges:(1) that Paoli was in communication with the Corsican republican refugees in Genoa and France, and (2) that Paoli was asserting that through his influence with George III he would be able to take the Viceroy's place and put Colonel Moore in military

command. Two days later Elliot wrote to William Wind-
ham, Secretary at War, that "Paoli is throwing off the mask,
and we are in a most critical and difficult situation." He
added that Colonel Moore "is related to the father of all
mischief. But this is not official, and is between ourselves."
A few weeks later he made an "official" request that Moore
be removed from the island to another post, either by
transfer or promotion.[85]

Shortly after the Viceroy's return to Bastia, Moore recalled that "he had long promised to pay General Paoli a
visit, but had hitherto been prevented." He now decided to
head for Rostino in the company of Lord Huntly of the
Gordon Highlanders, Colonel Oakes (an officer whose
friendship with Moore went back to their days in America),
and the commander of the Corsican battalion in Bastia,
Lieutenant Colonel Giampietri. Moore surely knew that at
the time chosen such an expedition could not have pleased
the Viceroy (the day after the group departed Elliot wrote
the letter asking for Paoli's recall), but it was entirely consistent with his policy of constantly acquainting himself at
first hand with the situation in the island. While at Rostino
the visitors learned that Pozzo di Borgo and Colonna had
been burned in effigy in all the villages of the area. The
party passed two days very pleasantly with Paoli, who received them with "great kindness and politeness." The
General spoke frankly and, in Moore's view, "with great
moderation" of the Viceroy's "want of judgement," which
was a "misfortune to his country."[86]

Upon returning to Bastia early in August, Moore found
the Viceroy highly excited by the state of "insurrection" of
the Corsican troops in Bastia. To Moore the town appeared perfectly quiet. Walking home with Oakes in the
evening, he met Elliot, who assured them that "the Corsican battalion was disaffected, and meant to come out and
burn Pozzo di Borgo; that Giampietri was a great scoundrel; that guards were at all gates to fire upon any body of
men coming from the country." Moore was later visited by
Major Murati of the Corsicans. "He came to ask me what
was the matter; they are afraid, he said, of our battalion,
and 'all the English are under arms against us. Our people

are asleep in their barracks!' I told him that it was impossible to account for such folly; . . . I hoped that the Corsican officers would behave like men, keep quiet, and take no notice of what they saw." The next morning Trigge gave Moore orders to direct the Corsican battalion to march to Corte on the following evening, 5 August. This the battalion did without the least disturbance. Moore observed: "Few corps would have suffered their barracks to be surrounded as theirs were with sentries, more especially as they knew that if they had sent out into the country they would have been supported by whatever number of men they chose."[87] From Lucca Lady Elliot wrote of the "insurrections" which prevented her husband from making the usual summer move from the governor's mansion at Bastia to more comfortable quarters inland. "There is so much discontent and disaffection that Sir Gilbert's situation is perilous. He cannot venture into the country, and must stay and roast at Bastia and face all the evils of heat and disease."[88]

As the narrative has been demonstrating, Moore was now on a different footing with the Corsicans and their leader than he had been during his first months in the island. The Corsican soldiers, while they doubtless never could measure up to trained English troops, he now saw as a dependable, serious lot when accepted on their own terms. As for Paoli, Moore's short experience as a British M.P. had never prepared him for anyone like the General. Whatever he had previously thought of Paoli's shortcomings, Moore now found in him a political leader whose absolute hold over his people, particularly in view of the open means by which it was obtained, demanded deep and unqualified respect. For his part Paoli found in Moore an extremely able officer in whom he could place his trust for the defense of Corsica.

Moore analyzed the situation clearly, not without a sense of puzzlement:

> [The Corsicans'] great veneration for Paoli made them feel every affront that was offered to him. They were so incensed against Pozzo di Borgo and Colonna that, did not Paoli endeavour to restrain them, they would probably ere

now have put these gentlemen to death. . . . I did not see
the use of what the Viceroy was attempting, that of making
a party against Paoli. He would have done better to have
governed through his influence. It was with him that the
original agreement was made by the Viceroy himself, and
through him we were received into the country, and to
break with him seemed to me perfect folly. If we had not his
goodwill and that of the people, the sooner we made our retreat the better. . . . By a series of rash, absurd actions he
committed the troops as far as depended upon him. Had
the Corsicans been equally intemperate, and one shot fired,
we must have been driven out of the country. The fact is,
that the people in general have great goodwill to us individ-
ually. Paoli's party, the one Sir Gilbert quarrelled with, wish
to be united with us as a nation, and dread the misconduct
of Sir Gilbert as most likely to bring about a rupture.[89]

A few days later the Corsican Administrative Council
advised the Viceroy to dismiss Pozzo di Borgo and to call
Parliament together as the only means of quieting the people. As Moore heard it, Elliot "said he would rather die
than give up his friend. . . . It is thought by the counsellors
(I have spoken to several of them) that the Viceroy will
stick to Pozzo di Borgo at all events. He is, they say,
directed by him like a child."[90] Elliot assured his wife that
reports of his danger were greatly exaggerated. At the
same time he displayed signs of weariness and disgust. After he received the sanction and authority to dispose of
Paoli and Moore, he wrote to his wife, he would settle matters and return to a better life.[91]

Paoli, sickened at the turn of events, nevertheless continued his efforts to calm his people. Prior to the episode
at Bastia he had come to the conclusion that Pozzo di
Borgo wished to provoke the appearance of insurrection to
make Elliot rely upon him absolutely. In these circumstances the convening of Parliament could be delayed and
the island governed by decree. On one occasion the government ordered an expedition of about one thousand
men to proceed from Ajaccio against the malcontents of
Mezzana. The remonstrances of the people of that area,
together with a letter by Paoli addressed to them but also
providentially presented to the commander at Ajaccio,

caused the expedition to be deferred. A similar order was then given to the troops at Bastia. Two Corsican officers resigned rather than obey; the troops were not asked to march. This episode, not mentioned by Moore, might properly have suggested to Elliot the existence of "disaffection" in the Corsican battalion.[92] Paoli warned that he and the Corsicans would refuse to be provoked. "Do not expect it; there will be no rebellion. The people, united and loyal, will make known the injustice of him who slanders them because they show themselves discontented with the abuse of authority. The war will be with the pen, and the indisputable facts will convince." The turning of English cannon on the Corsican barracks at Bastia moved Paoli to say that the English eyes at home were "blindfolded."

> When they learn in London that the cannon have been turned toward the city . . . the stones themselves will say *tyranny, tyranny*. They represent the people as being in a state of insurrection, and perhaps in great part they attribute the cause of it to me. My zeal and my innocence provide me a breastplate of bronze. I am determined to defend myself and to attack, but with legal means. I cannot betray the confidence of the people. I have cooperated in giving this constitution to them, and while I live I will not silently suffer them to be oppressed under it. Nor will they be able to make use of the bogey that the English will abandon us. This bogey is equivalent to the assertion that the King can betray his oath and his interests.[93]

Elliot, however, did not relent. "If affairs do not take a turn for the better," wrote Paoli, "and the Viceroy continues to accuse me as the author of the movements which he calls insurrections, I will find myself obliged to write him a letter, and have that portion of it printed which is directed to the public. . . . The King is just, and has no other means to make his will known than the laws. There is another tribunal in England, which is formed by public opinion; and this is not governed by the selfish views of the few. A great disinterested people weighs things; it examines reports with the good sense which is natural to it."[94] Far from responding to Elliot's telepathic and still confidential wishes, Paoli felt more than ever that it was his

duty to stay on. "I more than any other have the obligation
to see that the government of our King is esteemed and revered by all. . . . [and to make sure that the Corsicans] do
not reproach me for having subjected *la patria* to the despotism of miserable favorites."[95] With a definite time set for
the reconvening of Parliament—15 November—he found
occasion to pursue his efforts to subdue unrest by
addressing a long letter to his "Fellow Citizens, Most
Beloved Compatriots." Essentially, what he asks is that the
people believe in and act under the British and Corsican
system of government, no matter what the provocations,
which he does not minimize. In making petitions addressed to the Viceroy "there is no doubt that they have
made use of a right solemnly preserved in the constitutional contract. . . . I fear some demands are inopportune,
others disrespectful." But when the people express their
wishes in conformance to the laws and with due respect to
the dignity of him who must take them under consideration, "I will be with you. . . . You must have faith in the wisdom of your representatives, and in the just and
magnanimous heart of his Majesty."[96]

As time ran out Paoli was reduced to clutching at straws.
He knew that Frederick North, third son of his old acquaintance, Lord North, was due to occupy the post of the
English Secretary of State in the Viceroy's Cabinet. If only
North could be persuaded to "travel in the interior he
would be able to see the loyalty of the people, the treachery
of evil advisers, and the obstinacy of the one who continues to lend them his ear and his confidence." When
North arrived the Paolists immediately sought him out to
enlighten him on the true state of affairs in the island, to
show how the government failed to observe the articles of
the constitution, and how it accorded undue influence to
the party of the aristocracy against the party of liberty.[97]
North of course had not come with a mandate from London to overturn the policies of his superior. On the contrary, he had been thoroughly briefed in London by
Portland, and upon his arrival in Bastia had received the
further benefits of the Elliot-Pozzo view of affairs.

North, it turned out, was to be the messenger in breaking the news to Paoli. Elliot's dispatch to Portland of 31 July, asking for the recall of Paoli, had been laid before the King by Portland as a "most painful part of his official duty. . . . He has to represent to your Majesty the ingratitude and unworthiness of some who owe their very existence to your liberality and protection. . . . The state of the Island of Corsica as represented by the Viceroy should seem to require the immediate adoption of firm and vigorous measures." In replying, George III demonstrated that he had been King long enough to deal appropriately with such a situation. "I quite concur with the Duke of Portland that it is absolutely necessary that the conduct of Paoli and his adherents should meet with the rigour from Government which alone can give a due tone to authority when far removed from the seat of the Supreme Government." What followed, however, revealed George III as more shrewd than his Minister. "At the same time I am sorry to see in all Sir Gilbert's letters a degree of jealousy that I had hoped had not been a part of his character."[98]

In a letter dated 3 October 1795 North requested that Paoli be kind enough to consent to a meeting at Ponte Nuovo, since the road beyond required riding on horseback, a feat his gout would not permit.[99] North carried with him a letter from the King. "Your presence in Corsica worries your enemies and makes your partisans audacious. Come to London, where we will know how to reward your fidelity, and will welcome you to a place in our family."[100] Before leaving for his third exile from Corsica, Paoli wrote a letter to the Viceroy recounting his past life devoted to securing the liberty of his country and his inward satisfaction at seeing his labors in the process of fulfillment. "If any believe themselves more concerned than I with the good of my country and the glory of our sovereign I look upon them as presumptuous and worthy of my contempt."[101] Wishing to avoid contact with the Viceroy, Paoli applied to Admiral Hotham for a frigate, and then went directly to San Fiorenzo. Elliot nevertheless came to visit him twice and, according to Paoli's later account to Moore, "showed him the most servile attention, forced his aide-de-camp upon him to attend him on his journey, and paid him the most abject flattery. Paoli said he did not think an Englishman could have had so little pride."[102] Paoli should not have been surprised. In their recent joint public appearances Elliot had found it expedient to treat Paoli with some obsequiousness—maintaining good public relations, in modern terms. Paoli took ship for Leghorn on 13 October 1795. The multitudes who lined the shore entertained deep feelings of sorrow, feelings already being succeeded by those of doubt and indignation concerning the motives of their protectors.

Elliot's plans to rid himself of Moore bore fruit at virtually the same instant. On 1 October Moore was informed that his connection with the people of the island who opposed the Viceroy's measures, and countenance and support he gave them, helped to thwart the Viceroy's actions and made it impossible for him to carry on the government. The Secretary of State at home, informed of these facts, had empowered Elliot to send Moore home. However, records Moore, Elliot made it clear that if "I broke off my connection with the people who opposed him, and in future as far as I could supported his government," well then, I might stay on. No approach by Elliot could have been more calculated to arouse Moore's indignation. Their interview on 2 October was immediately followed by a letter from Elliot to General Trigge stating that it was "his Majesty's pleasure" that Moore "should quit the Island in eight and forty hours, or as soon after as a passage can be obtained for him."[103]

Moore did not scurry about. First, he went to Corte to pay a visit to his regiment. "The attention I received from almost every individual in the army showed many marks of friendship from the Corsicans. The battalion at Corte waited upon me in a body, as also the Supreme Council." As he was preparing to leave Corte, Moore, who did not yet know that Paoli was also essentially under orders to leave, wrote a brief letter to the General. "I feel I am incapable of an improper or unbecoming action. I hope the person who is the cause of my leaving Corsica may upon his return be able to say as much. I cannot take my leave of you, General, without returning you many thanks for your politeness and kindness to me upon every occasion. I trust you will yet see better times, and that the treaty you made with Great Britain will turn out in the end as useful to England and fortunate for Corsica as it promised in the beginning." Upon his return to Bastia, Moore received a letter from Paoli informing him that the General was also going to England, and proposing that Moore accompany him. Moore, though he did not trim his behavior to curry favor, saw no reason at this moment to appear to support Elliot's charges of conspiracy. In his journal he recorded his surprise at the departure of Paoli, although he recognized that this had been Sir Gilbert's "great object" for a long time. "I fear the consequence will be the reverse of what he expects. I think General Paoli's presence curbed his countrymen and prevented their acting with the violence to which they were inclined from their dislike to the Viceroy and his measures. I think it probable that upon Paoli's departure there will be immediate confusion."[104]

Paoli and Moore went their separate ways from Italy to Germany, and accidentally crossed paths at Cuxhaven. Detained by contrary winds, they had two long conversations. In one Paoli expressed a fear bordering on conviction that Pitt intended to give up Corsica. "He says Dundas is a man without morals, and from Pitt's intimacy with him he suspects also his principles."[105] Paoli did not arrive in London until 24 December 1795. Since Moore had been able to take ship from Cuxhaven on 20 November and land at Yarmouth on 24 November, unfavorable winds cannot have accounted for Paoli's stay of a month across the channel.[106] The delay invites a moderate amount of speculation.

During the five weeks of roundabout travel necessary to reach Cuxhaven, Paoli had time to enjoy the sensations of being free from importunities of friends, imperatives of conscience, orders from superiors; time also to sense ever more strongly that his position was that of an officer called

home in disgrace, and to feel withal a deep weariness of
body and spirit. An additional month was not too long an
interval for the old General to recover his purpose and resolve upon a course of action. That the Duke of Portland
had seen to the free circulation of stories of the ungrateful
leader "whose misbehaviour has instigated others to acts of
disaffection and disturbance," Paoli had no doubt; no
doubt also that the stories were given credence in high
places. Yet great delicacy in countering these stories in a
campaign by a foreigner—even though a loyal English
subject—was an absolute necessity. Corsica was a part of
the British Empire, and the Ministers were those of a British King to whom Paoli was deeply devoted. Therefore
there would be no ammunition for open attacks by Opposition leaders such as Fox and Sheridan. The campaign
would be carried out in letters to and conversations with
friends who might have some influence in modifying the
views on Corsica held by parliamentary figures as well as
the general public. Paoli would be emphatic in stressing
the devotion of the Corsicans to Britain, and just as positive
in explaining the need for the British rulers in Corsica to
return to actions showing respect for the provisions of the
constitution.

With this much decided, he could more happily dwell on
the pleasure of again seeing his old friends. Some of his
own generation, like Reynolds, had died. The death of
Boswell, however, had come as a shock. The General now
certainly wished he had taken time to answer more fully
Boswell's last letters—rather foolish they were, and therefore endearing as well as saddening. Boswell had encountered Masseria in late November 1793, a month after he
had received from Paoli the news that the independent but
endangered government of Corsica had sought the protection of Great Britain; he therefore was not wholly surprised to see an emissary of the General in London. On
17 March 1794 Boswell wrote to his old acquaintance Henry
Dundas, Home Secretary in Pitt's cabinet, suggesting that
he be considered for the appointment of British "Minister
or Commissioner" to Corsica. On the same day he wrote to

his son Alexander: "I indulge hopes of being again with General Paoli in that illustrious Isle. It would renew my youth." Dundas was thus once more enabled to frustrate Boswell's political ambitions, in "a cold Ministerial letter" which informed Boswell that his "services in Corsica could not be accepted." Boswell goes on to confess that "I had begun to shrink from the thoughts of quitting London and going among foreigners."[107] By 31 March we find Boswell recovered, and in a letter to Paoli exclaiming "how much am I now elated" by what has happened since Paoli's last letter. "I trust the Corsicans will now be a free and independent people allied with us, and consequently entitled to our protection. Masseria has been frequently with me. But I do not agree with him in his projects of sinking the brave Islanders under the dominion of this country." After telling Paoli of his rejection by Dundas, he continues: "Permit me to request of your Excellency, that in case a connection shall be formed between Great Britain and Corsica, you may be pleased to mention me for consideration in such manner as may seem best to you" (L 1025). That Masseria is not acting on his own surely is obvious to Boswell; to Paoli, Boswell's disingenuousness can only seem unworthy of a friend.

Early in 1795 Boswell again writes to Paoli, acknowledging receipt during the previous months of "several packets and letters, the last of which was a joint epistle to me and my brother." None of these materials survives among the known Boswell papers. One letter, possibly the earliest, doubtless was written just after the Consulta had finally approved the new constitution by which the King of Great Britain became the sovereign of Corsica also. At this time, 27 June 1794, Paoli wrote a letter to Burnaby with which he enclosed a copy of the new constitution as well as several "other interesting papers." Paoli goes on to ask Burnaby, apparently as one of several other friends in England, to do what he can to assist and guide the four special Corsican deputies. Boswell, after six months at Auchinleck, arrived in London in January 1795. In the aforementioned letter he expresses pleasure in having time briefly to enjoy the company of three of the Corsican deputies, one of them [Galeazzi] having already left "on account of the climate." The "climate" may have had something to do with the dressing down administered by the Duke of Portland. "I do not fully rejoice at Corsica being sunk into the territories of another country, though under our own King," Boswell points out sternly. He nevertheless wishes he could join the deputies, who set out "tomorrow morning for my favourite Island, for which I retain as warm and fond an affection as I felt almost thirty years ago. . . . I do not hesitate to say in plain terms that the Ministry of this country has shewn both gross negligence and ingratitude in not naming me to one of the appointments there under the new government."[108] Perhaps Paoli found time to reply, but with the turn affairs were taking in Corsica it seems unlikely. He no doubt expected eventually to explain the realities of the politics of power when he met Boswell in England. Now, with his wayward friend dead, he would find comfort with the children and their uncle T. D.[109]

Paoli could look forward to seeing many other friends in England; indeed, as he acknowledged in letters to Burnaby, most of his friends were in that country. Their identities, professions, interests, are named or foreshadowed in Boswell's journals and letters. Military men, political figures (not primarily those enshrined in history books), writers, explorers and scientists who usually had been recognized by the Royal Society, and artists composed the main body of his friends. The last group, who in any case had always provided figures of interest to the General, usually shared the additional attraction, no matter what their origins, of a comforting fluency in Italian. Without Boswell, Paoli in his letters becomes our chief informant, with assistance from the Farington Diary with respect to artists.

Within the above groups there were individuals who, though their interests and achievements were inseparable from their characters and therefore from their appeal to the General, were so intimate, so valued in being trusted with Paoli's heartfelt thoughts, that they should not really be classified. Not gallantry alone brings first to mind his

dear Maria Cosway, who had returned to England from
her interrupted pilgrimage. Paoli had taken time to answer
her letters in the midst of the turmoil of his second generalship in Corsica. Andrew Burnaby of course eagerly
awaited the return of his friend. With Burnaby, Tiberius
Cavallo (1749–1809) enjoyed the pleasure of receiving
Paoli's letters in Italian. Born in Naples of a physician
father, Cavallo left at an early age to settle in England. It
was not long before he distinguished himself as a "natural
philosopher," and was admitted to the Royal Society at the
age of thirty. His ingenious experiments in chemistry and
physics, his investigation of the influence of light and air on
plant growth, establish him as one of the eminent scientists
of his time. From our perspective we see him as being more
than once on the verge of but never making wholly original
discoveries or expressing productive theories. His position
was solid enough; the *Complete Treatise on Electricity*, first
published in 1786, was a standard, authoritative work for
some time. Boswell's journal reveals many meetings with
Cavallo, but a letter from ten-year-old James Boswell, Junior, to his mother, dated 5 December 1788, somehow de-
tains the eye. On 3 December we dined at General Paoli's,
he writes, "where was one Tiberius Cavallo, an exceeding
curious man as can be."

Appropriately, two generals may be said to bring up the
rear: Sir George Howard (?1720–1796), made a field
marshal in 1793, and Robert Melville (1723–1809), both
mentioned by Boswell. Howard sat in Parliament for
Stamford until his death, achieving a reputation as
"republican." Melville was a man cut to Paoli's measure.
First, to be sure, he was a general, but not a mere general.
His interest in antiquity happily was not confined to books,
as Paoli's was of necessity; he actually travelled the routes
of the ancient armies and examined the sites of those battles Paoli had read about from early youth. Like Paoli he
was a Fellow of the Royal Society, and as befitted a member
of that body he extended his curiosity to other matters also,
in particular distinguishing himself as an investigator of
botanical phenomena.

CHAPTER V

LAST EXILE, 1795-1807

Following his arrival in London at the end of 1795 Paoli
was to survive another eleven years, but by 1798 his health
was declining so rapidly that he was forced to curtail his
physical activities. On 16 March 1796 Farington notes that
Paoli is sitting for a bust by Flaxman, and despite his age
"looks remarkably well." In the same entry is recorded
Paoli's comment to Flaxman that he once weighed 300
Italian pounds (225 pounds in current measure), but was
now down to 140 Italian pounds. Two months later Poggi
tells Farington that he has been with General Paoli, "who
is become very thin and so much altered. Poggi thinks his
mind is affected by circumstances which have happened in
Corsica." Inasmuch as Paoli tells Burnaby the following
year that "I continue to enjoy tolerably good health," the
reader is forced to conclude that Poggi has seen Paoli for
the first time since his departure from England in 1790.
The Paoli of the 1780s is hardly recognizable in Dance's
drawing of the late 1790s, but most of the decline took
place in Corsica. Flaxman's bust is of course no representa-
tion of the subject posing. The sitting was a courtesy to the
General, the bust itself being that of a man twenty years
younger—although the artist, with the aid of a portrait like
Cosway's, might well have sought and found clues to the
General in his prime.[1] Withal, Paoli continued to see a
number of his friends and to correspond with a good many
more. Until it was too late—that is, until the latter part of
1796—he was unremitting in his efforts to help his Corsicans; and after the abandonment of the island by England he kept an open table for his countrymen and helped
financially as much as circumstances permitted.

For the first year the public Paoli, the man who felt a
continuing obligation to use what influence he had to keep

the Corsican-British union intact, can sometimes be separated from the private Paoli. He recognized that he could do little to affect the behavior of the Corsicans; more than he realized, he was not even kept fully informed of events on the island. London was the area of contest. The Ministry would have been pleased to have Paoli retire quietly from sight, but the General lost no time in having the Gentleman of the Chamber present him to the King. "His Majesty recognized me, and spoke to me with his usual goodness." Again, on 6 January 1796, Paoli returned to Court, when George III once more greeted him graciously. Never one to defy British protocol, Paoli had also on his arrival requested a conference with the Duke of Portland, who, he wished to believe, was poorly informed or else trapped by a pledge to support Sir Gilbert Elliot at any cost. Portland's tactic with Paoli, as it had been with Moore and was to be with Elliot, was to agree with the visitor and suggest that any difficulties were the result of a misunderstanding. In this instance, the King's rather casual opinion had been wrongly interpreted as an order. Paoli answered "that whatever might have been the motive for my being summoned here, the intention of his Majesty will always be obeyed by me with the greatest pleasure and respect."[2]

Stubbornly desperate to improve relations between the British and the Corsicans, he confided to Burnaby that "there is no doubt that in England, where I have such sincere and honest friends, I shall be able to live in peace and contentment"; but he would never be able to enjoy peace, much less contentment, "in any place on earth" so long as the condition of *la patria* was unstable and its affairs poorly directed.[3] To become effective he had first to erase the picture of himself as the ungrateful pensioner who provoked, nay, even led, insurrections against his Majesty's Government. Here he believed himself successful. "I do not regret having come here," he wrote in February 1796. "The calumny has been repudiated at my arrival. . . . On the contrary . . . the way which they have taken to do me evil has done me greater credit."[4] No action by the Admin-

istration in London actually supported this belief, and
Paoli did not get direct information from his Corsicans until October, when he learned of military actions taken by
Elliot against the islanders. By this time rumors had been
spreading that the British were going to abandon Corsica.[5]
Not only English officers but female correspondents of Lady Elliot were asking, as early as June 1796, when Corsica
was to be given up. To Paoli this threat had always been Elliot's unconcealed ace to play when it became necessary to
keep the Corsicans in line. Actually, Paoli was now being
unfair to Elliot, who, mindful of the successes of the
Corsican General of France, wrote to one of the Ministers:
"You cannot keep Corsica against the will of the people.
You ought not, if you could; but if you can spare a sufficient number of British troops to hold the strong places of
the Island, with the aid of the fleet, against all external attacks, the knowledge that you can do so will keep this
people steady to your cause. If we are weak we shall be set
at naught. If we are strong weak powers will cling to us."
Elliot added that the Admiral, Sir John Jervis, and Commodore Nelson supported his views.[6]

At first Elliot's response to the new "insurrections" was
sensible and mild. He listened to the demands of the insurgents, reduced taxes, even sacked Pozzo di Borgo. But
with the successive triumphs in Italy of the French armies
under Naopleon the task of governing became more difficult. Measures were taken which appeared to show fear,
or what was worse, an indifference to the Corsicans' state
of mind which suggested an indifference to their ultimate
fate. The institution of trial by jury was abolished (twelve
Corsicans could not be found who would convict another
Corsican, Elliot affirmed); control of the schools was
turned over to the Church, a measure which not only sub-
stituted conservative scholasticism for liberal education but
also implied that education was no longer a concern of the
government; unauthorized public assemblies were forbid-
den; and a measure was passed to reward with five
thousand francs the apprehension of any secret Republican emissary from France. By August 1796 North

reached the point of ordering the prohibition of public political discussion of any kind.[7] In the previous month Nelson had been ordered by Admiral Jervis to move from San Fiorenzo to institute a blockade of Leghorn. At this time Napoleon was collecting in that area a body of refugee Corsican troops with Gentili at their head. He had already taken precautions to send agents to lead uprisings in the Island—precautions which turned out to be quite unnecessary.[8]

By the latter part of August Nelson's informants told him that Corsican troops, with wives and children, were also coming from Nice. They were to be carried in small vessels from several ports along the coast. "If each takes eight or ten, it is almost impossible we can stop any of them; but if they are sure of being taken care of when they land in Corsica, the part of the Kingdom where they are so concealed or assisted must be rotten at heart."[9] Nelson, anxious to fight the French at Leghorn rather than wait for them to reach Corsica, learned that the 100th Regiment had been recalled from Corsica. "Whatever fears we may entertain for Corsica," he wrote to Elliot, "it is certain Government at home have none, by taking so very respectable a part of your force away." Without the means to prevent the large numbers of small boats with men, women, children—and arms—from reaching Corsica, Nelson and his Admiral began to fear that the island was moving towards a state of revolt. Elliot, however, as Nelson wrote to Jervis, "apparently has no fears for Corsica: his information, I must suppose, is good, and that he knows of every additional scoundrel who sets foot on the Island" (3 September 1796). Elliot apparently was satisfied that, since claims for rewards of five thousand francs were so rare, the people were loyal. His isolation from the native population appears to have been complete, even though he was obliged to send forces against Bocagnano and the vicinity of Ajaccio. His advisers presumably persuaded him that the uprisings were local and insignificant.[10]

The British Ministry, faced with the collapse of Italy and anticipating Spain's declaration of war, dispatched orders

on 31 August 1796 for the immediate abandonment of
Corsica and the withdrawal of the fleet to Gibraltar. The
Duke of Portland's phrasing of the order conveyed an attitude which many Englishmen no doubt felt, and which
the Corsicans knew they felt. The Government, Portland
wrote, intended "to withdraw the blessings of the British
Constitution from the people of Corsica," who apparently
had been entertaining "the blessings unawares."[11] Elliot received the order on 28 September 1796, but did not reveal
its contents to the Corsicans for a fortnight. He immediately convened, in Paoli's words, "the best subjects in
the nation" at Corte—*not* Bastia—and undertook to establish a commission for the defense and security of the
country. At the head of this commission were placed "the
most zealous and esteemed patriots." This expedient so
disconcerted the French party that many of them took cover and others were delivered up to the police. The an-
nouncement two weeks later of the British intention to
leave Corsica made the earlier action seem designed only
to add to the despair and even to the danger of the Corsican leaders.[12]

Gentili's troops landed at Capo Corso on 18 October
1796. Early on 20 October Nelson disembarked every last
man safely despite a heavy gale, and sailed briskly from
Bastia to Elba, which he reached before night. The Spanish
fleet, which was cruising off Capo Corso, did not succeed
in molesting Nelson's squadron, nor did it later engage the
fleet of Admiral Jervis, who remained off San Fiorenzo
several days longer. (Nelson joined him here on 24 October.) Ironically, at this time Elliot and Jervis received coun-
ter-orders to hold Corsica; if the evacuation had already
taken place, they were to establish themselves at Elba,
which under their own independent orders the British had
earlier taken.[13]

For Gentili the retaking of Corsica proved to be the
"military parade" Napoleon had envisioned prematurely
in late 1794. Gentili, a fair and decent man, was soon asked
by Napoleon to lead the French expedition to the Ionian
Isles. His successor as administrator was for a time the vin-

dictive Saliceti. Saliceti and his successors were guided for a brief period by the orders of Napoleon, who granted an amnesty to the Corsicans from which he excluded only the heads of those families who had opposed him under Paoli.[14]

So much for military decisions affecting Corsica, upon which Paoli, as he bitterly realized, had not the slightest influence. We are free now to make use of the few clues which tell us of the remainder of his life in England. For Maria Cosway the general's affection of course remained unchanged. He had understood the needs which urged her south from England even when her child was very young. The kindest comment of the gossipers was that of Walpole: "Surely it is odd to drop a child and her husband and country all in a breath." One story had it that Maria had become enamored of the Italian castrato, Marchesi, when her husband was painting him, and then trailed him all over Europe. Mrs. Piozzi, who as a former victim of gossip should have been reluctant to credit all she heard, confided to *Thraliana* that "Mrs. Cosway ran madding all over Europe after a castrato, leaving her husband and new-born baby at home here . . . a prey to almost infernal passions, or appetites strangely depraved."[15] Marchesi may have been one of Maria's travelling party for a period; Paoli, like Richard Cosway, of course knew better than to heed the ridiculous stories. In fact, Cosway sent money for Maria's support even as she sought to get into a convent; her letters to him meanwhile were full of instructions for their daughter's proper education as a Catholic.[16] Maria's first venture to enter at least an anteroom of the Church came to an end in 1794, when Richard became ill and she returned to care for him and their child.[17]

The death of Maria's daughter, on 29 July 1796, came as a heavy blow. Walpole, writing to Mary Berry, says the mother is "so afflicted for her only little girl that she shut herself up in her chamber and would not be seen. The man Cosway does not seem to think that much of the loss belonged to him: he romanced with his usual vivacity."[18] For "romanced" one must keep in mind an old meaning;

as Walpole said on another occasion, "Cosway abounds
with good nature, but never speaks a word of truth." Cosway was really deeply moved, but in ways only Sweden-
borgians and other cultists could pretend to understand.
He kept the embalmed body of his daughter in the living
room in a marble sarcophagus elaborately decorated by his
sculptor friend Nollekens. Maria, when she finally re-
gained her strength, put an end to the impious nonsense
and gave her child a proper burial.

The impressions once held, that Maria was coquettish,
flighty and unstable, physically fragile, prove unsubstantial
when examined. The former impressario of grand concerts and the now indefatigable seeker of proper labor for
her Lord must be seen as a woman of durable faith with a
body, if not robust to the eye, having great reserves of
strength.[19] For a few years, before it was easy to travel to
Paris and terrritories under French dominion, Maria
added to her reduced wifely duties renewed activity as an
artist, exhibiting at the Royal Academy and annoying
many of that body's members by attempting to promote
the election of various Italian artists. Her relations with
Paoli quite naturally changed, the father returning to his
role as comforter of the daughter at the time of painful
loss, but otherwise being an object of care as he grew older
and more enfeebled while she gained confidence in her
will and maturity. In a letter written two weeks after the
death of Maria's child, Paoli expresses regret at having just
missed the Cosways before their forthcoming departure
from London. He wishes Maria had stayed just a little
longer, giving her more time to find relief from her "real
afflictions" and him an opportunity to be in her company.
There would still be time, had he not then a friend at
home, and the next day an engagement with his "fellow
Corsicans" at Blackheath, the military parade and review-
ing ground. Paoli did not forget, nor would he allow the
world to forget, that he was a General, freely chosen by a
proud and independent people. In the same letter he expresses himself in ways which the protective father of only
a few years earlier would have found unthinkable. "Do
spend your time enjoyably and pity your friend that he

cannot do as much. . . . Oh God! what misfortunes I foresee for my poor homeland. I thought I had made its condition firm and secure: now it appears that I had subjected
it to the oppressions of the most jealousy-ridden of
regimes. . . . If you can find consoling news, do remember
it to raise somehow the oppressed spirits of your friend. "[20]

A chart of the state of Paoli's health during his last years
in England would show it constantly declining; not so his
spirits, which reached their lowest level of despair in 1797
and thereafter recovered considerably and appeared to
stabilize. The reasons for the intensifying depression are to
be found in events in England and abroad. Paoli's early belief that he was succeeding in his efforts to influence British
opinion was shattered as he began to receive fresh and
authentic news from the island. To Burnaby he tried to explain his feelings upon hearing of England's plan to abandon Corsica. On the one hand was his strong sense of
obligation which demanded loyalty to England, and the
actual attachment he felt for that country irrespective of
what might in honor be required; on the other, his self-
respect, damaged beyond the hope of repair because of
what he still owed his country, which had done so much for
him and had trusted absolutely in him. Viewing from afar,
incapable of helping, he endured "the furies of hell." If only he were in Corsica he would be able to unite his people
and adopt measures to preserve independence and neu-
trality. In these circumstances, with the coastal fortresses in
their hands, they would be in a "better situation than that
of '68 and '69." Paoli realized that he had made very
personal disclosures. "I cannot have any secret from you,
who have always given me good advice, and comfort for
my afflictions."[21] Here is an old man voicing complaints
and sorrows, not a statesman exercising judgment.
Burnaby no doubt refrained from asking, "Do you recall
what happened in '68 and '69, when an army much less
resolute and powerful opposed you, and when your country was not torn by divisions?"

Writing again to Burnaby on 10 December 1796, Paoli
tried to view the fate which had befallen his country in historical perspective, and to console himself with the thought

that he had never lacked good intentions. At this time he was indirectly informed that the order to evacuate Corsica had been countermanded, but that the dispatches had not arrived in time. It was "almost insinuated" to him that a move to expel the French might be undertaken, and for this the English would want Paoli's support. He would not, he wrote, be party to a civil war in Corsica for the purpose of reestablishing a government which had lost the people's affection and esteem. A pension was hinted—almost as if, "now that I can no longer be useful to the King, I am worth the trouble of being bought." He criticized the British for not having notified the Corsicans in time for them to organize and set up defenses. Even so, the Corsicans did not feel resentment. "Good Englishmen" would therefore see clearly that a great wrong was done to the Corsicans by "representing them as insubordinate, disloyal, and barbarous."[22]

As winter wore on Paoli felt himself an object of attack from all sides. Any uprising or sign of discontent on the island was attributed to the influence of the General, who continued to be reported as soliciting aid from England. In England, Paoli still wished to believe that the Ministers blamed Elliot, but he realized that the latter's friends "and the secret agents of the Ministry do not fail to insinuate that my conduct here and in Corsica was the reason for this abandonment. . . . I must suffer the calumny and injustice in silence until the spring makes it possible for me to retire someplace where I can no longer either hear or see abuses of justice, good faith, and morality."[23]

Elliot now benefitted from the fact that he literally arrived on the wave of good news, of the battle of Admiral Jervis' fleet of fifteen sail of the line against a Spanish fleet of almost twice its size, in which the British inflicted heavy losses. While still at anchor off the coast of England, Elliot wrote excitedly about the "most famous sea fight that ever was fought, at which I had the superlative good fortune to be present. . . . Sir J. Jervis is immortalized and Commodore Nelson a hero beyond Homer's."[24] England's otherwise gloomy winter was lighted by its heroes' exploits, which for a time stilled the fear of an invasion of Ireland. A grateful nation advanced the admiral to the peerage as Earl St. Vincent, and, besides making Nelson an admiral bestowed upon him the honor of Knight of the Bath.

For Paoli the year 1797 was one of almost uninterrupted sadness. His apartments in the monastery of Rostino were sacked. He regretted the burning of his writings and his books, but took some consolation from the fact that his sister was not molested. "All things considered," he wrote to Burnaby on 2 April, "the contempt which they show toward me here no longer gives me so much pain. I am old; my principal concern must be to leave the memory of my character. . . . I must place my consolation in the hope that posterity will be more just to me, or at least more indulgent. In the spring, if it is possible to go to Naples I will leave this country. The climate does not make me feel strong in my old machine." As for the affairs of the world, he knew no more of them than was reported in the periodicals. "If I had to form a judgement, I would say that there is no likelihood of peace. . . . I strongly fear that this war . . . will spread and endure as long as that which ended in the peace at Westphalia." In the same letter Paoli noted that Elliot had brought Pozzo di Borgo to England with him, and that both had been presented to the King by the Duke of Portland.

Elliot confidently expected recognition for his work in Corsica and Italy. Paoli saw things differently: "Pozzo di Borgo may be well paid for having ill served," he wrote on 3 July 1797, "but, be sure that he as much as his master is believed the author of much dishonor at this Court. . . . Nothing is decided concerning the promotion of his master. It may well come about, but it will provoke satire because he has no merit and no importance. However, anything can happen."[25] The insupportable was to happen, and without provoking satire. On 26 July 1797 Paoli addressed a letter to George III. The current situation in Corsica, he wrote, had made him "lose all hope of being of any use in his Majesty's service." He wished to retire to some neutral country of Germany, since it could not be

Italy, "in order no longer to serve as a pretext for harass-
ments and for threats of confiscation of the properties of
my friends and relatives." Even as he sought a "retreat for
the remainder of an existence fallen and truly filled with
bitterness and pain" because of the evil consequences of all
the measures which he had believed "the most appropriate
for consolidating the liberty and happiness" of his homeland, and for adding to the glory and the service of his
Majesty, he affirmed that, whatever the reasons for abandoning Corsica, no one could attribute it "to any lack of
loyalty to your sacred person. My affection, Sire, and that
of my compatriots for your Majesty was unshakable and
equal to any test. . . . As for me, I will forget the ills visited
upon me by people interested in sullying the loyalty and
uprightness of my principles: they will be sufficiently pun-
ished by their conscience, and by the judgment of the im-
partial public."[26]

On 20 September Paoli wrote to Burnaby that he had
received his passport, but that in the current state of military and political affairs it was impossible to determine
whether he would leave London for Hamburg or for Bath.
A month later he wrote of his decision to wait—it was impossible to conjecture what place would "be safe from the
armies or the influence of the French." Thus it was to be
Bath for that winter. In the same letter Paoli discussed the
problem of his pension. It is surprising to discover that the
pension supposedly granted to Paoli two years earlier was
not yet being disbursed. The pension had been officially
recommended by Elliot, but Paoli did not wish to accept a
pension if it was granted as a favor requested by that man.
It was communicated to Paoli that the whole was merely a
formal matter, and that he must accept or refuse the pension. Paoli found it possible to view the reward as coming
from his Majesty, even if the Duke of Portland and Sir Gilbert Elliot participated in signing papers.[27]

That Paoli possessed independent means is a fact not
mentioned by the General's biographers; but a letter to
Burnaby dated 2 April 1797 makes it clear that the next
spring, if it were possible to go to Naples, he planned to
leave England and be on his own. In Italy he would be able

to live "decently and comfortably" on the little which remained of his financial resources; further, the change in
climate would improve his health. He then mentioned his
investments and income, with no reference to a possible
pension which certainly would have made it possible for
him to live "decently and comfortably" in London. The
previously mentioned letter to George III three months
later, then, perhaps brought matters to a head. Paoli most
certainly had need of the pension by the time he received
it. To Burnaby early in 1798 he wrote: "At this time of
common desolation I have the added burden of supporting many people in Tuscany. Fortunately, however, the
person who has charge of my money there apparently does
not wish to defraud me of it. If he had sent it to me I already would have spent it; and now I would be in the
greatest distress for the sustenance of my people."[28]

Elliot received his reward, being created Baron Minto of
Minto on 20 October 1797. The new Baron wished to exercise his creative talents in designing his arms. The Duke
of Portland duly transmitted and endorsed Elliot's request
for his Majesty's license "to bear in chief as an augmenta-
tion to his family arms, the arms of Corsica, by way of
indication of the reasons which he conceives to have induced your Majesty to confer on him the honor of the
peerage."[29] The request was granted. The design, as described by Debrett, carries "above all a chief of augmenta-
tion argent, and thereon a Moor's head sable, being the
arms of the island of Corsica." What Corsican, least of all
Paoli, could be pleased at having his country's flag incorporated into the arms of its betrayer? But of course the
Ministry had never for a moment accepted the Corsican
view. Elliot had been a successful negotiator and coordi-
nator of military and political affairs. As for the Corsicans,
what reason was there to expect them to behave better
than the Americans or the Irish? Further, the Ministry was
aware of its share of responsibility for the actions, and inac-
tions, in the Mediterranean.

The beginning of 1798 found Paoli disturbed by the
"horrible oppressions" practiced on the island by the lackeys of Saliceti and Arena. His own nephews were obliged

to escape to Tuscany. Wholesale confiscation of property, imposition of high taxes, and the oppression of the Church contributed to new insurrections.[30] Later this same year Paoli discussed the apparent disinclination of Burnaby's sons to participate in the war in Europe. "At my age I can no longer consider any war just which is not . . . for the defense of one's own country: and when this is in danger, indifference or inaction in your sons becomes culpable." However, Paoli believed France incapable of invading England.[31]

After Napoleon's accession to power Paoli hoped for an improvement in the lot of the islanders. He did not blame Napoleon for his treatment of the Paolists; but did wish that the conqueror would show that he remembered his native land. I value him nevertheless, Paoli wrote, "because he has shown that the inhabitants of that oppressed and abused Island, once freed from the cold hands of a tyrannical government, know how to distinguish themselves in every career. He has made our vendettas against all those who had been the cause of our humiliation. Our destiny is now determined. I hope that our people will learn how to take advantage of the opportunities which they have in common with the French, so that they may prosper in commerce and in agriculture."[32]

During this period the ministrations of Maria, who was concerned for the state of Paoli's soul as well as of his mind and body, undoubtedly comforted the old man. For his part, Paoli writes that he is "altogether disposed to follow your wise, good, and saintly counsel . . . so that you will no longer doubt my orthodoxy." As for his health, "the air of Bath is not so good as that of Clifton. After the holidays I shall perhaps return there from being busy." In another letter Maria writes: "I send you a book, but not as a gift, only as a loan; until you find one you are always immersed in philosophy or literature, but this is the greatest of all." It takes no effort of the imagination to conclude that Maria is attempting to draw Paoli away from his too worldly interests. She goes on: "If you have no engagement this morning, and would go with me to Mr. Nollekens, you

would give me pleasure and see some fine engravings. My
servant will come and tell you in which chapel I shall be,
and if you will fetch me you will do me a favour. Are you
coming to Mass today? The feast of All Saints; that we may
meet among them some day is the hope of your friend."
Paoli, pleased with the scolding, capitulates uncritically,
demonstrating the true source of Maria's influence upon
him: "I will read the book because you recommend it. I
have not yet opened it to see who is the author. The carriage is at your disposal. Name the hour, because I would
not come to your chapel, but after Mass at the Portuguese
Chapel I will come and fetch you wherever you are."[33]
Maria apparently was to make use of the General's coach,
with or without its owner, much as Boswell had many years
before. In the Farington Diary for 18 January 1799 it is
noted that Maria Cosway took the Italian painter Bonomi
to Loutherbourg's "in General Paoli's coach." On 23 November of this year the diary records that Nollekens went
to Benjamin West's the previous night and found him in
his bedchamber. "General Paoli and Mrs. Cosway were
there."

The search for health continued. A passage in one of
Euphemia Boswell's letters, apparently written late in October 1800, reads: "I had lately a very beautiful and kind
letter from General Paoli. He has been at Bristol for his
health. He is now wonderfully better, thank God."[34] At
what precise time Paoli became virtually immobilized it is
difficult to determine. He was present at the Royal
Academy Dinner on 25 April 1801; and in the summer of
the following year was believed by Burnaby to be well
enough to join him in the country at Baggrave Hall. Paoli
was forced to decline the invitation for fear of exposing
himself en route to another attack of a disorder "which so
nearly threatened my life. . . . I fear that I will not even be
able to go to Clifton as they advised me; a trip which I
would have been able to make slowly with my own carriage."[35] It is of interest that in the same letter he speaks of
one of his compatriots who had arrived at his house a few
days earlier, and needed his help. To the very end the

General felt responsible for all the Corsicans who had lost
relatives or property under what he called his "administration." Bed and board, letters, any possible verbal appeals,
all that was in his power he gave to the end.

With the peace of March 1802 friends expressed hope
that Paoli would be permitted to return to Corsica. "Even
if I were permitted," he replied, "my advanced age will not
allow me the pleasure of seeing once again *la patria*. Because of a cruel destiny I have always had to leave when I
most believed myself to be of some usefulness. Now I am
old. . . . I greet everyone. . . . I do not hate anyone."[36] In
another letter he asked that it be made known "to all those
who took part in the stripping of my possessions in
Morosaglia or in Pastoreccia that I pardon them. . . . May
they continue to enjoy them as if they were their own."[37]
He was cheered to hear that soon schools and colleges were
to be opened in Corsica. "These considerations enrich the
few days of life which remain to me."[38] Improvements,
however, were slow in coming. Paoli lived long enough to
recall the truth of an observation he had made earlier, that
the abuses by local government officials were likely to lead
to some form of "colonial regime" for Corsica."[39]

Unable now to undertake the project he once entertained of writing a work on Corsica, a work in which he no
doubt intended to give an account of his stewardship, Paoli
gladly assented to a proposal by Burnaby that he publish
letters and other documents which the General had sent
him. Paoli imposed no conditions: "It has been my inviolable custom in corresponding with my friends to speak of
things as I see them, to express my opinions with simplicity
and frankness; nor did I ever keep copies of my private
letters. You have complete authority to make use of those
which you have as you see fit; especially if in some way they
can communicate clearly the observations which you made
when you visited my unhappy country, upon which some
things have recently been written, but by people biased
and uninformed." Burnaby thus became the authorized
custodian of Paoli's reputation, playing Horatio to Paoli's
Hamlet, and telling his "story" in Paoli's own words:
Journal of a Tour to Corsica in the Year 1766 . . . with a Series

of Original Letters from General Paoli to the Author. Although Burnaby's book was not published until 1804, it comes to a close with Paoli's letter to him of 13 July 1802.

In a "Conclusion" Burnaby wrote that "the sole object of this selection [of documents and letters] is to vindicate General Paoli's character from the aspersions and misrepresentations of envy and detraction." By the year 1804 Paoli was less likely to be maligned in England than to be ignored, but envy and detraction had done their work upon him. Perhaps it was in large part to assuage his friend's pain and take away the bitterness of thoughts of failure that Burnaby provided for the small printing of his work. For the remainder of his time Paoli lived quietly in London, and at peace. He had accepted Corsica as a part of France. What he wrote earlier he would maintain now. "My love for liberty has always been the same; I have declared it free from any personal interest. *La patria* is now free like the rest of France; why should I not be content? From whatever hand it may derive, may it be blessed! Are the Corsicans free? *Hoc erat in votis.* [Thus it was in my prayers.] I will close my eyes in the great sleep, content, and without remorse for my political conduct. May God forgive me the rest." In 1806 Paoli wrote: "I have lived enough: and if I were permitted to begin life again, I would refuse the gift if it were not accompanied by the perceptions and knowledge gained from my past life, so that I could correct the errors and the follies which accompanied it."[40]

General Pasquale de Paoli died on 5 February 1807 after what the periodicals described as a long and painful illness. The instructions in his will were followed: "I ask that my body might be buried in the churchyard of St. Pancras, where foreigners of any creed are buried. I wish to be led there with dignity but without ostentation or display, at the fall of night in a hearse followed by my carriage. I wish my coffin to be simple, and I should like to be placed in a vault in order to ensure that surgeons might not use my body for anatomy lessons." The will provided five hundred Florentine zecchini for the "foundation and perpetual maintenance of three university professorships." In addition

Paoli gave a token of his "particular affection and gratitude" to the parish of Rostino where he was born, by providing for the foundation of a normal school where the young would learn to read and write, and to master the rudiments of Latin and of arithmetic. For the sustenance of a capable master he allotted the annual sum of one hundred zecchini.[41] A cenotaph to Paoli was afterwards erected in the south aisle of Westminster Abbey, over which was placed the white marble bust by Flaxman. Paoli's testamentary wishes suffered the fate of his earlier hopes. No university was established in Corsica; Paoli created in 1763 the only one the island has ever known.[42] Napoleon appears to have confirmed if not established the French policy which has prevailed since: namely, that no department of the country is to be neglected more than Corsica.

The disorders from which Paoli suffered appear from the little evidence available to have involved the central nervous system. A specific reference to sciatica was quoted in an early letter, and this term is helpfully modern. Today the slipped, perforated, degenerative, swollen or bleeding disc would account for most of Paoli's specified complaints. The numbness and pain in his arm and hand indicate not only difficulties in the main spinal column but also in the higher vertebrae. Paoli's efforts to seek a cure or even relief, if this diagnosis is correct, would have been as completely fruitless as the surviving letters suggest.[43] The immediate cause of death is revealed in a passage in the Farington Diary for 6 June 1807, a passage by James Boswell the Younger which fittingly concludes the present account of Paoli's life: "He [J. B. the Younger] spoke of the death of General Paoli, his old friend. He died at the age of 82 of a suppression of urine, to which he had been long subject. He had a pension of 2000 pounds a year from our government, but had many Corsican friends to assist for whom he had an open table. His figure had undergone a great change: from being very large and stout he had become very thin; but his spirits were good."[44]

The prominent Corsicans surviving Paoli were Carlo Andrea Pozzo di Borgo, now in the service of Tsar Alex-

ander I, and Napoleon. In 1814, after Napoleon's down-
fall, Pozzo as a general in the Russian army was among the
first to reenter with the allies the Palace of the Tuileries.
For over twenty years he had never lost the scent of his
quarry. He had most nobly observed the custom to which
his country had given birth, the vendetta. It was Royalist
France which honored Pozzo with the title of Count, and
primarily to that country he owed the considerable fortune
he ultimately amassed.[45] Pozzo lived long enough to hear
the hours-long ringing of bells and firing of cannon which
marked the ceremonies of Napoleon's burial, in December
1840, "on the banks of the Seine, in the midst of the French
people that I love so well." Pozzo died not long after, no
less a Frenchman. His descendant bought a wing of the
Palace of the Tuileries after that structure had been burnt
down following the deposition of Napoleon III, and trans-
ported the numbered stones to Ajaccio in order to construct, beginning in 1886, an enhanced replica now known
as Château de la Punta. It stands on the shoulder of a
mountain above the city and all its memorials to Napoleon.
The Duke Pozzo di Borgo has opened it to the public, who
can view the richly furnished interior and gaze upon
David's portrait of Napoleon as well as Gérard's of the first
Count Pozzo di Borgo. Thanks to the art which survives
life, the expressions of the men staring at each other are
startlingly devoid of enmity. Their remains are far away,
but over the mountains, at Morosaglia, Paoli is to be found
entombed in the little family chapel in the house where he
was born.

Although Paoli had spent more of his adult life in England rather than in Corsica, and properly deserves the full
entry in the *Dictionary of National Biography*, his British
friends knew as well as the islanders that the General was
quintessentially Corsican.

> Ev'n from the tomb the voice of Nature cries,
> Ev'n in our Ashes live their wonted Fires.

As the stones were being assembled for Pozzo di Borgo's
château, Corsicans throughout the island raised a con-

Aspinall: *The Later Correspondence of George III,* ed. A. Aspinall, vol. II, Cambridge, England, 1963.

Boswelliana: Boswelliana, the Commonplace Book of James Boswell, ed. Rev. Charles Rogers, London, 1874. Additional sayings by and about Paoli are to be found in the Boswelliana MS in the Hyde Collection. Of marginal interest, they have not been used in the present work.

BP: See item (1) under "JB Journal."

Bulletin: Bulletin, Société des sciences historiques et naturelles de la Corse, Bastia, 1881–1911.

Burnaby: Andrew Burnaby, *The Journal of a Tour to Corsica in the Year 1766 . . . With a Series of Original Letters from General Paoli to the Author . . . 1766 to 1802,* London, 1804. Letters usually identified by date only.

De Witt: Cornelis de Witt, *Thomas Jefferson,* 3rd edition, Paris, 1861.

Corsica: James Boswell, *An Account of Corsica, The Journal of a Tour to That Island, and Memoirs of Pascal Paoli . . . the Third Edition, Corrected,* London, 1769.

Foladare, *Corsica:* Joseph Foladare, *James Boswell and Corsica,* Yale dissertation, 1936 (University Microfilms, Ann Arbor, 1970).

Fortescue: *The Correspondence of King George the Third from 1760 to December 1783,* ed. Sir John Fortescue, 6 vols., London, 1927–1928.

Fournier: August Fournier, *Napoleon I,* trans. A.E. Adams and H.A.L. Fisher, 2 vols., London, 1912.

Giamarchi: F.M. Giamarchi, *Vita Politica di Pasquale Paoli,* Bastia, 1858.

Howard: *Letters and Documents of Napoleon,* selected and translated by John Eldred Howard, vol. I, London, 1961.

JB Journal or JB Letter: Boswell's journal entries, memoranda, and letters. Those already published are identified only by the date of the entry or letter, which does not always coincide with the date of the event. They may be found in one or more of the following: (1) *Private Papers of James Boswell from Malahide Castle, in the Collection of Lt.-Colonel Ralph Heyward Isham,* ed. Geoffrey Scott and F.A. Pottle, privately printed, 18 vols., 1928–1934; index vol., 1937; (2) trade or reading edition of Boswell's papers published by the McGraw-Hill Book Company, Inc., and William Heinemann, Ltd., 1950–; (3) *Letters of James Boswell,* ed. C.B. Tinker, 2 vols., Oxford, 1924; (4) research edition of Boswell's papers, published by McGraw-Hill and Heinemann, 1966–. In the footnote references no distinction is made between Boswell's fully written journal entries and his notes or memoranda.

Unpublished materials are identified by dates and in addition by catalog numbers from the forthcoming *Catalogue of the Yale Editions of the Private Papers of James Boswell,* to be published by McGraw-Hill and Heinemann. A star indicates that the item had a provenance outside the Boswell archives.

Life: James Boswell, *The Life of Samuel Johnson,* ed. G.B. Hill and rev. L.F. Powell, 6 vols., Oxford, 1934–1964. References usually are only to dates as published by Boswell.

Mahan, *Fr. Rev.:* A.T. Mahan, *The Influence of Sea Power upon the French Revolution and Empire, 1793–1812,* 2 vols., Boston, 1894.

Mahan, *Nelson:* A.T. Mahan, *The Life of Nelson: The Embodiment of the Sea Power of Great Britain,* 2 vols., London, 1897.

Minto: *Life and Letters of Sir Gilbert Elliot, First Earl of Minto,* ed. Countess of Minto, 3 vols., London, 1874. The Countess of Minto's work overlaps in large part the *Correspondance de Sir Gilbert Elliot,* trans. and ed. Sébastien de Caraffa, published in *Bulletin,* fascicules 133–138, 177–179. The letters for the French edition were transcribed in 1868, chiefly by Philippe de Caraffa, from the originals in the possession of Sir Henry George Elliot.

Moore: *Diary of Sir John Moore,* ed. J.F. Maurice, 2 vols., London, 1904.

Nelson: *Despatches and Letters of Lord Viscount Nelson,* ed. N.H. Nicolas, 7 vols., London, 1844–1846.

Pottle, *Earl. Yrs.:* Frederick A. Pottle, *James Boswell, The Earlier Years, 1740–1769,* New York, 1966.

Pottle, *Lit. Car.:* Frederick A. Pottle, *The Literary Career of James Boswell,* Oxford, 1929.

Ravenna: Leona Ravenna, *Pasquale Paoli,* Florence, 1928.

Renucci: F.O. Renucci, *Storia di Corsica,* 2 vols., Bastia, 1833-1834.

Rota: Ettore Rota, *Pasquale Paoli,* Turin, 1941.

Shelburne MSS: Manuscript collection of the Earl of Shelburne now at the Clements Library, Ann Arbor, Michigan.

Thrasher: Peter A. Thrasher, *Pasquale Paoli: An Enlightened Hero,* London, 1970.

Tommaseo: Niccolò Tommaseo, *Lettere di Pasquale Paoli,* in *Archivio Storico Italiano,* vol. XI, 1846.

Villat: Louis Villat, *La Corse de 1768 à 1789,* 2 vols., Besançon, 1924-1925.

Walpole, *Correspondence:* Horace Walpole, *Correspondence,* ed. Wilmarth Lewis and others, New Haven, 1937-.

NOTES

Introduction

1. Available in London 13 Feb. 1768; entered in Stationers' Register 15 Feb. 1768. Pottle, *Lit. Car.*, p. 61. I shall refer to the entire work as *Corsica*, to the first section as *Account*, and to the second (*Journal* plus *Memoirs*) as *Tour*. Page numbers are from the third edition, 1769.
2. *Journal of the Rev. John Wesley*, ed. Nehemiah Curnock (London, 1909–1916), V, 292–293; François René Jean de Pommereul, *Histoire de l'Isle de Corse* (Berne, 1779), I, 8. For the reception accorded the book see Pottle, *Lit. Car.*, pp. 61–62; Foladare, *Corsica*, pp. 119–151; Pottle, *Earl. Yrs.*, pp. 356–368.
3. F.O. Renucci, *Storia di Corsica*, 2 vols. (Bastia, 1833, 1834); Arrigo Arrighi, *Histoire de Pascal Paoli*, 2 vols. (Paris, 1843); F.M. Giamarchi, *Vita Politica di Pasquale Paoli* (Bastia, 1858); J. D'Oria, *Pasquale de' Paoli* (Genoa, 1870); C. Bartoli, *Histoire de Pascal Paoli* (Bastia, 1889–rev. of a shorter 1866 work); Leona Ravenna, *Pasquale Paoli* (Florence, 1928); Ettore Rota, *Pasquale Paoli* (Turin, 1941); Peter A. Thrasher, *Pasquale Paoli: An Enlightened Hero* (London, 1970). I have omitted some works of lesser importance.
4. Boswell's journal for the Corsican tour has not survived; we are given clues to its contents by a running outline which he made in organizing it for publication. See Foladare, *Corsica*, pp. 104–118.
5. Boswell did publish, unsigned, an account of Paoli's tour to Scotland with the Polish Ambassador, Count Burzynski, August-September 1771, for the *London Magazine*, XL (1771), 433–434. I ignore other contributions to periodicals and the essays which he wrote for *British Essays in Favour of the Brave Corsicans* (London, 1769). Boswell's efforts after the publication of *Corsica* were directed toward securing British aid, even military intervention, on behalf of the islanders. They add very little of significance to his portrait of Paoli in *Corsica*.
6. Foladare, *Corsica*, esp. pp. 61–118, 647–714. See also Pottle's earlier account in *BP*, VII, 205–245.
7. *Earl. Yrs.*, p. 259.
8. The Italians did not have much success in propagating this notion in Corsica during World War II.
9. I shall not attempt to append a comprehensive bibliography, which would be quite long, for students of Paoli. Rota and Thrasher are sufficiently thorough in this respect. I shall, however, note particular additional sources when necessary.
10. So wrote Walpole to the Duchess of Choiseul. Chatham made the speech on 25 Jan. 1771. Choiseul had demonstrated his mastery

of the arts of duplicity in 1761, when manipulating the concurrent negotiations between France and Spain and between France and Britain (*The Letters of Horace Walpole,* ed. Mrs. Paget Toynbee (Oxford, 1904), VIII, 10; Z.E. Rashed, *The Peace of Paris* (Liverpool, 1951), esp. pp. 68–114).

11. Minto, esp. pp. 200–201, 207; Nelson, II, 286, 287; Maurice Jollivet, *Les Anglais dans la Méditerranée (1794–1797): Un Royaume Anglo-Corse* (Paris, 1896), pp. 294–297.

12. Fournier, I, 132; Camille Piccioni, *Histoire du Cap-Corse* (Paris, 1923), p. 208; P. to Burnaby, 10 Feb. 1798. The writers dealing with this period, depending upon which side they espouse, agree roughly that the number of Corsicans expelled by the French was of the same magnitude as the number previously driven out by the Paolists. Andrew Burnaby (?1734–1812) became chaplain to the British factory at Leghorn about the year 1762, and in the absence of John Dick discharged the functions of the consulate with the title of proconsul. In 1766 he made a tour to Corsica and gained the lasting friendship of Pasquale Paoli. Burnaby made available to Boswell the manuscript of his tour, which extended from 3 to 22 August 1766, to use as he wished. Boswell fully acknowledges his indebtedness in the preface to *Corsica,* pp. xvii–xviii. (For an extensive notation of Boswell's borrowings see Foladare, *Corsica,* pp. 72–75 and Appendix VIII. Boswell says he has "freely interwoven" Burnaby's journal into his own work; I assumed that the journal Burnaby later published did not differ in text from that of the manuscript he lent Boswell.) In 1769, soon after he returned to England, Burnaby was nominated to the vicarage of Greenwich. In 1786 he was presented the archdeaconry of Leicester in the Lincoln diocese. He succeeded to large paternal estates in Huntingdonshire about 1767, but Baggrave Hall, Leicestershire, the inheritance of his wife (m. 1770), became his favorite place of residence. In 1804 Burnaby published his journal of the tour together with letters that Paoli addressed to him in the years 1766–1802: *Journal of a Tour to Corsica in the Year 1766 . . . with a Series of Original Letters from General Paoli to the Author.*

13. Thrasher, pp. 170, 278–279. Napoleon on St. Helena needed no encouragement from his visitors to speak of the "nation of shopkeepers," yielding the opportunity to enhance his reputation as a phrasemaker to the pleasure of adding to the discomfiture of the hated enemy by giving credit to their Paoli. What, if anything, Paoli said to Napoleon on this subject it is impossible to know.

14. 27 Oct. 1777. As Mrs. Thrale recognized, Johnson, who had no patience with the professed, gushing sincerity then in fashion, was toying with irony; she probably sensed also that Johnson now longed to communicate as they frequently did when together.

15. JB Letter, 28 Dec. 1764.

Chapter I

1. Boswell used 6 April as the date for celebrating Paoli's birthday, but this matter, like many concerning Paoli, has been the subject of considerable disagreement. The epitaph under Flaxman's bust in Westminster Abbey gives "April 5th." The General signed himself Pasquale de Paoli. Boswell's adoption of "Pascal" as "more agreeable to an English ear" (*Corsica*, p. 154n) must surely have annoyed Paoli, but he characteristically refrained from correcting his young friend. Some blame may be attached to Lord Hailes, who wrote to Boswell, 29 Aug. 1766, "*Paschal* is more pleasing to the English ear than *Pasquale*." Boswell continued the usage for some years (see his letter to Garrick, 18 Sept. 1771). His journals and letters ultimately conformed to the style of "General Paoli" (*Lond. Chron.*, 5 April 1768; Francesco Guerri, *Corsica Antica e Moderna*, I [Leghorn, 1932], "La data di nascita e la data di morte di Pasquale Paoli [6 aprille 1725–5 febbraio 1807]," 64–69, and "L'atto di battesimo di Pasquale Paoli," 193–195).
2. Joseph Chiari, who was born in Corsica, constantly compares the terrain and social structure of the island to that of Scotland. Thrasher not only adopts "clan" but also invariably uses "glen" to describe the Corsican valley (Joseph Chiari, *Corsica: Columbus's Isle* [London, 1960].)
3. *The Political State of Great Britain*, vol. 52, 1736. For an account of the differences among the chiefs which were to plague Corsica, and of England's relations with Corsica in the ensuing years, see André Le Glay, *La Corse pendant la Guerre de la succession d'Autriche* (Paris, 1912), pp. 140–149, 180–190.
4. Genovesi's later reference to "our Paoli" need not indicate more than a fellow Italian leader's pride. See Rota, pp. 47–56. Rota, and Thrasher after him, derive their information concerning Paoli's Italian period from studies by Ersilio Michel in *Archivio Storico di Corsica*, especially "Pasquale Paoli ufficiale dell'esercito napoletano, 1741–1755" (Leghorn, 1928), p. 85f.
5. Boswell, *Tour*, p. 351.
6. In the full text of the later 1763 proclamation this action is referred to as having been ordered by George II in council on 10 May 1753 (*Annual Register for the Year 1763*, p. 213). Gaffori was not assassinated until October of the same year.
7. Many close paraphrases suggest that Boswell is also indebted to Burnaby, unless—and this is remotely possible—Burnaby modified his text to conform to Boswell's before printing it. Matthieu Fontana makes considerable use of Boswell's book in *La Constitution du Généralat de Pascal Paoli en Corse, 1755–1769* (Paris, 1907), pp. ix, 2, 18, 42, 57, 98, 116.
8. "Hotels are heavily staffed with continentals, and modern farm labor is performed largely by salaried North Africans" (Robert Cairns, "Sunny Corsica," *National Geographic*, Sept. 1973, p. 416).
9. Out of the two hundred thousand people in free Corsica, Paoli estimated that he could put forty thousand armed men into the field (Boswell, *Account*, p. 253; Shelburne MSS, vol. 40, pt. ii, no. 24).

10. By early 1766 Burnaby found that the number of professors had increased to twelve, with "more than 150 students" (Burnaby, p. 16).

11. The Rousseau-Buttafoco correspondence, which extended from 31 Aug. 1764 to 19 Oct. 1765, has been printed many times in editions of Rousseau's letters. After the project of going to Corsica had been abandoned—and with it certainly the notion that the Corsicans wanted him as lawgiver—Rousseau occupied himself with continued work on a constitution, filling three notebooks. See Ernestine Dedeck-Héry, *Jean-Jacques Rousseau et le projet de constitution pour la Corse* (Philadelphia, 1932), chaps. X and XI.

12. *Lettres de M. Buttafoco à M. Paoli et à d'autres particuliers dans l'isle de Corse* (Paris, undated but usually placed in 1791).

13. For an account of Buttafoco and the Buttafoco-Marbeuf-Choiseul correspondence see Colonna de Giovellina, "Les Buttafoco," *Revue de la Corse* (Paris, 1932), XIII, 57–65, 114–120, 184–197. Those who refer to the son of Carlo Buonaparte as Napoleone Buonaparte will choose the spelling, Matteo Buttafuoco. Napoleon styled himself Bonaparte by 1796; Buttafuoco used the mixed form, Matteo Buttafoco, when writing to superiors in the French army; and he was referred to as M. Buttafoco when later serving as a deputy for the nobility of Corsica at meetings of the Estates-General and then the National Assembly. The family, in Corsica or in Italy, continued to use Buttafuoco. I shall use Buttafoco.

14. Boswell, *Account,* p. 166. The full text of Rousseau's letter to Deleyre, dated 20 Dec. 1764, was first published in the trade edition of the Boswell papers. Thrasher (p. 97) quotes the passage in Boswell's book but places it four years later and changes the occasion: "Rousseau's affection for the island led to an indignant outburst in 1768, when war at last broke out between Corsica and France." Boswell's *Corsica* appeared some months before the French attacked the Corsicans.

15. *Jean-Jacques Rousseau et le projet de constitution pour la Corse* (Philadelphia, 1932). For additions and commentary see Foladare, *Corsica,* pp. 633–646.

16. Thrasher writes that Paoli "had no intention, as he admitted later to Boswell, of submitting the island to the rule of Jean-Jacques" (p. 97). I find no evidence of such an admission. Boswell apparently took the ideas concerning Paoli's "true" intentions from Burnaby's journal of his tour, and Burnaby phrases these ideas as inferences: "I am persuaded that General Paoli had no intention. . . . Such were the views, I have reason to believe, of the General in desiring the presence of Monsieur Rousseau" (Burnaby, pp. 20–22). Some years later Rousseau's part in the episode dwindled in Paoli's mind to an incidental anecdotal comment to Fanny Burney: "[Boswell] fetched me some letter of recommending him."

17. All the material now taken from Boswell is to be found in the *Tour,* pp. 315–372, and is not footnoted. Spelling and punctuation are modernized.

18. "La testa mi rompa." In the *Tour* Boswell gives Paoli's original, Italian or French, and then translates; only his translations are given here. Boswell's running outline for this section does not contain "la testa . . ." but, with reference to Paoli's difficulties in writing, "sudo anzi," "I only sweat," a comment which Boswell evidently decided was too vulgar to be attributed to his hero.

19. Aspinall, II, 604.

20. For a list see *Tour*, p. 321n, and Foladare, *Corsica*, p. 528n.

21. Neither Paoli's answers nor his criticism of Swift have survived in manuscript. Boswell printed one of the answering letters in the *Tour*, pp. 395–397.

Chapter II

1. Pottle, *Earl. Yrs.*, pp. 244–261, 284–286, 303–308, 323, 337, 356–368, 378–386, 389–397, 409–410. For another account see Foladare, *Corsica*, pp. 11–60, 152–196.

2. The characterization of Paoli by Pitt is from the last paragraph of the published *Tour*; the observation on Genoa and France occurs in a cancelled portion of the first draft of the book (M2). Boswell probably deleted the passage so as not to "hurt Paoli with the French," as John Dick phrased his concern (C 1024).

3. Villat, I, 19–22.

4. The post eventually was to go to Buttafoco. The entire correspondence between Choiseul and Paoli has been printed by L'Abbé Letteron, *Bulletin*, fascicle 69, pp. 441–596.

5. *BP*, VII, 216–217; P.R.O., Chatham MSS, viii, 94 (dated 31 Jan. 1767).

6. Lord Fitzmaurice (E.G. Petty-Fitzmaurice), *Life of William, Earl of Shelburne* (London, 1912), I, 282–283.

7. See John Brooke, *The Chatham Administration, 1776–1768* (London, 1956). The quoted phrases are from pp. 79 and 112. For the letter from Chatham, below, see JB Journal.

8. John Brooke in the work cited above describes the negotiations with the Rockinghams and Bedfords in considerable detail, for the most part withholding judgment. The ramifications of Britain's policy toward Europe, which was never to prove intelligible to Paoli, are examined by Michael Roberts in *Splendid Isolation, 1763–1780* (Univ. of Reading, 1970). For the general reader Steven Watson, *The Reign of George III, 1760–1815* (Oxford, 1960), is a helpful introduction. To go further without abandoning oneself to a guide in one of the various camps is to invite confusion. For example, Brooke in a work more recent than that listed above, *King George III* (London, 1972), writes: "Few of the followers of Chatham were men of character. Had they been, they would not have been followers of Chatham" (p.157). Similarly, partisans of Paoli who wish to read extensively on Shelburne or Burke must be prepared for rough shocks.

9. *Bulletin,* fascicle 69, p. 534. See also *Lond. Chron.,* 8 Sept., 10 Sept., 29 Sept., 7 Nov. 1767.

10. Correspondence between Choiseul and Boyer, French Minister at Genoa, and between Choiseul and Sorba, Genoese Minister at Versailles, extending from 27 July 1767 to 12 March 1768. John F. Ramsey, *Anglo-French Relations, 1763–1770: A Study of Choiseul's Foreign Policy* (Berkeley, 1939), pp. 185–186. Hereafter cited as Ramsey.

11. *Bulletin,* fascicle 69, pp. 529–531, 534–535. In many of the letters of this period Choiseul takes offence at the "tone of equality" assumed by Paoli.

12. Cornelis de Witt, *Thomas Jefferson,* 3rd ed. (Paris, 1861), p. 420. Hereafter cited as de Witt.

13. *Bulletin,* fascicle 69, pp. 582–586.

14. Ramsey, p. 186.

15. *Bulletin,* fascicle 69, p. 594.

16. Shelburne MSS, 40, ii, 34. Many of the Shelburne manuscripts relating to Corsica were used by Lord Fitzmaurice (E.G. Petty-Fitzmaurice), *Life of William, Earl of Shelburne* (London, 1912), I, 363–385. The Shelburne correspondence dovetails exactly with the French correspondence, in Affaires Etrangères, *Correspondance Politique, Angleterre,* vols. 478–481, cited by Ramsey, pp. 186–190, 258–259, and de Witt, pp. 438–442.

17. Ramsey, p. 187.

18. See Shelburne to Rochford, 8 April and 13 May 1768, Shelburne MSS, 40, ii, 50; and 40, ii, 64. Commodore Richard Spry, English Commander in the Mediterranean and Minister to Genoa, was instructed to obtain full information from officials of the Republic. Among items in his expense account is one which reads: "To [be] paid to a certain great person, as a reward for giving me secret intelligence of what was transacting in the Senate [of Genoa] respecting the cession of Corsica to France, 200 pounds" (Great Britain, State Papers Domestic, *Calendar of Home Office Papers,* vol. III, no. 196. See also ibid., vol. II, nos. 911, 923, 927, 934).

19. Shelburne to Rochford, 8 April 1768; Châtelet to Choiseul, 8 April 1768. Shelburne MSS, 40, ii, 50; Ramsey, p. 187.

20. Châtelet to Choiseul, 6 May 1768. Ramsey, pp. 187–188.

21. Rochford to Shelburne, 5 May 1768; Choiseul to Châtelet, 12 May 1768; Shelburne to Rochford, 13 May 1768; Shelburne to Rochford, 27 May 1768. Shelburne MSS, 40, ii, 60, 64, 68; Ramsey, p. 188.

22. Rochford to Shelburne, 2 June 1768. Shelburne MSS, 40, ii, 69. Choiseul did not permit the publication of Boswell's book, apparently fearing intensification of sympathy for the Corsicans. French translations from other countries did become available. The text of the treaty between Genoa and France is printed by Villat, II, 423–428.

23. For indications of the unpopularity of Choiseul's Corsican policy among the French see Walpole, *Correspondence,* vol. 4, p. 202; James Harris (1st Earl of Malmesbury), *Letters, 1745–1820* (London, 1844), I, 163–166; J.H. Jesse, *George Selwyn and His Contem-*

poraries (London, 1882), II, 362; Shelburne MSS, 40, ii, 1 and 69; *Correspondance Litteraire . . . par Grimm, Diderot, Raynal, etc.,* ed. A.A. Barbier (Paris, 1814), IX, 64–65.

24. De Witt, pp. 438–439.
25. Ibid., p. 439 (20 June 1768).
26. Extract of intercepted letter from Marquis Caracciolo to Marquis Janucci, London, 27 May 1768, in Shelburne MSS, vol. 35, no. 14.
27. Châtelet to Choiseul, 10 June 1768. Ramsey, p. 189.
28. Duke of Grafton, *Autobiography,* ed. Sir W.R. Anson (Oxford, 1898), p. 204.
29. Fitzmaurice, I, 375 (Rochford's letters written 14 and 21 July). Châtelet had embarked at Dover on 10 July, according to *Lond. Chron.* of 12 July 1768.
30. Grafton, *Autobiography,* pp. 204–205.
31. Shelburne MSS, 40, ii, 1.
32. P to Burnaby, 5 Aug., 6 Sept., 1 Nov. 1767.
33. *Archivio Storico Italiano* (Florence, 1888–1897), series V, vol. 5, pp. 275–276.
34. *Bulletin,* fascicles 146–147, p. 276. *La patria* is translatable —fatherland, native land, homeland—but letting it stand in Paoli's utterances often seems obligatory.
35. Ibid., p. 277.
36. Shelburne MSS, 40, ii, 22.
37. Letter by Paoli in cipher, undated. *Archivio Storico Italiano* (Florence, 1888–1897), series V, vol. 5, p. 239.
38. Grafton, *Autobiography,* p. 207.
39. Stewart to Shelburne, Shelburne MSS, 40, ii, 24, dated at Florence, 14 Aug. 1768. The first conference with Paoli had apparently been held on 7 Aug. Stewart, who travelled under the name of Murray, was paid one thousand pounds for his service. At the end of August Sir Horace Mann sent to Shelburne a description of the "exact situation" in Corsica, an account of which he had just received from Paoli. "The sum total of it," he wrote to Walpole, "is that so long as he [Paoli] has the least glimpse of hopes of being assisted by England, he will oppose the French, but when he despairs of that, his people in defiance of him will submit to them" (Great Britain, State Papers Domestic, *Calendar of Home Office Papers,* vol. II, no. 968 and vol. II, p. 436; Walpole, *Correspondence,* vol. 23, pp. 51–52).
40. Stewart to Shelburne, 20 Aug. 1768. Shelburne MSS, 40, ii. 25.
41. Fortescue, vol. II, no. 642 (13 Aug. 1768).
42. Grafton, *Autobiography,* pp. 203–209.
43. Fortescue, vol. II, no. 652 (15 Sept. 1768) and no. 653 (16 Sept. 1768).
44. Intercepted letter by Caracciolo, in Shelburne MSS, vol. 35, no. 14.
45. Pottle, *Earl. Yrs.,* pp. 378–382, 389–390, 394–397, 409–410. See also Foladare, *Corsica,* pp. 189–194.
46. Rota, p. 140.
47. Ibid., p. 141.

48. Choiseul to Bedford, 13 Oct. 1768; Bedford to Choiseul, 1 Dec. 1768. *Correspondence of John, Fourth Duke of Bedford . . . with an Introduction by Lord John Russell* (London, 1842–1846), III, 402–407.

49. The speeches on the address of thanks for the King's speech and those made later during the debate on Corsica, below, are taken from Sir Henry Cavendish, *Debates of the House of Commons* (London, 1841), I, 31–45 and 52–61.

50. Seymour's failure to give adequate notice of the "object" of his motion was looked upon as a conspicuous violation of custom. See P.D.G. Thomas, *The House of Commons in the Eighteenth Century* (Oxford, 1971), p. 101.

51. As Grenville appeared determined not to know, in some senses negotiations are never "completed" at a given moment—and revelations can always prejudice future negotiations. The basic issue was not easily settled. See Richard Pares, *King George III and the Politicians* (Oxford, 1953), pp. 201–203.

52. Dated 18 Nov. 1768. Walpole, *Correspondence*, vol. 23, p. 69.

53. Châtelet to Choiseul, 18 Nov.; Choiseul to Châtelet, 22 Nov. 1768. Cornelis de Witt, *Thomas Jefferson* (3rd ed., Paris, 1861), pp. 448–449.

54. P to Burnaby, 22 Dec. 1768.

55. *Bulletin*, fascicles 227–228, p. 163.

56. Foladare, *Corsica*, p. 528n.

57. JB Letter, 24 Aug. 1768; *Lond. Chron.*, 10 Dec. 1768. For an account of the fortunes of the shipment see Pottle, *Earl. Yrs.*, p. 390 and n.

58. On the *British Essays* see Pottle, *Lit. Car.*, pp. 76–84, and *Earl. Yrs.*, esp. notes to p. 395; Foladare, *Corsica*, pp. 174–178, 183.

59. Foladare, *Corsica*, p. 191n; Pottle, *Earl. Yrs.*, p. 369n.

60. P to Burnaby, 21 Jan. 1769.

61. *Lond. Chron.*, 26 Nov. 1768, 24 Jan., 14 Feb., 6 May, 9 May 1769; *Gentleman's Magazine* (letter signed "E.Y."), XXXVIII (Nov. 1768), 523.

62. Walpole, *Correspondence*, vol. 4, pp. 185–186, 203–204, 210, 234, 297–298; vol. 23, pp. 75, 78–79, 81, 84, 85, 87, 96, 107.

63. Ravenna, p. 141.

64. Duke of Richmond to Edmund Burke, 2 Sept. 1769. *Correspondence of Edmund Burke*, II, ed. Lucy S. Sutherland (Cambridge, England, 1960), 67–68. After the event Walpole wrote to Conway (29 Dec. 1770), "I feel much for Madame de Choiseul, though nothing for her *Corsican* husband" (*Letters of Horace Walpole*, ed. Mrs. Paget Toynbee [Oxford, 1904], VII, 431).

65. Paoli was given a pension of £1,200 per year; the group in Tuscany £1,000 per month. On 12 June 1772 Lord North informed Paoli that the payments to the exiles in Tuscany would be terminated in June of the following year (Fortescue, no. 1075). Ravenna (p. 140) and Rota (p. 149) place the number of Corsicans brought to Tuscany by British vessels at 340, including clergy. Those later supported in whole or in part by the British government probably numbered in tens rather than hundreds.

66. Undated, but probably shortly after the conquest of Corsica. *Mémoires du Duc de Choiseul,* ed. F. Calmettes (Paris, 1904), pp. 245–246.

67. The account of Paoli's concerns is taken from Burnaby, p. 69n, who offers it as an extended surmise. Inasmuch as Burnaby was in communication with Paoli and acted as his official shepherd during the first days in London, it may be taken as reasonably accurate.

68. Burnaby was not as alert as Margaret Montgomerie, who wrote to Boswell on 29 July: "I see by the papers your friend General Paoli is on his way to England." The *London Chronicle* for 29 July 1769 indeed had Paoli already landed and on his way to London. Perhaps Burnaby believed that the English heavily discounted accounts in newspapers.

Chapter III

1. Journal, 25 Sept. 1769. In 1770 appeared a pamphlet by an unknown admirer of Paoli, *A Review of the Conduct of Pascal Paoli,* which was drawn largely from newspaper sources.

2. Walpole, *Correspondence,* vol. 14, pp. 170, 174; *Journal of the Rev. John Wesley,* ed. Nehemiah Curnock (London, 1909–1916), V, 292–293.

3. See, for example, letter to *Lond. Chron.,* 5 Oct. 1769, which ends with the observation that Paoli's conduct proves "that he is an abject slave in the freest country in Europe."

4. G.P. Anderson, "Pascal Paoli, an Inspiration to the Sons of Liberty," *Publications of the Colonial Society of Massachusetts,* XXVI (1926), 180–181, 200, 204–205.

5. Samuel Vaughan, *An Appeal to the Public on Behalf of Samuel Vaughan, Esq.* (London, 1770), pp. 134–135. Vaughan, like Beckford and Trecothick (the evidence is not so clear on the last), answered to Johnson's description of the conspicuous advocate of liberty and freedom—the plantation owner who kept slaves. Further, Vaughan was involved in a charge of bribery brought by the Duke of Grafton, a circumstance likely to make his an extreme view. See Pottle, *Lit. Car.,* p. 314.

6. Mar. 1770, p. 231; Jan. 1770, p. 69.

7. *Memoirs of the Reign of George III,* ed. G.F. Russell Barker (London, 1894), III, 257–258. The granting of the pension to Paoli was generally credited to the influence of Boswell's book. The General never ceased to be grateful. See Pottle, *Earl. Yrs.,* pp. 429, 563; Foladare, *Corsica,* pp. 203–206.

8. *Journal of the Rev. John Wesley,* ed. Nehemiah Curnock (London, 1909–1916), V, 342.

9. Tommaseo, p. 182 (23 Sept. 1769).

10. Tommaseo, pp. 184–185. See also Boswell to Sir Alexander Dick, 3 Oct. 1769; R. Ambrosi's selections from a document written by Abbé Guelfucci, "Relation du voyage de Pascal Paoli d'Italie en Angleterre," *Revue de la Corse* (Paris), X (1929), 23–29.

11. Tommaseo, p. 181.
12. See S. Maccoby, *English Radicalism, 1762–1785* (London, 1955), p. 133; *Chatham Correspondence*, ed. W.S. Taylor and J.H. Pringle (London, 1839), III, 370.
13. The quotation dated 4 March 1770 is in a letter to Burnaby; the reference to "intolerable coldness" is also from a letter to Burnaby, uncharacteristically without date. Printing it over thirty years later, Burnaby guessed at a time near the end of 1771 (p. 80).
14. Fortescue, II, no. 1075.
15. Journal, 25 Sept. 1769. Information on Boswell during the remainder of his stay in London, 1769, comes from journal notes and memoranda, letters, and the manuscript of *The Life of Johnson*, the latter offering nothing significantly different from the published *Life* with reference to Paoli.
16. JB Journal, 27 Sept. 1769; JB Letter, 3 Oct. 1769.
17. The *Life* gives 10 October as the date for the first meeting between Paoli and Johnson. See Pottle, *Earl. Yrs.*, pp. 563–564, for evidence suggesting 31 October.
18. Contemporary Corsicans affect not to understand Italian, which they do, and are offended if Corse is called a dialect of Italian. Joseph Chiari believes its "roots seem to be, above all, vulgar Latin, Greek, and Arabic." Geoffrey Wagner notes that there are newspapers in Corse on the island, and that even French-language dailies print special columns in Corse. He also states that there is in progress an ambitious Corse dictionary which takes into account the various dialects (Dorothy Carrington, *This Corsica* [London, 1962], p. 46; Joseph Chiari, *Corsica: Columbus's Isle* [London, 1960], p. 147; Geoffrey Wagner, *Elegy for Corsica* [London, 1968], p. 75).
19. *Boswelliana*, p. 328 (entry dated 27 May 1783).
20. Anderson, "Pascal Paoli, an Inspiration to the Sons of Liberty," pp. 190–191.
21. *Life*, 14 July 1763; also in journal of same date.
22. Journal (brief), 23 Jan. 1790.
23. 12 May 1775.
24. *BP*, XIII, 302; JB Journal, 2 April 1775, 24 April 1778, 30 May 1781. The reference to Jupiter and Thetis occurs in the *Iliad*, I, 500–502.
25. Johnson's statement in a letter to Boswell dated 18 Feb. 1777, "Paoli I never see," no doubt refers to a period of weeks or possibly months.
26. Quotation from Paoli in letter to Boswell, 26 April 1782: C 2157; see also his letter to Boswell of 22 Jan. 1782: C 2156. No letter from Paoli to Boswell survives for the interval from 26 April 1782 to 24 January 1783. Paoli wrote at least one during the period, a letter of condolence to which Boswell replied on 18 Jan. 1783: L 1014.
27. *Diary and Letters of Madame D'Arblay*, ed. Charlotte Barrett (London, 1842), II, 186, 190; *Thraliana, the Diary of Mrs. Hester Lynch Thrale*, ed. Katharine C. Balderson (Oxford, 1942), I, 540–541.
28. Antonio Gentili to JB, 26 Aug. 1784: C 1362. In the *Life* Boswell

relates Johnson's decision and reprints the letter to Lord
Thurlow.

29. See Burnaby's note to Paoli's letter of 4 March 1770. Catherine
the Great wrote Paoli a letter on 27 April 1770 (Tommaseo,
p. 186).

30. Boswell did not actually stay with the General until May 1775; he
thereafter made Paoli's his headquarters when in London.

31. JB Journal, 18 March 1776. Boswell dates Paoli's remark 30
March 1776.

32. Very few letters to friends abroad survive for this period. Paoli
apparently was in indirect communication with Corsican leaders
in Italy and on the island, but not in control of particular events.
He specifically disclaimed complicity in the uprising prepared by
Pasqualini, with all its bloody consequences (Ravenna, p. 150;
Ambrogio Rossi, "Osservazioni storiche sopra la Corsica," *Bulletin*,
fascicles 181–185, p. 45). The most comprehensive study of the
period is Louis Villat, *La Corse de 1768 à 1789* (2 vols., Besançon,
1924–1925). Allowance must be made for Villat's pro-French
bias. Paoli wrote to Burnaby and to British "ministers" concerning
the sufferings inflicted on the Corsicans by the French, but he did
not dwell on them in speaking to Boswell. See P to Burnaby, 24
July 1770, 30 July 1771, 23 Aug. 1771, Letter 30 (undated; perhaps end of 1771). Burnaby, who for some time was the General's
only close friend in a position to communicate his views to appropriate individuals in government, published no later letters
from Paoli for the period of the first exile in England. If there
were any, they probably dealt mainly with arrangements for visits.

33. Tommaseo, p. 186.

34. *Lond. Chron.*, 23 Sept. 1769.

35. *Lond. Chron.*, 12 Oct., 17 Oct., 24 Oct. 1769; also J 21, 1 Oct. 1769.

36. Walpole, *Correspondence*, vol. 23, p. 150. Unhappily we cannot accept the story in the *London Chronicle* for 30 Nov., which had
Oxford honor the General with the degree of Doctor of Laws.

37. *Lond. Chron.*, 11 Nov. 1769. Many items in the *Chronicle* for this
period, though not written by Boswell, appear to be based on information supplied by him.

38. In a letter which Boswell prefixed to the third edition of *Corsica*
Lyttelton wrote: "If I were a few years younger, I would go in
pilgrimage to Corsica (as you have done) to visit this living image
of ancient virtue, and to venerate in the mind of PASCAL PAOLI
the spirit of TIMOLEON and EPAMINONDAS."

39. *Early Diary of Frances Burney*, ed. A.R. Ellis (London, 1889), II,
302, 316; *Diary and Letters of Madame D'Arblay*, ed. Charlotte Barrett (London, 1842), II, 155–156; *Autobiography and Correspondence of Mary Granville Delany*, ed. Lady Llanover (London,
1861–1862), V, 470, 545; *Elizabeth Montagu, Her Letters and
Friendships*, ed. Reginald Blunt (London, 1923), I, 229, 249, 251;
Croker's 2nd ed. of Boswell's *Life of Johnson* (London, 1835), IX,
252; William Roberts, *Memoirs of Hannah More* (London, 1834), I
212, 242, and II, 102; *Thraliana, the Diary of Mrs. Hester Lynch
Thrale*, ed. Katherine C. Balderston (Oxford, 1942), I, 389; C.B.

Tinker, *The Salon and English Letters* (New York, 1915), pp. 123–
165. The first reference to Paoli in *Thraliana* is dated 7 June 1779,
but Paoli met the Thrales at least as early as 20 Aug. 1774 and by
1779 he was on the footing of an informal visitor. See Johnson's
Welsh diary for 20 Aug. 1774 and his letter to Mrs. Thrale, 16
Oct. 1779; also A.M. Broadley, *Dr. Johnson and Mrs. Thrale* (London, 1910), p. 198.
40. *Boswelliana*, p. 321 (May 1781).
41. The gift had brought Boswell a letter of thanks "in elegant Latin"
from the University of Corte. P to Burnaby, 1 Nov. 1767; JB to
Rev. Wm. Temple, 24 Dec. 1767; Dr. Gregory to Mrs. Montagu,
21 Sept. 1771.
42. 9 Sept. 1771 (J 22). Boswell was irritated at the failure of the officials of Edinburgh to treat the illustrious vistors becomingly. See
in the trade edition *Boswell for the Defense*, pp. 22–23.
43. The Corsican "abate" is not identified by Boswell in the first journal entry, 19 March 1772, but he appears to be the Andrei who is
named 3 April 1775, 18 July 1786, and a week after this last entry
in a letter which Boswell wrote to Dr. Wall at Oxford. The French
and Italian biographical dictionaries and encyclopedias list
Antoine François Andrei (1740–1800) as a deputy from Corsica
elected to the National Convention in September 1792, and in addition to his political activities mention his poems in Italian and
his parodies in French of Italian operas. He is not given the title of
"Abbé," which he no doubt had reason to forget in Paris. Paoli
wrote to "Abbé Andrei" on 15 March 1793 of his discovery that his
letters to Andrei were being intercepted. Of the Corsican deputies
at the National Convention, Andrei was the only one to rise to
Paoli's defense in the debate over the warrant for Paoli's arrest issued by the Committee of Public Safety on 2 April 1793. He narrowly missed being accused himself. A selection from Paoli's
eloquent letter to Andrei of 19 April 1793 is printed at the appropriate place in the present work. See Giamarchi, pp. 294, 296,
298–299. Henry Angelo wrote that General Paoli was "very fond
of equitation" and during his stay in England was a constant at-
tendant at the senior Angelo's manège, frequently bringing with
him "a Corsican Priest, the Père André, an intelligent and shrewd
fellow" (*Reminiscences* [London, 1904], II, 40–41).
44. Burnaby, p. 71n.
45. Boswell had contributed the following to the *London Chronicle* for
11 Nov. 1769: "Last week James Boswell, Esq., presented Mr.
Garrick to General Paoli, who expressed great satisfaction at being acquainted with our Roscius; and, we hear, that a tragedy of
Shakespeare is soon to be performed before the General at
Drury-lane theatre."
46. Paoli was elected Fellow of the Royal Society on 3 Mar. 1774. Illustrative of his continued association with the curious and the
learned were the visits in 1785 of Pierre François Hugues (1719–
1805), known as D'Hancarville, author of a 5-vol. work on
Etruscan, Greek, and Roman antiquities first published in Naples
1766–1767, in both English and French. His *Recherches sur*

l'origine, l'esprit et les progrès des arts de la Grèce; sur leur connexion avec les arts et la religion des plus anciens peuples connus; . . . 3 vols. in 2, London 1785, which among other things asserted a relationship between ancient art and religious phallic worship, proved to be controversial. Hancarville (Boswell called him D'Ankerville or Dankerville; Jefferson, Danquerville) panted after Maria Cosway in Paris in 1786, at a time when her head and heart were as filled with Jefferson as that patriot's were with her (JB Journal, 19 April, 9 May, 3 June 1785; Fawn M. Brodie, *Thomas Jefferson* [New York, 1974], esp. p. 519, n. 26).

47. A quick count of the acquaintances of Paoli to be found in the early collection of Boswell's papers, published 1928–1934, yields over one hundred names.
48. JB Journal, 20, 23 March 1772; 18, 30 March 1776. If the portrait was completed it did not find a repository in any place listed in the standard dictionaries of art and artists.
49. Journal, 11 April 1776. Patrice Mac-Neny (b. 1712 or 1716, d. 1784), "graaf de Neny," was every bit as eminent as Boswell suggests and in addition authored a useful historical work. He was the descendant of an ancient family in Ireland which took refuge in Belgium after the reverses of the Stuarts.
50. According to Father Guelfucci, when the newly arrived Paoli party were seeking the Rev. Andrew Burnaby in London they met by accident Captain Medows, who had spent the previous month of April [1769] in Corsica ("Relation du voyage de Pascal Paoli d'Italie en Angleterre," *Revue de la Corse* [Paris], X [1929], 23–29).
51. Journal, 18 April 1776. Solander was a well-known botanist. The other three are famous in the annals of the Royal Society.
52. See JB Journal, 16 March 1776 and 18 March 1778. Antonio Gentili (b. 1751, d. 1798 or 1799) was fourteen years old when Boswell met him at Sollacaro, and fifteen or a bare sixteen when he "took" Capraja. The young man may have distinguished himself in that action, which as Boswell himself had related in the *Account*, p. 258, was commanded by Achille Murati and Giovan Battista Ristori. The former, according to Napoleon on St. Helena, lacked only a vaster field to become a Turenne (Giamarchi, p. 370). Antonio Gentili is to be found in the standard French biographical dictionaries and encyclopedias. For additional information on him and his family—including the distant relative, Count Gentili—see Renucci, I, 238, 300, 311, 390, and II, 120; Camille Piccioni, *Histoire du Cap-Corse* (Paris, 1923), pp. 191, 208; Arrigo Arrighi, *Histoire de Pascal Paoli* (Paris, 1843), II, 57–59; *Revue de la Corse* (Paris), 1929, pp. 105–121, 177–187, and 1930, pp. 18–27; *Archivio Storico Italiano*, XI (Florence, 1846), pp. 315–316; Moore, I, 99; *Bulletin*, fascicles 133–138, p. 457, and fascicles 165–166, pp. 5, 12, 20.
53. Journal, entry of 2 April 1776.
54. Ravenna, p. 152.
55. JB Journal, 31 Mar. 1772.
56. Margaret Forbes, *Beattie and his Friends* (Westminster, 1904), p.

81; *Journal of the Rev. John Wesley*, ed. Nehemiah Curnock (London, 1909–1916), VI, 477 and VII, 30. Cosway's fine oil portrait, chosen as frontispiece by Paoli's three twentieth-century biographers, was first exhibited at the Royal Academy in 1798. However, the original drawing if not the final oil portrait itself appears to date from the period shortly before Paoli ended his first exile in England, March 1790. Cosway earlier had drawn a portrait of Paoli, also "in armour," which served as the original for an engraving published by Charles Townley in 1784.

57. *Diary and Letters of Madame D'Arblay*, ed. Charlotte Barrett (London, 1842), II, 155–156; A.M. Broadley, *Dr. Johnson and Mrs. Thrale* (London, 1910), p. 198; *Thraliana, the Diary of Mrs. Hester Lynch Thrale*, ed. Katherine C. Balderston (Oxford, 1942), II, 858. I am indebted to Professor James L. Clifford for information from Mrs. Piozzi's diaries of 1788–1790.

58. Minto, II, 222; Moore, I, 47.

59. Walpole, *Correspondence*, vol. 23, pp. 142, 150, 159. See also *Memoirs of the Reign of George III*, ed. G.F. Russell Barker (London, 1894), III, 257–258.

60. Walpole, *Correspondence*, vol. 12, p. 63; vol. 25, p. 242.

61. Ibid., vol. 15, p. 332; vol. 23, p. 140.

62. *Journal . . . Wesley*, VII, 30.

63. JB Journal, 19 April 1772. See also entry for 29 March 1778: "Horace was a little soul . . . Virgil a great soul."

64. William Roberts, *Memoirs of Hannah More* (London, 1834), I, 242. See also Paoli's reference to *3 Henry VI* in JB Journal, 8 April 1772.

65. JB Journal, 25 Sept. 1769; *Life*, 10 Oct. 1769. See also SJ's discussion with Paoli on the primitive signification of *macaroni*, JB Journal, 14 April 1778.

66. JB Journal, 28 April 1778; somewhat modified in *Life*.

67. George C. Williamson, *Richard Cosway, R.A., and His Wife and Pupils* (London, 1897), p. 75.

68. JB Journal, 22 March 1772, 9 May 1776, 2 April 1783; *Boswelliana*, p. 321. Johnson in exercising his right to the last words on the possibility of Reynolds achieving eternal fame as a sculptor presents an unflattering analysis of his friend's ambitions: "Ay, but by his portraits he makes present money."

69. For the printing press in Corsica see Foladare, *Corsica*, notes to p. 436.

70. *Diary and Letters of Madame D'Arblay*, II, 155–156. An illustrative example from Boswell is found in the journal for 29 April 1783: "Went with the General to Langton's. By the way, while he restrained my vivacity, he said, 'You're like my mare, when I put on the curb, she dance.'"

71. William Roberts, *Memoirs of Hannah More* (London, 1834), I, 242.

72. Symonds to JB, 3 Oct. 1767: C 2634.

73. JB Journal, 22 Sept. 1769, 18 Dec. 1785; Rota, p. 153; *Journal of the Rev. John Wesley*, ed. Nehemiah Curnock (London, 1909–1916), VII, 30.

74. JB Journal, 14 May 1776, 16 and 18 Sept. 1777; P to Maria Cosway, 30 March 1798, in Williamson, *Richard Cosway*, p. 74.
75. "Memorabilia Paoli," 27 May 1784: M 211.
76. JB Journal, 11 April 1778; *Boswelliana*, p. 320; JB Notes, 18 April 1775.
77. Frank Brady, *Boswell's Political Career* (New Haven, 1965).
78. JB to P, 14 March 1780: L 1007; P to JB, 31 March 1780: C 2152; P to JB, 3 June 1780: C 2153. I am unable to account for the complete absence from the Boswell collection of Boswell-Paoli letters for the period 1769–1780. From March 1780 onwards all but a few do survive.
79. JB to P, 18 Sept. 1780: L 1008; P to JB, 2 Oct. 1780: C 2154. Burke made his speech on 9 Sept.
80. For evidence of SJ and P being together see JB Journal, 9 May 1781; Mary Hyde, "Not in Chapman," in *Johnson, Boswell, and their Circle: Essays Presented to Lawrence Fitzroy Powell* (Oxford, 1965), p. 314.
81. L 1012; C 2157. Boswell was to be disappointed again. See Brady, pp. 93–96.
82. L 1013; L 1014.
83. JB to P, 18 Feb. 1783: L 1015; P to JB, 28 Feb. 1783: C 2159.
84. Masseria certainly lived apart from Paoli some of the time. See P to JB, 8 Nov. 1786: C 2166.
85. JB to P, 9 Feb. 1784: L 1017; P to JB, 20 Feb. 1784: C 2161.
86. P to JB, 27 July 1784: C 2163; Gentili to JB, 26 Aug. 1784: C 1362; SJ to JB, 11 July 1784. The full text of Johnson's letter to Boswell and of another he wrote to Sir William Forbes show how grudgingly Johnson acceded to Boswell's wishes. See David Buchanan, *The Treasure of Auchinleck* (New York, 1974), pp. 323–326.
87. JB to P, 14 Feb. 1785: L 1019; P to JB, 26 Feb. 1785: C 2164.
88. Journal, 6 July 1786, 6 May 1787.
89. JB to P, 7 Nov. 1786: L 1020; P to JB, 8 Nov. 1786: C 2166.
90. P's letter of condolence in *BP*, XVII, 164–165 (transl. fr. Italian); JB to P, 10 Dec. 1791: L 1023.
91. Walpole, *Correspondence*, vol. 25, p. 646; vol. 33, pp. 510–511.
92. Maria and the General were certainly good friends by the summer of 1784. How much earlier they first met I have been unable to determine.
93. For Maria Cosway see Williamson, *Richard Cosway*, pp. 15–75; [Michael] *Bryan's Dictionary of Painters and Engravers*, rev. G.C. Williamson (London, 1903–1904); Helen Duprey Bullock, *My Head and My Heart: A Little History of Thomas Jefferson and Maria Cosway* (New York, 1945), esp. pp. 13–97; Fawn M. Brodie, *Thomas Jefferson* (New York, 1974), esp. pp. 200–254.
94. Williamson, p. 15; Brodie, p. 201 and n. 10. I am indebted to Diana G. Wilson, who is presently engaged in a full-length study of Richard Cosway, for calling my attention to the unreliability of much that has been written on the Cosways.
95. Bullock, p. 14. Gouverneur Morris found Maria "vastly pleasant"

even in the trying summer of 1789 (*Diary and Letters,* ed. A.C. Morris [New York, 1888], I, 148, 150).

96. Walpole, *Correspondence,* vol. 12, p. 213.
97. I am here taking strong exception to the interpretation of the Walpole and Wolcot passages given by Professor Brodie. She quotes only the first eight lines of Walpole's poem, introducing these with the comment: "Horace Walpole composed for the *Morning Chronicle* a poem of mixed derision and praise." Even these eight lines, with their reference to a painter's palette covered by "colours in confusion" which appear as a "chaotic mass," contain no element of derision; the "lovely artist" with her "imagination" and "grand visions" creates art from these materials—like any other painter. The remaining thirty-two lines are uniformly encomiastic. As for Wolcot, there is indeed no mistaking the meaning of "two fools" in the first stanza quoted, and Brodie correctly states that he writes "maliciously of both the Cosways." Brodie, however, omits the last four lines of the poem, which are in her source, Williamson. These lines virtually nullify all that goes before, with their praise of Richard Cosway's painting and Mrs. Cosway's "merit," whatever that is (Brodie, pp. 201–202; Williamson, p. 34; Horace Walpole, *Anecdotes of Painting in England (1760–1795),* ed. F.W. Hilles and P.B. Daghlian [New Haven, 1937], V, 127–129).
98. Bullock, p. 13; Brodie, p. 203.
99. Bullock, p. 52.
100. Brodie, pp. 222–227.
101. 14 Oct. 1789; Brodie, pp. 225, 242.
102. Tommaseo, p. 569, p. clxxxiii.
103. In the conclusion to the book Burnaby states that he "has known and been in habits of intimacy with General Paoli for nearly forty years" (p. 173). A surviving letter from Burnaby to Boswell, 30 March 1778 (C 703), does indicate that the two were on visiting terms, or at least familiar enough to exchange invitations.
104. Frank Brady, *Boswell's Political Career* (New Haven, 1965), pp. 103–106.
105. *Boswelliana,* pp. 301–302.
106. *Journal of the Rev. John Wesley,* ed. Nehemiah Curnock (London, 1909–1916), VII, 30.
107. Paoli once succeeded in silencing Wilkes in absentia. The General had evidently become acquainted with Wilkes' daughter, for whom her profligate father at all times displayed an extreme fondness. In the midst of one of Wilkes' denunciations Boswell repeated a judgment he had heard from Paoli: "I forgive the father for the sake of the daughter." Wilkes could only reply, "You never told me that before" (Journal, 15 May 1781).
108. *BP,* XIII, 301 (7 May 1781).
109. *Thraliana,* I, 389, (7 June 1779); JB Journal, 1 Oct. 1769: J 21; Journal, 18 May 1778. "Going from one room to another" may seem an odd way of describing the step from minor military officer in Italy to Generalship of Corsica; but, as Paoli had told Bos-

well in the *Tour* (p. 351), "from his earliest years he had in view the important station which he now holds."

110. Alternates were, for the clergy, Joseph-Marie Falcucci; for the nobility, Gaffori (Buttafoco's father-in-law); for the third estate, Arena and Chiappe (Villat, II, 366, 369–386). Five years later Pierre-Paul Colonna de Cesare Rocca was to appear in the Corsican delegation to George III as Pietro Paolo Colonna-Cesari-Rocca.
111. Villat, II, 347, 413–419.
112. Villat, II, 350–352.
113. Villat, II, 402–405.
114. Tommaseo, p. 322. The ancient city of Chalcedon, opposite Byzantium at the entrance of the Euxine, was founded before Byzantium. In Paoli's figure it had the virtues of simplicity and dignity as compared with the needless elaboration and complexity of the latter.
115. Arrigo Arrighi, *Histoire de Pascal Paoli* (Paris, 1843), II, 58–59.
116. The letters of recommendation, dated 26 March 1790, are C 2170 and C 2171. For Giacomo Pietro see P to JB, 7 Oct. 1791: C 2177. The list of guests for Boswell's dinner was first published in *BP*, XVIII, 29–30. Besides Boswell and Paoli the following were present: the Minister from Sardinia [Count St. Martin de Front], the Minister from Portugal [?Chevalier d'Almeida Mello y Castro], Sir John Dick, John Osborn, Sir Joseph Banks, Richard Cosway, T.D. Boswell, Lord Macartney [George Macartney, 1st. E.] Now in the Boswell collection are items which Boswell starred as his contributions to the *Public Advertiser* (P 117). The dinner is described in the issue of 2 April 1790, with the final statement: "The Bishop of Carlisle and Sir George Howard, who were to have completed this select party of General Paoli's friends, were unluckily engaged."
117. Giamarchi, pp. 230–231.
118. Burnaby, p. 82. The letter, dated at Bastia 2 March 1790, is signed by Panattieri, Belgodere di Bagnaja, Raffaele di Casabianca, and Pietro Paolo Morati. In the Boswell collection there are two letters addressed to Paoli begging the Father of their Country to return, one from Isola Rossa, dated 14 Jan. 1790 (C 832) and signed by a committee of which Arena is the President; the other from Bastia, dated 7 Feb. 1790 (C 763), from Francesco Casa-Bianca, stressing the need for haste to forestall anarchy. In an item in the *Public Advertiser* (P 117) Boswell indicates that Paoli set out on 29 March 1790.

Chapter IV

1. Tommaseo, pp. 329–330; Renucci, I, 265.
2. Tommaseo, p. 332; P to Burnaby, 4 May 1790.
3. P to Burnaby, 14 June 1790.
4. Dated at Toulon, 12 July 1790 (C 2175). Burnaby prints no letter for this period, but may well have received one. "The sole object

of this selection [of letters] is to vindicate General Paoli's character from the aspersions and misrepresentations of envy and detraction," Burnaby writes in the conclusion to his book. He undoubtedly omits much purely personal correspondence.

5. R.R. Palmer, *The Age of the Democratic Revolution* (Princeton, 1964), II, 27–31.
6. Ravenna, pp. 156–157; Giamarchi, pp. 230–231.
7. Giamarchi, pp. 231, 245.
8. Tommaseo, p. 350; Giamarchi, p. 247.
9. P to Burnaby, 30 June 1791.
10. Ibid. (postscript 4 July).
11. *Observations de M. Buttafoco sur la résponse de M. Saliceti* (Paris, undated, but usually placed in 1791). At approximately the same time Buttafoco published *Lettres de M. Buttafoco à M. Paoli et à d'autres particuliers dans l'isle de Corse.*
12. *Lettre à Matteo Buttafoco* (Ajaccio, 1791). See also Fournier, I, 31–32, and Ernestine Dedeck-Héry, *Jean-Jacques Rousseau et la projet de constitution pour la Corse* (Philadelphia, 1932), p. 102.
13. Howard, I, 31, 32.
14. Ravenna, p. 162; Giamarchi, p. 271; Fournier, I. 45–49.
15. Giamarchi, pp. 274–283; Fournier, I, 47.
16. Giamarchi, pp. 266, 267.
17. Ibid., pp. 283, 285.
18. Ibid., p. 288 (dated 18 March 1793).
19. Fournier, I, 47–48.
20. Giamarchi, p. 289.
21. Fournier, I, 48.
22. Giamarchi, pp. 298–299.
23. Tommaseo, p. 404f.
24. Giamarchi, pp. 311–312.
25. Ibid., pp. 321, 322.
26. Ibid., p. 362.
27. Ravenna, p. 172; Giamarchi, p. 367.
28. Paoli wrote to Francis Drake, British agent at Genoa, and to Admiral Hood. In his letter to Boswell, Paoli gives the "last days of August" as the time of his appeal; in that to Burnaby he gives 1 September as the date of his message to Hood. The slight discrepancy may simply be the difference between the time of decision and that of execution (P to JB, 12 Oct. 1793: C 2179; P to Burnaby, 11 Oct. 1793; *Cambridge History of British Foreign Policy,* ed. A.W. Ward and G.P. Gooch [New York, 1922], I, 553–554).
29. The publications surviving in the Boswell collection (P 35– P 40) date from January and February 1793. Their burden is the firm, sometimes angry rejection of calumnies and slanders against the Corsicans and their leader, along with strong protestations of devotion to the ideals of liberty and equality and the constitution which guarantees them. The papers supposedly by Paoli—he may well have delegated the tasks of writing them—show none of the characteristic force and directness of his letters of the time.
30. The letters to Burnaby and Boswell reveal that Admiral Hood, lying off Toulon, before he received the appeal from Paoli had al-

ready sent three warships and one or two frigates to attack the French at Calvi, San Fiorenzo, and Bastia—all this contrary to published histories and biographies.

31. P to Burnaby, 19 Aug. 1794.
32. Fournier, I, 51–55; Mahan, *Fr. Rev.*, I, 92; Mahan, *Nelson*, I, 106–107; Howard, I, 9, 44; Watson, p. 367.
33. Minto, II, 162 (17 Sept. 1793), 165.
34. Mahan, *Fr. Rev.*, I, 105; Howard, I, 45.
35. Minto, II, 206–207.
36. Mahan, *Nelson*, I, 116–118.
37. Minto, II, 209–210.
38. Ibid., II, 214–215. Koehler is spelled *Kochler* by Moore and several other contemporaries.
39. Moore, I, 44–45. For "poor rag," below, see P to Burnaby, 30 July 1771.
40. Ibid., I, 44–47.
41. Minto, II, 214–215.
42. Moore, I, 81, 83, 94–99; Nelson, I, 397–401, and II, 6, 8. Nelson hoped that the success against Bastia would be looked upon as a naval victory, with his command of marines a decisive factor. "I am scarcely mentioned," he complained.
43. George III, aware of the delicacy of the situation, wrote on 24 April 1794: "I trust Mr. Dundas will not fail to hint to Stuart the necessity of keeping up harmony with the Commander of the Fleet, and as Sir Gilbert Elliot seems to have some weight with Lord Hood, by that means to cultivate that desirable object. I know Stuart is a zealous and active officer but not wanting of high feelings; therefore a little caution recommended may avoid future trouble" (Moore, I, 67–68, 152; Aspinall, II, 198–199).
44. Moore, I, 99; Burnaby, p. 119. In justice to Gentili it should be noted that the French *Représentant* in Corsica, Lacombe St. Michel, had left Bastia for France, "to hasten the succours which had long been promised." The army and townspeople, however, had good reason to believe that they had been abandoned. For a circumstantial account of the siege of Bastia see Carola Oman, *Sir John Moore* (London, 1953), pp. 100–109, or Oman's chief sources, Moore, I, 65–99, and Nelson, I, 362–401, II, 6, 8.
45. Calvi did not fall until 10 Aug. 1794. The British navy blockaded the port, and Corsican and British troops attacked by land. Whereas the siege of Bastia had been largely static except for the rather useless lobbing of shells, that at Calvi involved extensive action by troops, and purposeful bombardment. On examining the port after its surrender Moore commented: "It is inconceivable the destruction our fire has occasioned; there is literally not a house which has not been damaged by shot or shell." Malaria took the greatest toll, however, of both seamen and troops. It was at Calvi on 10 July that Nelson received his serious injury to the right eye. Again he believed that his part and the part of the navy in the action were insufficiently recognized (Moore, I, 103–117; Nelson, I, 440, 442, 446–448, 464, 475–478; Mahan, *Nelson*, I, 137–148, 151–154).

46. Texts in Burnaby, pp. 107–115.
47. Minto, II, 255–257.
48. Giamarchi, p. 394.
49. Except for the use of hyphens, Giamarchi (p. 406) and Ravenna (p. 175) are in agreement in the spelling of the names of the deputies: (1) Pietro Paolo Colonna-Cesari-Rocca, (2) Giovan Francesco Galeazzi, (3) Giuseppe Ottavio Nobili-Savelli, (4) Francesco Maria Pietri. For the first, Colonna, Cesari, and Rocca are apparently accumulated family names; the last of them in some sources is omitted. Pietri spent some time in England during Paoli's first exile; and later was one of the Corsican deputies to the French Legislative Assembly. In August 1772 he and Pozzo di Borgo left France for Corsica in anticipation of a break between the Republic and Paolist Corsica. In 1796 Pietri left Corsica and turned up in England; how long he stayed I do not know. Paoli wrote to Burnaby that he himself would have followed the deputation had not the war and the uncertainties of the government kept him at home. "I would have liked to present my homage to the King, to embrace my friends, and then retire to Bath, far from affairs and intrigues" (P to Burnaby, 27 June 1794 and 18 Oct. 1796; Minto, II, 259–260).
50. Giamarchi, p. 405; Minto, II, 257.
51. Minto, II, 261–264. The English text of the Corsican constitution is reprinted in the *Annual Register for 1794,* pp. 103–109.
52. P to Burnaby, 19 Aug. 1794; Tommaseo, p. 486.
53. Minto, II, 237–238 (7 April 1794).
54. Ibid., II, 268–271 (7 Aug. 1794).
55. Ibid., II, 271 (6 Sept. 1794).
56. Aspinall, pp. 232–233; P to Burnaby, 10 Dec. 1796. The letter by Paoli, taken together with that he wrote to Burnaby on 18 Oct. 1796, constitutes his summary of British mistakes in Corsica. He adds a footnote in his letter of 10 Jan. 1797.
57. Aspinall, p. 232 (22 Aug. 1794); Burnaby, p. 165.
58. Minto, II, 314. R.R. Palmer incorrectly states that Paoli accused Elliot of stealing the diamonds ("The Kingdom of Corsica and the Science of History," *Proceedings of the American Philosophical Society,* vol. 105, no. 4 [Aug. 1961], p. 357).
59. Burnaby, pp. 170–171 (29 Nov. 1794). That Paoli found significance in the event beyond what Palmer calls a "comical misunderstanding" is indicated by his reference in the account of British misrule and by his later giving Burnaby the correspondence concerning the incident and sanctioning inclusion of the material in an appendix to Burnaby's edition of his letters to Burnaby.
60. P to Burnaby, 10 Dec. 1796; Minto, II, 276; Aspinall, II, 259.
61. R.R. Palmer, *The Age of the Democratic Revolution* (Princeton, 1964), II, 286. Palmer had made the same statement in "The Kingdom of Corsica and the Science of History," *Proceedings of the American Philosophical Society,* vol. 105, no.4 (Aug. 1961), p. 357.
62. Minto, II, 282–283.
63. Ibid., II, 294–295.
64. P to Burnaby, 24 Jan. 1795.

65. Moore, I, 124, 131, 134.
66. Ravenna, p. 177.
67. Minto, II, 317.
68. Giamarchi, p. 423; Ravenna, p. 177.
69. Moore, I, 121, 138.
70. Giamarchi, p. 429.
71. Moore, I, 141 (10 March 1795).
72. Howard, I, 51-52.
73. Nelson, I, 501-502.
74. Fournier, I, 62; Minto, II, 298-299; Nelson, II, 10-26; Mahan, *Fr. Rev.,* I, 189-192; Mahan, *Nelson,* I, 161-173.
75. P to Burnaby, 10 Dec. 1796. Paoli wrote the above after he had arrived in England for the second exile; but many earlier letters indicate that little was lost upon him as it happened.
76. R.R. Palmer simplifies matters somewhat in stating that "the aged patriot Paoli . . . became a rallying point for the anti-French and anti-revolutionary elements" (*The Age of the Democratic Revolution* [Princeton, 1964], II, 284).
77. Moore, I, 139.
78. Ibid., I, 124 (5 Oct. 1794); R.R. Palmer, "The Kingdom of Corsica and the Science of History," *Proceedings of the American Philosophical Society,* vol. 105, no. 4 (Aug. 1961), pp. 356-357. Palmer's figure is "two or three hundred thousand dollars today." My allowance for the inflation of the British pound (and the American dollar) may be excessive.
79. Moore, I, 147; Tommaseo, pp. 541, 543.
80. Minto, II, 318; Burnaby, p. 140; Moore, I, 151 (16 May 1795).
81. Moore, I, 153; Minto, II, 300-301.
82. Moore, I, 157.
83. Tommaseo, p. 538. See also Moore, I, 159-160 and 164-169; Minto, II, 319-321.
84. Minto, II, 319-320 (2 Aug.).
85. Minto, II, 322; Carola Oman, *Sir John Moore* (London, 1953), p. 126.
86. Moore, I, 160. Lord Huntly was George Gordon, Marquis of Huntly, afterwards fifth Duke of Gordon. Oakes was later fully styled Lieutenant-General Sir Hildebrand Oakes.
87. Moore, I, 162-163. Thrasher's statement that Moore "feared greatly for the safety of his troops" is a gross exaggeration, as puzzling as his reversal of chronology. Thrasher has the Corsican troops march to Corte upon Elliot's orders, and then puts Moore on the road to Paoli at Rostino, "possibly to pacify him" (p. 307).
88. Minto, II, 323.
89. Moore, I, 161-163.
90. Ibid., I, 163.
91. Minto, II, 325 (17 Aug. 1795).
92. Giamarchi, p. 444.
93. Ibid., pp. 434-435, 441.
94. Ibid., pp. 440-441.
95. Tommaseo, p. 539.
96. Burnaby, p. 132.

97. Giamarchi, pp. 441, 443.
98. Aspinall, II, 395 (30 Aug. 1795) and 396 (31 Aug.)
99. Burnaby, pp. 171–172.
100. Giamarchi, p. 446; Renucci, II, 73.
101. Giamarchi, p. 447; Tommaseo, p. 544.
102. Moore, I, 178–179.
103. Ibid., II, 172–175.
104. Ibid., I, 175–176; British Museum, Add. MS. 22688, ff. 114–115. Moore left Corsica on 9 October, four days before Paoli.
105. Moore, I, 178. Dundas' unscrupulousness had frequently been called to Paoli's attention by Boswell.
106. Moore, I, 179; Burnaby, p. 133. Thrasher (p. 313) writes of "Paoli's arrival in England with Moore."
107. JB Journal, 26 Nov. 1793; 2, 8 Jan. 1794; 24, 26 Mar. 1794; also JB Letter, 17 Mar. 1794.
108. JB to P: L 1027—undated, but probably written in early March 1795. See also P to Burnaby, 7 Jan. 1796.
109. In the letter from Paoli to Sir William Forbes, London, 17 Jan. 1796, in the hand of T.D. Boswell except for the signature, Paoli acknowledges: "Mr. T.D. Boswell has delivered to me a mourning ring left to me by James Boswell, Esquire, which I shall ever preserve and esteem as a mark of the regard of my deceased friend" (National Library of Scotland, MS.Acc.4796, box 87).

Chapter V

1. The Farington quotation from Poggi is dated 12 May 1796. These entries and two later brief references to Maria Cosway are taken from "The Windsor Typescript."
2. P to Burnaby, 7 Jan. 1796. The Gentleman of the Chamber was Henry Belayse, 2nd Earl Fauconberg. Thrasher (p. 314) has Dundas inform Paoli "that the King no longer wished to see him," and leaves the reader with the distinct impression that Paoli did not go to Court.
3. P to Burnaby, 7 Jan. 1796.
4. Tommaseo, p. 552.
5. P to Burnaby, 18 Oct. 1796; Minto, II, 345.
6. Minto, II, 344.
7. Ibid., II, 265; Giamarchi, pp. 454–455; R.R. Palmer, "The Kingdom of Corsica and the Science of History," *Proceedings of the American Philosophical Society*, vol. 105, no. 4 (August 1961), p. 359.
8. Mahan, *Fr. Rev.*, I, 213.
9. Nelson, II, 256.
10. Ibid., II, 258–259. See also Mahan, *Nelson*, I, 238–239; Burnaby, p. 136; Maurice Jollivet, *Les Anglais dans la Méditerranée (1794–1797): Un Royaume Anglo-Corse* (Paris, 1896), pp. 240–249.
11. Minto, II, 354–355.
12. P to Burnaby, 10 Jan. 1797.
13. Mahan, *Fr. Rev.*, I, 216–217, and *Nelson*, I, 247–251; Minto, II, 360–361; Jollivet, pp. 280–282; Nelson, II, 285, 303.

14. Fournier, I, 132; Camille Piccioni, *Histoire du Cap-Corse* (Paris, 1923), p. 208.

15. Walpole, *Correspondence*, vol. 11, p. 285 (letter dated 8 June 1791); *Thraliana, the Diary of Mrs. Hester Lynch Thrale,* ed. Katharine C. Balderston (Oxford, 1942), II, 875. The quotation from Walpole is usually found without the introductory statements to Mary Berry: "I am glad Mrs. Cosway is with you; she is pleasing."

16. Contemporary accounts have Maria "enter" or "retire to" a convent in Genoa in 1793. Mrs. Piozzi in a footnote to her *Thraliana* entry for 29 Mar. 1794 properly corrects her assertion, noting that Mrs. Cosway "went en Pension—She did *not* take the Veil" (Angelica Church to Thomas Jefferson, 19 Aug. 1793; Bullock, p. 137; Brodie, p. 254).

17. Before he had left for Corsica, Paoli presented Maria Cosway with a casket of precious stones which had been sent to him in 1774 by the Elector of Saxony, Frederick Augustus III, as a mark of friendship. Maria ultimately presented the casket, along with Cosway's portrait of Paoli, to the Uffizi. George C. Williamson, *Richard Cosway, R. A., and His Wife and Pupils* (London, 1897), p. 72. In addition to passing on a valued heirloom Paoli possibly was giving Maria some security in the event that her behavior might deprive her of her husband's support.

18. Walpole, *Correspondence,* vol. 12, p. 203 (letter dated 16 Aug. 1796).

19. An enduring monument to Maria Cosway is the Collegio di Maria SS. Bambina, Lodi, Italy. Maria at last found her vocation in establishing and overseeing a school—*collegio*—for Catholic girls which might bring to her charges the sense of fulfillment and happiness which she experienced in her youth. By 1830 she was able to make her college into a religious house and attach it to the church of Santa Maria della Grazie. Francis I, Emperor of Austria, asked Maria to accept the rule of the educational religious order *Dame Inglesi,* which she did in 1831. In 1834 the Emperor paid Maria Cosway a visit and created her a baroness of his empire. The Baroness died 5 Jan. 1838 (Williamson, pp. 54–55).

20. P to Maria Cosway, 14 Aug. 1796: *C 2181. Paoli addresses Maria as his "comare" and refers to himself as her "compare." I translate both loosely as "friend," but the first actually means "godmother" and the second "godfather." Paoli probably adopted the terms after he was chosen to act as godfather to Maria's daughter; they suggest a familial tie, and affection.

21. P to Burnaby, 18 Oct. 1796.

22. The criticism of the mode of British withdrawal is amplified in Paoli's letters to Burnaby of 10 Jan. and 2 April 1797.

23. P to Burnaby, 10 Jan. 1797.

24. Minto, II, 377–378; Mahan, *Nelson,* I, 268–272, 284–285.

25. Giamarchi, p. 495.

26. Aspinall, II, 604.

27. P to Burnaby, 23 Oct. 1797.

28. P to Burnaby, 10 Feb. 1798.

29. Aspinall, II, 638 (14 Nov. 1797). See also Minto, III, 2.

30. P to Burnaby, 10 Feb. 1798.
31. P to Burnaby, 12 July 1798.
32. Giamarchi, p. 499; Ravenna, p. 183.
33. Williamson. *Richard Cosway,* pp. 74-75. Paoli's first letter is dated 30 March 1798.
34. Letter to Sir William Forbes, National Library of Scotland, MS.Acc.4796, box 88.
35. P to Burnaby, 13 July 1802. A list of those attending the Royal Academy Dinner is given in a newspaper clipping pasted in the Farington Diary immediately following the entry for 25 April 1801.
36. Tommaseo, p. 577 (18 May 1802).
37. Ibid., p. 579.
38. Ibid., pp. 579-580.
39. Giamarchi, p. 500 (4 Feb. 1802).
40. Ibid., pp. 502-503.
41. Joseph Chiari, *Corsica: Columbus's Isle* (London, 1960), p. 52; Ravenna, pp. 185-186; Tommaseo, p. 587; Henry B. Wheatley and Peter Cunningham, *London Past and Present* (London, 1891), III, 16-21.
42. L. Cristiani, *Pascal Paoli* (Ajaccio, 1956), p. 37.
43. The disorder which "so nearly threatened" Paoli's life, noted in the letter to Burnaby of 13 July 1802, probably had a different origin. On 12 July 1798 he wrote to Burnaby from Clifton: "I do not leave my immediate confines, although I am now in the hands of doctors for treatment of a powerful and threatening rheumatism of the head." He expected to return to London soon to consult some eminent physician about his illness, "which until now is resisting the remedies prescribed for me, and the change of climate." On 10 Jan. of the previous year he wrote to Burnaby that the rigors of winter had brought him but slight symptoms "of that catarrh which in this season always persecutes me." The powerful "rheumatism of the head" answers to the modern description of a congestion and infection of the sinuses.
44. Entry of 6 June 1807 in *The [Joseph] Farington Diary,* ed. James Greig (London, 1923-1928), IV, 147.
45. For Pozzo di Borgo see P.K. Grimsted, *The Foreign Ministers of Alexander I* (Berkeley and Los Angeles, 1969), pp. 183, 219-221, 243-244, 281-284, 297-298, 351, 352. The Pozzo di Borgo family has not made the founder's papers available to the public. The official biography, Pierre Ordioni's *Pozzo di Borgo* (Paris, 1935), is therefore not of great use.
46. The renovation required to convert Paoli's former home into what is now called the Paoli Museum was not extensive. For a description of the house as it appeared in 1867 see Léonard de Saint-Germain, *Itinéraire Descriptif et Historique de la Corse* (Paris, 1869), p. 397.

INDEX

This index includes, in addition to the persons mentioned in the text, several who appear in footnotes which are essentially expansions of the text. Many minor references to Paoli and to Boswell are omitted. Sovereigns and British princes of the blood are entered under their Christian names; noblemen and Lords of Session under their titles. Abbreviations used are D. (Duke), M. (Marquess), E. (Earl), V. (Viscount), B. (Baron), Bt. (Baronet), JB (James Boswell), P (Paoli), SJ (Samuel Johnson).